Bread
from
Bethlehem

A daily devotional on the book of Ruth

John M. O'Malley

Bread from Bethlehem

This four-chapter book of the Bible is set in the time of the Judges. It was a time when men did what they felt was right in their own eyes. Great leaders led God's people from rebellion to reform. Men like Samuel, Gideon, and Samson stood for God and truth in untoward times.

The book is more than just a story; it is God's sovereign hand in the process of mining a Gentile gem to place in the royal crown of His Son, Jesus. The story has tragedy and triumph, discouragement and delight, funerals and a wedding. Its pages contain every element in life that we encounter. It is a story with which we can identify with in many ways.

As you read Ruth's story and this companion devotional, you will notice many spiritual lessons that will apply to your life. Let the Word of God speak to your heart each day as you read.

God gave me this simple outline as a road map through the book of Ruth. It may help you as you read through the book of Ruth and this devotional guide.

Chapter 1	God's Cultivation of a Gentile Gem.
Chapter 2	God's Care of a Gentile Gem.
Chapter 3	God's Cleansing of a Gentile Gem.
Chapter 4	God's Coronation of a Gentile Gem.

May God bless your reading of His Word,
John M. O'Malley

Foreword ...

Nestled in the midst of the Old Testament we find one of the most beautiful stories of holy writ. The Holy Spirit records for us in the Book of Ruth man's failures through sin and God's provision of a kinsman Redeemer. Within its pages is displayed through the persons of Elimelech, Naomi, Boaz and Ruth, the wayward wandering of Israel, Israel's return, and a Groom Who finds a precious bride. What a tremendous presentation of the Gospel!

God has given John O'Malley a wonderful insight to the character and spirit of this God inspired story. He has marvelously been able to share his study in a daily devotional format, Bread From Bethlehem, which is excellent to use for personal time in the Word, family devotional time or by any serious student of the Word of God. We recommend to the reader that he take each day with thoughtfulness and meditation, allowing the Scripture to speak to him. One will grow in his appreciation for the God Who has brought him out of "Moab" to "Bethlehem-judah" and to the Saviour Who has become his "Goel" kinsman Redeemer.

Dr. Larry M. Groves
Faith Baptist Church,
Indianapolis, Indiana

Sojourning in Moab . . .

Ruth 1:1 *Now it came to pass in the days when the judges ruled, that there was a famine in the land. And a certain man of Bethlehem-judah went to sojourn in the country of Moab, he, and his wife, and his two sons.*

Sojourning in Moab should be a startling phrase for the believer! Elimelech, an Israelite, felt it necessary to leave the famine in Bethlehem for the land of Moab. Scripture indicates that his plan was just to sojourn in Moab. When one sojourns he desires to be a temporary resident in a place. The verses following reveal that Elimelech's family first continued in Moab (vs. 2), and then continued dwelling in Moab about ten more years (vs. 4).

It was a temporary famine that made Elimelech leave Bethlehem. Yet, his family did not leave Moab when death, disappointment, disease, disaster, and discouragement came to their home. Odd, isn't it? He left a famine in the land and ended up with a famine in his soul. When a man takes himself out of God's will, he will end up losing far more than he ever intended to give.

What would make a man leave the "House of Bread" (*Bethlehem*) in the "Land of Praise" (*Judah*) for the land of the incestuous son of Lot (*Moab*)? Who could make a man believe that bread in Moab would be better than a tough time in the Promised Land? The answer is simple - no one else but Satan!

Satan still convinces people that a sojourn in Moab is better than staying in God's will and watching God provide. Has your sojourn in Moab led you to continue dwelling there? Time in Moab saddens the heart, drains the soul, and skews the thinking. Even if you have to come back empty, find the prayer train out of Moab and come back to Bethlehem today.

Think about it . . .

My God is my King . . .

Ruth 1:2 *And the name of the man was Elimelech . . .*

Many times in our study of the Bible, we search for the meaning of people's names to help us identify their character. In the book of Ruth, one of the central figures is a man named Elimelech. Elimelech's parents chose a name for their child that meant, "My God is King." Each time their son heard his name he would have to contemplate that his name indicated his parent's desire for his life.

Yet, I notice a disparity between what his name meant and how he lived his life. The book of Ruth tells us that when a famine arose in the land, Elimelech, the one whose name means, "My God is King," departed for Moab.

We, as Christians, are named after our Saviour. We are to be like Him in our decisions, our determinations, and our declarations. What do we do when the spiritual drought time comes? Famines should never make us look toward Moab. Famines should never make us long for Moab. Famines should never make us leave for Moab. Pastor Charles Spurgeon said, "Better poverty with the people of God, than plenty outside of the covenanted land."

Our God is our King. Why would we go to sojourn in Moab? Elimelech faced a famine and went to sojourn in Moab. He said, "My God is King, but I am still going to sojourn in Moab!" Perhaps he went to Moab to look for provision, or prosperity, or a new promise. I remind you, dear reader, Elimelech found none of these things in Moab. He only found his death.

If your God is King, why not live in His place, with His people, under His promises? If God is your King, why seek to provide for yourself? If God is your King, why endanger and expose your family to life apart from God's will?

Think about it . . .

And she was left . . .

Ruth 1:3 *And Elimelech Naomi's husband died; and she was left, and her two sons.*

Death is an unannounced visitor to most homes. He comes and brings no housewarming present; but rather, he always takes far more than he brings. In our verse today, Death's visit has orphaned and widowed three people in Moab. These are three people who should not have been in Moab for any reason. Elimelech had let famine drive him from his home. His death has now left his family in Moab with only bitter memories.

Left alone to raise two sons in Moab - the very thought is overwhelming. Naomi faces the choice forced upon every widow, "What do I do now?" She makes her choice, not based upon her faith relationship, nor upon her family relationship, but seemingly upon her feelings. Naomi's feelings clearly influenced her decision.

One can almost hear the decision process in her mind: *"Well, my boys HAVE grown up in Moab; and my husband IS buried here. The boys are interested in a couple of girls here. What is left in Israel to which I can go back? It is a 67-mile trip; I am just not ready for that. There have been so many changes in my life; I just want to keep things normal right now. I believe I am going to stay."*

"And she was left . . . " says it all. Moab is not the Promised Land. Maybe a famine drove you into Moab; maybe a death has stranded you in Moab. If you find yourself in Moab, GET OUT!!! Under Satan's influence, Moab will continue to take from you and leave you empty. You say, "There is no way that I can get any more empty!"

Friend, if you read ahead, you will see that Moab will also take Naomi's two boys and a daughter-in-law. Though Moab can threaten to leave you alone and take everything from you, Moab cannot take away God's guiding hand. God's hand can bring you home again from Moab.

Think about it . . .

Taking wives from Moab . . .

Ruth 1:4 *And they took them wives of the women of Moab; the name of the one was Orpah, and the name of the other Ruth: and they dwelled there about ten years.*

There is a danger in thinking that our decisions to sin affect only ourselves. In the case of Elimelech, he didn't realize that when he moved to Moab, he gave his sons with the impression that if it was alright to move to Moab, it must be OK to marry Moabites.

Oh, how quickly personal standards will drop when we move from the place of God's will to the place of our choosing. All Israelites knew that they were not to marry anyone outside of the children of Israel. Why did Mahlon and Chilion choose to marry apart from God's law?

Clearly, the opportunity to sin came because they were living outside of God's will, as a result of their father's decision to move to Moab. Elimelech's sin of compromise by sojourning in Moab bred two sins of compromise in his sons: They sinned in their marriages and in maintaining a spiritual life in Moab.

Friend, you may be continuing in a sin that you have held onto for years thinking it only affects you. You are wrong. It WILL affect those around you too! Have you moved to Moab? Pack your bags today and move back into God's will. Did someone else bring you to Moab?

Move back into God's will, today! Moab will take you further, keep you longer, and cost you more than you ever planned.

Think about it . . .

Alone in Moab . . .

Ruth 1:5 *And Mahlon and Chilion died also both of them; and the woman was left of her two sons and her husband.*

There is no feeling of loneliness like the one following the death of a loved one. Our hearts grow accustomed to our loved ones always being with us. Parents anticipate watching their children grow; yet, they ache with loneliness when, they stand by the grave of a child, to whom they say "good-bye." True loneliness is felt when a husband or wife, who is determined to grow old with their companion, attends the funeral of their soul mate, they are left feeling like an appendage has been severed and they cannot stop the bleeding. When a child stands by the grave of a parent and bids "adieu," the ache of loneliness shudders their soul as the casket and the earth entomb the one who gave them counsel, comfort, and confidence.

Loneliness must have had its icy grip on the empty heart of Naomi. Was it possible for her to be wrung out any more? When she stood by the sandy graves of Moab, she must have felt an overwhelming sense of loneliness. When her husband died, she felt alone; yet, she did have the comfort of leaning upon her boys. However, now buried in the family's plot in Moab are her husband and her sons. She must have stared at the sand with loneliness as she buried her two boys. Mahlon and Chilion were two grown men whose deaths left two childless wives and a widowed mother.

Yes, loneliness moved into Naomi's heart and home like an unwelcome guest. She was left alone by the death of her family; however, the Heavenly Father had not left her alone. The next verse begins, "Then she arose . . . " The opening phrase certainly stands in contrast to this verse (v.5). Loneliness had extended its grip on her heart. Death had taken her husband and children, but she was determined that she would not be left alone in Moab.

Though loneliness may reach to grab your heart today, determine not to yield to his icy grip. You may be lonely, but isn't it time to move on?

Think about it . . .

Going home . . .

Ruth 1:6 *Then she arose with her daughters-in-law, that she might return from the country of Moab: for she had heard in the country of Moab how that the LORD had visited his people in giving them bread.*

Naomi, now widowed and coping with the loss of her two sons, determines that Moab will take nothing more from her. She left Bethlehem full, and is now leaving Moab empty. She has experienced emptiness in her home, her heart, and now also in her home going. She determined in her heart that her days would be better spent in Bethlehem.

Her determination was kindled when news out of Bethlehem indicated that God had visited His people in giving them bread. Moab was quite a distance from home (67 miles), but news from home has a way of finding its way to you when God sends the messenger. She heard news of bread. It would not be the bread that would bring her home, but rather, she would leave Moab because of the Baker.

The news reminded her of the
> Glory of the LORD. *"The LORD"*
> Grace of the LORD. *"Had visited"*
> Guardianship of the LORD. *"His people"*
> Goodness of the LORD. *"In giving them bread"*

How long has it been since His glory was revealed in your life? Are you living with an awareness of His grace? Have you wandered away from His guardianship? When was the last time that you sensed His goodness? Moab makes people forget how good home really was.

Dear reader, if you have made Moab your home, back in Bethlehem you will experience His glory, grace, guardianship, and goodness. There is one way to come back; it is found in the third word in the verse. Why don't you arise and get back?

Think about it . . .

The journey home . . .

Ruth 1:7 *Wherefore she went forth out of the place where she was, and her two daughters-in-law with her; and they went on the way to return unto the land of Judah.*

Sometimes, in Scripture, we are prone to bypass the biographical, historical, and geographical details in a verse in order to get to the bigger elements of the story. Our focus verse would be easy to overlook, but this verse makes me consider three things. It helps me consider Naomi's trials, her testimony, and her trip.

Consider with me Naomi's trials. *"Wherefore she went forth out of the place where she was"* The child of God would do well to note that no matter how far you have gone from God's will,

YOU CAN COME HOME! This thought should be both precious and pleasant to all readers. Moab had been a chain around the family of Elimelech, and the day Naomi walked out, that chain was broken. Your trials are never permanent; they end when you start to head home.

Then, contemplate Naomi's testimony. *"And her two daughters-in-law with her"* Naomi, though in Moab, must have lived a life of some spiritual value. She maintained enough of a testimony before her daughters-in-law that one of them converted to the true God. Her testimony was evident through the disappointments of Moab and the death of her husband and sons. Ruth saw enough light and truth in Naomi to come to the faith.

Now look at Naomi's trip. *". . . They went on the way to return unto the land of Judah."* Three women begin the journey home to Bethlehem. The 67 miles would be long, arduous, and heavy-hearted, however, though the conditions were adverse, the comfort would come in knowing that Naomi was headed home. Reader, never allow your trials to affect your testimony; you see, you are headed home!

Think about it . . .

Thank God for friendship . . .

Ruth 1:8 *And Naomi said unto her two daughters-in-law, Go, return each to her mother's house: the LORD deal kindly with you, as ye have dealt with the dead, and with me.*

The old preacher said to the younger preacher, "If in this life's course you are given five real friends, you will be most blessed." Truly, real friends are hard to find. Their value cannot be assessed with money. God is so good to allow us to make friends and be a friend.

Naomi had made friends with Ruth and Orpah. Ruth and Orpah were certain of one thing; Naomi had been kind to them in Moab. They had lost their husbands, yet, Naomi had lost both her husband AND her sons. There was a quality about Naomi that they appreciated, and the two responded with kindness. The widowed sisters-in-law, standing somewhere near Moab's border, paused to hear Naomi's words. What would she say to them?

Naomi looked at these two girls who had been through so much. They had lost their husbands and now did not know what to do. Ruth and Orpah, numb from their loss, contemplate heading to Bethlehem with Naomi. Their mother-in-law, aching with loneliness, turns and utters these words, "Go, return each to her mother's house: the LORD deal kindly with you, as ye have dealt with the dead, and with me."

Reader, you may be going through a hurt or a problem right now. Do not allow yourself to become so absorbed in your grief that you miss the treasure of your friends. You say, "I have no friends to tell my woes and worries to right now." Remember, *"There is a friend that sticketh closer than a brother."*

Think about it . . .

The hardship of goodbye . . .

Ruth 1: 9 *The LORD grant you that ye may find rest, each of you in the house of her husband. Then she kissed them; and they lifted up their voice, and wept.*

The type of ministry with which we, as a family, are involved, places upon us the necessity of saying goodbye every week to friends. Some of those friends we will get to see again in a matter of months or even a year. Yet, there are others we may not see again. Saying "Goodbye" is not our favorite thing to do; we would much rather only say "Hello."

Naomi, on her outward-bound journey from Moab, reaches a place where she knows that her daughters-in-law should return to their people, culture, gods, and ways. She bids farewell to her daughters-in-law. Her bidding farewell to them brought tears from the eyes and the heart. She kissed them and told them to go home.

The goodbye was sorrow-filled that day. Naomi wished God's best for their future as young widows. She bid them farewell and wished God's best for them to find peace in their hearts and at home. This peace and rest is something that Naomi had not had in a long time. This farewell was sorrowful, but she had days ahead in Bethlehem of many "Hellos."

Reader, you may have to say goodbye to a loved one or a lost one. Those goodbyes are never easy. Yet, we know that there will come a day where we will never say goodbye again. A day when we will only say "Hello!"

Think about it . . .

"Thy people" is not enough . . .

Ruth 1:10 *And they said unto her, Surely we will return with thee unto thy people.*

Ruth and Orpah were faced with a difficult decision. They had to choose either to go to Bethlehem with their deceased husband's mother, Naomi; or go home and live with their families. They were making the choice of Naomi's people or Moab's people. This difficult decision ultimately revealed their spiritual condition.

These two daughters will say, "We will return with thee unto thy people." Yet, we know only one daughter-in-law would go with Naomi. Orpah seemingly spoke the right words but saw it only as identification with Naomi's people. Yet, when Ruth spoke alone, she not only repeated what Orpah said, but expanded it and said, "Your God will be my God."

Many will make decisions to follow because of others, but they never finish the journey. Dear reader, making our decisions to follow God based solely on human relationships is not the right and lasting way. We must make our decisions to follow God based on our relationship to Him.

Why not be a Ruth kind of follower and follow God because of your relationship with Him and not your relationships to others.

Think about it . . .

Questions from a hurting heart . . .

Ruth 1:11 *And Naomi said, Turn again, my daughters: why will ye go with me? are there yet any more sons in my womb, that they may be your husbands?*

Sometimes the heart just hurts so badly, we misunderstand the deeds of others and can only see our own hurt. The daughters-in-law are struggling with empathetic emotions for Naomi. They know, in part, what she is going through. The girls are reaching out to Naomi with their statements of being willing to follow her home. They want to help Naomi.

Naomi is wrestling with her guilt of living in Moab apart from God's design. She told the girls to go home. She asked them why two young widow girls would want to come with her. She asked them if they thought she could bear any more children for them to have husbands according to God's law. Her questions reveal that her hurting heart felt so empty that she could not give fellowship, friendship, or a future to Ruth and Orpah.

Ruth and Orpah were not looking for what Naomi could provide for them. They were looking to be a balm to their mother-in-law's aching heart.

Do you have any friends with a hurting heart? Today, find a way to get to their side and let them know you have come, not to take, but to give your prayers and presence. Stand with your friend in this hour, for they need you more than they realize at this moment.

Friend, are you the one with the heart that aches? Your friends are not coming to hear your heart's guilt in having nothing to offer; But rather, they are coming to give you the friendship and fellowship you need.

Ponder this poetic thought . . .

> Friend, have you a hurt that runs so deep,
> that it's all that you can see?
> I, your companion, am here for you
> kneeling upon prayer-bent knee.
>
> I do not come for your provision,
> nor for your humble protection.
> I am come to be your friend
> and offer you my compassion.

John M. O'Malley

Think about it . . .

Looking at tomorrow . . .

Ruth 1:12 *Turn again, my daughters, go your way; for I am too old to have an husband. If I should say, I have hope, if I should have an husband also to night, and should also bear sons;*

Naomi knows her sin has cost her more than she ever thought she would have to pay. The guilt overwhelmed her as she spoke to Orpah and Ruth. She faced the surging tide of guilt due to her husband's name being extinguished. She held great empathy for Ruth's and Orpah's loss of their husbands.

She perhaps blamed herself for the loss of her three men, and now, her daughters-in-law potential separation from their families in Moab. She saw herself as too old to be able to secure a husband and bear children. She saw herself as going into her golden years not having grandchildren to hold and help along in life. Guilt certainly reigned in her heart.

This day was difficult. She contemplated her future in view of today's dilemmas. She saw herself as too old to have a husband; too old to have children; too far past hope to have hope for anything. Yet, today's dilemmas must not interpret the future. Today and tomorrow are both held in God's hand. Little did she know that 67 miles away was a place to live, a husband for Ruth, restoration of her husband's name, friends who would love her, and a grandson she would hold and nurse.

Are you guilty of governing your life with Naomi's nature? Do you interpret the future by today's dilemmas? I urge you to cease this fruitless, fearful, faithless way of living and look at today and the future as being in God's hand. He is able to make them work together for good!

Think about it . . .

The hand of the Lord is against me . . .

Ruth 1:13 *Would ye tarry for them till they were grown? would ye stay for them from having husbands? nay, my daughters; for it grieveth me much for your sakes that the hand of the LORD is gone out against me.*

Naomi looks at her girls, Ruth and Orpah. She sees the reasons they ought not follow her to Bethlehem. Naomi realizes that if she could provide sons to them, would they be willing to wait? Would the girls be willing to keep these boys from marrying any other? She saw the impossibilities and improbabilities and said, *"Nay, my daughters; for it grieveth me much for your sakes that the hand of the LORD is gone out against me."*

Naomi knew that her choice to stay in Moab cost her the death of her two sons. It was no small grief to her that the girls were being affected because of her errors. She viewed this as the Lord's hand being against her, and she saw how it affected them. Naomi is forcing the girls to consider the implications of coming with her. She gave them no bright prospects, only words of dismay.

Was the Lord's hand really against her? Did He not have her best interests at heart? Yes, His hand can be against us, but God is really for us. Remember God's disciplining hand is also His gracious hand.

Think about it . . .

They wept, again . . .

Ruth 1:14 *And they lifted up their voice, and wept again*

Agony has no fitting words. This mourning trio can only lift their voices and cry out. Their heartfelt expression, by custom and culture, was done by the repeated smiting of their hands on their breasts or on the tops of their heads while crying out in anguish. These sisters in suffering, struggles, and sorrow now weep from their hearts.

Oh, what a pitiful sight they must have been. Sorrow buried in the heart is, oftentimes, hard to relate to others in words. Orpah, Ruth, and Naomi pause to consider the emotional precipice of the moment. This mournful day will be long remembered by all involved.

Our trio wept as they realized they were leaving their memories and mates buried in the sands of Moab. They wept again, when thoughts of being homeless, husbandless, and hopeless entered their sphere of thinking. The phrase that captures my focus is, "They wept, again" The three were not hindered by the fact that a few moments earlier they had just wept.

I know it would be easy to discount the continual weeping because the three were women. Weeping, and weeping again, is not an exclusive right of women. Men must learn that tears can be the words that speak the hurts of their heart.

When sorrow visits, and then visits again the homes of our friends, remember a child of God is commanded to " . . . *weep with them that weep.*" (Romans 12:15)

Are you doing your job?

Think about it . . .

The moment of decision

Ruth 1:14 . . . *and Orpah kissed her mother-in-law; but Ruth clave unto her.*

The personal decision to depart from Moab had stirred the hearts of Orpah and Ruth. They had by the rules of compassion, custom, and culture, escorted Naomi to the border of Moab. Naomi had encouraged these girls to go home. Naomi reminded them of their mothers and fathers; she spoke of the peace and rest they would have by being home. Naomi prayed the Lord's blessings on her daughters-in-law because they had been kind to her. Naomi urged them to go away from her dark cloud of judgment from God.

Orpah and Ruth each had to make a decision. Do we go with Naomi and face uncertainty with her in Bethlehem; or do we stay home with our people? If this were solely a legal decision, then they would be free from HAVING to go to Bethlehem. If this were an emotional decision, then they were choosing between returning home to Dad and Mom and going with Naomi, the sole connection to their deceased husbands. If this were a financial decision, they were choosing between a hard life in Moab and a hard life in Bethlehem.

This decision was not an emotional, financial, or a legal issue on which to deliberate. This moment was a spiritual moment, with an invitation to make a decision. "Do I choose the ways of Jehovah or refuse them altogether?" This was the question to answer.

Reader, are you at a similar place of decision? Your response is either to kiss or cleave. Once and for all, why not forsake Moab's ways and cleave to the truth of God's Word? Those who try to play in Moab and worship in Bethlehem, fail.

Think about it . . .

Gone back . . .

Ruth 1:15 *And she said, Behold, thy sister-in-law is gone back unto her people, and unto her gods: return thou after thy sister-in-law.*

Naomi and Ruth stand as a pair in misery watching Orpah return to Moab; the moment is overwhelming. Discouragement's trio has become a duet; the remaining pair watching Orpah's departure in agony. Naomi said to Ruth, "Behold, thy sister-in-law is gone back." Naomi encourages Ruth to do as Orpah and just go to her home.

Orpah went back to Moab's people, principles, and priorities. She left the ways she had been around for more than ten years. Orpah determined that she would be more comfortable with the ways she once knew, than to really convert to another way.

Today, there are some people who are like Orpah. They once stood with God's people in righteousness and truth. They used to sing the songs, pray the prayers, walk the walk, and talk the talk; and now they are gone. When the Orpahs depart, it has an affect on the remaining people.

The message of this verse does not solely rest in Orpah's departure to Moab, but rather in Ruth's decision to stay with Naomi and go to Bethlehem. Sometimes the departure of an Orpah forces us to a place of personal decision about our own "stick ability." However, we must remember this one principle; never permit the departure of an Orpah to affect you.

Think about it . . .

"And Ruth said . . ."

Ruth 1:16 *And Ruth said . . .*

Naomi's testimony in Moab was on display for her family and friends there. Though both girls viewed Naomi's testimony, only one was drawn to the Lord. Every day in Moab, Ruth and Orpah watched Naomi's devotion, dedication, and decisions. Each daughter-in-law made up her own mind about the God of the Hebrews as portrayed by Naomi.

These girls had only known Moab's idols and gods. Yet, on the trip out of Moab, one girl had seen and heard enough about God that she was convicted of her own nature and converted to Israel's God. When I read Ruth's testimony, I am convinced of these six things.

Naomi's testimony drew Ruth
    to her heart. vs. 16 *"entreat me"*
    to her hope. vs. 16 *"goest"*
    to her homeland. vs. 16 *"lodgest"*
    to her home folk. vs. 16 *"people"*
    to Him. vs. 16 *"God"*
    to Heaven. vs. 17 *"diest"*

Each believer sojourning here in Moab (*the world*) must be aware of his testimony before the lost and the Lord's people. What would someone say of your testimony on this earth? The world watches your actions and reactions as you sojourn here. Your life is a reflection of the God in whom you say you believe. Will people convert to God because of your testimony?

Think about it . . .

Here to stay . . .

Ruth 1:16-17 *And Ruth said, Entreat me not to leave thee, or to return from following after thee: for whither thou goest, I will go; and where thou lodgest, I will lodge: thy people shall be my people, and thy God my God: Where thou diest, will I die, and there will I be buried: the LORD do so to me, and more also, if ought but death part thee and me.*

Ruth begins the testimony that marks her conversion to Israel's one true God. On two recorded occasions her mother-in-law has told her to go home to her culture, gods, and people. Naomi thought Ruth's desire was emotional, not spiritual. However, unbeknownst to Naomi, the convicting power of God was at work in Ruth's heart.

Ruth made it completely clear to Naomi, "Don't ask me to leave anymore; I am here to stay. The gods of Moab cannot draw me back; I am here to stay. The culture of my people cannot draw me back; I am here to stay. The friends I once had cannot draw me back; I am here to stay."

Ruth knew her conversion had to come with conviction. She had a conviction to the way, words, and will of the one true God. Remember, her decision was not made in the comfort of Bethlehem, but rather in the deserts of Moab. She determined in the hard place that she would live for the one true God and Him alone.

Dear reader, you should notice Ruth's conviction to stand on God's will, words, and ways and compare them to the believers of today. It seems we have fewer 'Ruth' believers today than ever. We have many who trek between Bethlehem and Moab with only a conviction to yield to the will of self. We even have believers who have moved within Moab's borders. These same believers spend their time convincing anyone who will listen to them that it is OK to be a spiritual drifter.

Today, we need believers who will say, "Don't ask me to leave any more; I am here to stay!"

Think about it . . .

Drawn to your heart . . .

Ruth 1:16-17 *And Ruth said, Entreat me not to leave thee, or to return from following after thee . . .*"

Ruth spoke of 6 things to which she was drawn because of Naomi. Consider the first comment: *"Entreat me not to leave thee or to return from following after thee."* It was as if Ruth was telling Naomi, "Your testimony has drawn me to your heart."

The companionship and compassion of Naomi had become very precious to Ruth. Ruth did not want their hearts to become separated. She wanted no emotional, physical, or spiritual separation between them now.

Clearly, she thought that since the days of Moab were ending and the return to the Promised Land was their next step, she wanted to be there. Their hearts, once melded together by disappointment, death and disaster, now were melded together because of faith's fellowship.

How about the 'Ruths' whom God has placed around you? Are they drawn to your heart? Has your Christian walk been consistent enough for them to receive a clear signal of your testimony?

Covenant with the Lord today that you will make the effort needed to send a strong signal of salvation's message at the next encounter God provides you.

Think about it . . .

Drawn to your hope . . .

Ruth 1:16 *For whither thou goest, I will go . . .*

Hope is the sole possession of Naomi. She no longer has a husband; death came and took him. She no longer has her sons, for death visited her home and took them. She is down to one daughter-in-law after the departure of Orpah. She will leave gravesites and grief in Moab. She seemingly is both empty-handed and empty-hearted.

How can hope be her sole possession, you say? Her circumstances and conditions indicate on the barometer of hope that a storm is here. Yet, you must recall that she had heard in Bethlehem that the Lord had visited His people once again with bread.

You may say, "It must be a very special bread to make her walk 67 miles home." No, my friend, she is not headed home for the bread, but rather for the Baker of the bread. Hope has been kindled in her heart once again.

Ruth catches a glimmer in Naomi's hope-filled eye and states, "Wherever you are going, I want to go. Your hope in the Bread-giver is the kind of life I want."

I wonder about us. Do many people see the hope of eternal life in our eyes or only the despair of the moment? Do many people see the hope of an ever-present help in our time of need or only the helplessness of our current crisis? I dare say, my friend, let the hope be seen.

The inhabitants of this hopeless world need to see people who have hope. How this hope would attract people to our Saviour!

Think about it . . .

Drawn to your homeland . . .

Ruth 1:16 *And Ruth said, . . . and where thou lodgest, I will lodge . . .*

Home. For most people the very word stirs hearts and elicits a warm feeling within the bosom. During the Christmas holidays, a friend called me in the middle of unwrapping presents and heard such laughter and rejoicing as my four siblings and their spouses and children opened gifts. He asked me, "Can I come over?" He was content and enjoying the day with his own family, yet, when he heard the thrill and joy in my "homeland," he asked to be a part.

Naomi must have had many a conversation about the Promised Land in Ruth's presence. Perhaps it was the stories of a land that flowed with milk and honey. Maybe it was the account of the grapes of Eshcol that grew so large in their clusters that two men would have to carry them. Was it the incidents of days when seas parted and rivers stood on end to allow God's people to move about? No matter the specific occasion, clearly Naomi had spoken enough about home that Ruth determined that she wanted to lodge wherever Naomi lodged.

What would happen if we began to speak more about our home in Heaven? What if we told of streets of gold, or gates of pearl, or even of a place where sorrow, death and tears are never present and will never be allowed access? What if we told of a land of rest and reunion that never ends? What if our conversation included tidbits of Heaven? You know, if it did, perhaps our testimony would draw people to our homeland. Remember, we are merely strangers, aliens, and pilgrims on this earth; our homeland is just beyond the veil of this life.

Think about it . . .

Drawn to your home folk . . .

Ruth 1:16 *And Ruth said, . . . thy people shall be my people . . .*

Ruth's testimony of her conversion included an interesting phrase. She told Naomi, "I want to be a part of your people." Certainly, Ruth had been listening to the last ten years of Naomi's conversation about her people. This phrase demands an investigation into the content and tone of Naomi's conversation about her home folk.

Ruth's statement includes two apparent thoughts. First, Naomi maintained a distinction from being a Moabite. No matter how long she spent in Moab, she never became a Moabite. We note this from Ruth's confession that said "thy people." Secondly, it is critical to note that though Naomi knew "all the dirt" on the home folk, she spent her time speaking of a people that were different because of their God, not because of their idiosyncrasies. Not one word that Naomi spoke during Ruth's ten years of listening drove Ruth from God, but rather drew Ruth to God's people.

Ruth wanted to meet a people who had God to fight their battles for them. She wanted to meet the people that had provision made for them in the wilderness and in famines. She wanted to meet the people who had escaped Egypt, marched around walls, and seen miracles in battle. She wanted to become one of those people.

How are you doing when it comes to your conversations about the people of God in your church? Have your conversations drifted to cynical, sarcastic, and shadowy gossip? Will this draw your lost family members to Christ? I think not! Let us maintain a standard in our conversations that is biblical. (Phil. 1:27; 1 Pet. 2:12)

Think about it . . .

Drawn to Him . . .

Ruth 1:16 *And Ruth said, . . . and thy God my God.*

The testimony of Naomi's life in Moab had drawn Ruth to her heart, hope, homeland, and home folk. Now Ruth stands at the exit from Moab and the entrance to the Promised Land and says, "Your testimony has drawn me to Him. The gods of Moab are nothing and have no hold on me."

Ruth indicated, "I have heard about His passion for His people. I have heard about His power for His people. I have heard about His provision for His people. I have heard about His pardon of His people. Naomi, your testimony has drawn me to Him. You have spoken so much about God; I want Him to be my God."

Growing up as a little girl , all Ruth had known were the gods of Moab. Those gods were lifeless, man-made objects, deified by Moabites. Now having heard of the one true and living God, she declares, "Naomi, your testimony has drawn me to Him."

Dear reader, do you have a testimony in Moab? How are you doing in making Jesus known in Moab? Have you become so self-absorbed that you are telling others of your woes, worries, and wants and are no longer speaking of the wonders of Calvary? Have you become so intoxicated on your own problems that your testimony is virtually silenced? I urge you today, break out of this pattern and look around you at the Moabites who are your neighbors. Go find one and declare to him the wonders of the Christ of Calvary.

God's mercy reaches Moab. Why not tell a Moabite today?

Think about it . . .

Drawn to Heaven . . .

Ruth 1:17 *Where thou diest, will I die, and there will I be buried.*

The statement must have resounded in Naomi's ears. "Wherever you die, that is where I want to be buried." Ruth had just stated the intentions of her faith. She had heard so much about God and His people that she told Naomi, "I just bought a one-way ticket and I am here for the duration."

Where would Naomi die? Does a believer in God ever die??? NO!!! We who believe in Him will never die! (John 11:26) Ruth's soul had been drawn to Heaven by one who lived in Moab but never let Moab live in her soul.

It was as if Ruth was saying, "Naomi, I want your leaving place to be my leaving place." Ruth wanted Naomi's launching place of death to be her launching place. Ruth wanted Naomi's landing place in Heaven to be her landing place.

Death is a leaving place for the believer. Like Ruth left Moab, death will let us leave the Moab of earth. Death for the believer is a launching place. When a believer dies, they launch out of this world without the help of NASA. Death for the believer means that the landing place is Heaven. Oh, don't you want to go?

Dear reader, these last few devotions have dealt with a testimony in Moab. How is your testimony? When last did a Moabite come up to you and say, "Wherever you are going when you die, that's where I want to go?"

Think about it . . .

Knocked out of the race . . .

Ruth 1:17 . . . *The LORD do so to me, and more also, if ought but death part thee and me.*

Several years ago, an Olympic runner was knocked down in his race. The crowd gasped as his hopes for winning were crushed. The crowd of runners all passed him by, but he determined to get up and finish. Certainly he would have been justified to get out of the race, because he would not WIN the race. Truly, he would not win, but that runner ran on because his determination was to FINISH the race he started.

In our passage, Ruth is beginning her race as a believer. Obstacles and obstructions certainly were before her. So, she concluded with determination that she was entering the race to finish. She determined that day, that she would finish her course.

She stated this with the strongest declaration she could make. Ruth said that nothing short of death would knock her out of the race. She went on to declare that she wanted God to give her worse than death, if she ever dropped out from this fellowship between herself and the only other believer she knew, Naomi.

The point is clear. Many of you are in a church, a local congregation and fellowship of believers. (*If you are not a member of a Bible-believing, local church, you should hang your head in shame; for your pride seems to be a stronger edict than God's Word.*) Setbacks, sufferings, and sin will take place in your walk with the Lord. I wonder what would it take to get you to quit His church?

There are those who have quit church because of the unfriendliness of believers. Others have quit church because of embarrassment over children or spouses. Even some believers have quit church because a high standard for personal holiness was upheld. I know of some who quit church because they didn't get their way in God's house. (*This has always perplexed me. Since it is God's house, shouldn't He get His way?*)

What would it take to make you drop out of church? Ruth knew when she started the race that it would be a race worth finishing. Have you made up your mind, like Ruth, to run and not drop out?

Think about it . . .

Steadfastly minded . . .

Ruth 1:18 *When she saw that she was steadfastly minded to go with her, then she left speaking unto her.*

The scene must have been incredible. Ruth broke her recorded silence with her profession of faith. This must have sent a clear signal to Naomi that Ruth was a genuine convert. Ruth's conversion silenced Naomi's insistence that Ruth go back to Moab.

You see, bitterness of the soul allows no rejoicing over the conversion of sinners. Naomi had not recognized that the sovereign hand of God was at work in her life. God had spared one from Moab's sinful grip, and yet, she still could not see God's almighty hand had been VERY good to her. This happens to many a believer. They think that all is lost and life is over; yet, God is NEVER bound by the circumstances of our lives.

Ruth, though a new convert, certainly had the mind of the apostle Paul. Paul stood before the brethren of Caesarea and they saw Paul could not be persuaded. Ruth, too, exhibited the proper mindset for a believer. This should serve as a call to steadfastness though our journey is long, though the way threatens to be hard, and though the future is not clear. Ruth clearly was steadfastly minded in her word, walk, and work. Are you?

Think about it . . .

Redemption in Bethlehem . . .

Ruth 1:19 *So they two went until they came to Bethlehem . . .*

The journey home finally begins. This journey had been in God's plan since before the day Elimelech's family left Bethlehem more than 10 years earlier. Naomi's strides toward Bethlehem are sure and steady. Heaviness and hope mark each footprint on this 67-mile journey. Their journey to Bethlehem should give a student of the Word of God much to contemplate.

Scripture indicates Bethlehem has certainly been a place where God has sought to conduct His divine work of redemption. On no less than three directly related occasions in Scripture, God has established his interest and wrought redemption in this tiny town of Bethlehem. The trip of Naomi and Ruth would be the first of three redemption journeys detailed in Scripture.

God began this trilogy with the redemption of a Moabitish girl named Ruth. He would use a man named Boaz who would stand in Bethlehem's gate and declare his intention of being the Kinsman Redeemer to Elimelech's name and Mahlon's widow. This redemption restored the birth line of the Messiah. The second incident of God's redemption in Bethlehem occurs in 1 Samuel 16:1. Saul, the King of Israel, has had his leadership terminated by God because of his pride. Samuel, the prophet, is told by God to go to Bethlehem and find David, the great-grandson of Ruth, the redeemed Moabitess. God sought on this trip of redemption, not the redemption of an individual, but rather the redemption of a nation, Israel.

The third occasion in the trilogy of God's redemption in Bethlehem occurs with a relative of David, the great-grandson of Ruth, the redeemed Moabitess. It will be about 14 generations later, and God will take an unlikely couple and send them to Bethlehem for the third episode of redemption in Bethlehem. They get to Bethlehem, and Mary gives birth to Jesus her first-born son, not of Joseph, but of the Holy Ghost.

Joseph and Mary's trek to Bethlehem was not for the redemption of an individual, nor for the redemption of a nation, but for the redemption of the world. Angels would herald to shepherds the good news, which was for ALL people. This good news was a Saviour born for the world. Yes, this would be the last of Bethlehem's involvement in God's plan of redemption. Bethlehem's story of God's redemption must be told and re-told. When last did you tell it?

Think about it . . .

Remembered in Bethlehem . . .

Ruth 1:19 . . . *And it came to pass, when they were come to Bethlehem, that all the city was moved about them, and they said, Is this Naomi?*

More than ten years had passed since Elimelech and his family left Bethlehem during a famine. Though a quartet left, only a duet returned. The townspeople were all abuzz with excitement and questions. "Is this Naomi?" was their chief question. The questions abounded and the answers were difficult, but her answer should have been, "YES, this is Naomi!"

She was not the same woman that had left this humble town. Naomi, who once was the wife of a mighty man of great wealth, is now the humble widow. What once all made sense to Naomi, now was confusing, as she reckoned that the Almighty had dealt bitterly with her. Yet the question, "Is this Naomi?" should have a lasting effect on the reader of God's Word. The effect namely is, the people of Bethlehem had long remembered Naomi as the one whose name and nature were pleasant.

How about your sojourn on this earth? The people you've met during the varied stages of your life; how do they remember your nature? Were you faithful and friendly? Were you a blessing or a burden? Were you a help or a hindrance? Though the testimony we have in the present is vital, the testimony we leave still speaks of us.

Having read this part of the verse, let us make sure the testimony we are leaving and the testimony we have left behind are both pleasing to the Lord.

Think about it . . .

"When sorrows like sea billows roll . . ."

Ruth 1:20 *And she said unto them, Call me not Naomi, call me Mara: . . .*

Naomi, whose name means "pleasant", has ended her 67-mile journey. The home folk are stirring about her and calling out to her. Naomi's very name seemed to haunt her. She blurted out an answer to those who called to her, "Naomi, is that you?" The question, oft repeated, began to haunt her empty soul. Her very name stood in contrast to her present feelings. Clearly, Naomi is drowning in a sea of personal crisis and agony.

She replies to her questioners with this mournful sentence; "Call me not Naomi, call me Mara: for the Almighty hath dealt very bitterly with me." This statement indicates to us that she was a woman self-absorbed in her misery. Had the Almighty dealt very bitterly with her? Is Naomi facing the consequences of her sinful choices since her husband died? Was she facing the providential hand of God as He orchestrated events to lead her in making the right choices in her life? Was it that she was blaming God for all that went wrong in her life?

Spafford, the hymn writer, penned these words after his own difficult experience in the song, "It Is Well With My Soul." He wrote "When peace, like a river, attendeth my way, When sorrows like sea billows roll; Whatever my lot, Thou hast taught me to say, It is well, it is well with my soul."

What do you say when the sorrows of your life seem to roll like the waves of the sea? Have you learned the Lord's lesson for Horatio Spafford in the sorrows that attend your way? Do you say in sorrow, "It is well with my soul?"

Dear reader, remember, your name is 'Christian', not 'bitter-one'. Let it not stand in contrast to the way you feel inside during each crisis.

Think about it . . .

The unjust accusation . . .

Ruth 1:20 . . . *for the Almighty hath dealt very bitterly with me.*

These words crossed the lips of Naomi in her bitter state of mind. The God of Israel now stands accused in the courtroom of Naomi's mind and soul. She hurled the unjust accusation toward Heaven in front of the spectators in Bethlehem. Eternity's witnesses had not been called to offer testimony; it was just one accuser who assessed the course of her life and said, "The Almighty hath dealt very bitterly with me."

Had she really meant what she said about Jehovah God? Were these just the words of a 10-year struggle with her decision to remain in Moab after her husband's death? Were these the words of a woman embarrassed by her situation in front of her home folk? Did she really believe that the Almighty had been dealing with her in a very bitter way?

It would be easy to judge her, but the careful reader would note that the end of the story reveals that God HAD been very gracious to her, to allow her to have her husband's and son's names restored, a grandchild to be born, and to have security in her old age. Did these hastily spoken words influence her family for generations to come? I would remind you of the words of her great-great-grandson; "*I have been young, and now am old; yet, have I not seen the righteous forsaken, nor his seed begging bread.*"

Believers, in times of trial, we may have occasionally repeated Naomi's unjust accusation toward God. Please remember, God will ALWAYS do the most gracious thing for His children. Before we say, "Shame on Naomi for her accusation," consider the times you have said the same thing.

Think about it . . .

It's all about me . . .

Ruth 1:20 . . . *why then call ye me Naomi, seeing the LORD hath testified against me, and the Almighty hath afflicted me?*

Naomi stands before her own people and seemingly cannot bear to hear her own name. This one, whose name meant "pleasant" or "delightsome", stood before her own people and said, "Call me not Naomi, but Mara."

The evidence she offers for this identity change is two-fold. She explained the God of Israel, Jehovah, had testified against her. The second reason offered is that El-Shaddai, The Almighty God, had afflicted her. Afflicted by the Almighty and testified against by Jehovah. Were these two factors enough to justify her renaming herself from Naomi to Mara?

God had brought her home again, but she could not yet, see the blessing of His providence. Presently, she could only see the hurts, hard times, and seeming hopelessness. She simply saw the burden of her punishment; however, as it usually is with God, the best was yet, to come. Her days of restored blessings were just around the corner.

Naomi did as most of us do. We believe that correction surely must make us unloved by God, and therefore, we should be unloved by all. However, God's correction is not solely an indication of His wrath, but rather an indication of His love. If He did not correct us, we would be classified as illegitimate children.

Instead of walking around mumbling the plaintive words of the song, "Its all about me," why not walk around determined and certain that, "Its all about Thee!"

Think about it . . .

Sin's effect on the believer . . .

Ruth 1:21 *I went out full, and the LORD hath brought me home again empty . . .*

Naomi reveals to us, in her answer to the townspeople's questions, the lessons she learned from her time in Moab. These lessons become our examples for today. When a careful look is made of Naomi's answer one can see four valuable life-lessons resulting from making "Moab mistakes."

Ruth recognized that confessed sin reveals God's forgiveness. Consider the words "I went out," and the counter phrase, "The Lord brought." Naomi saw her error in leaving the protection and provision of Bethlehem. She saw that, though she walked out, it was God who brought her home again. Friend, you may have left the place of God's will for your life. No matter how far you have gone, upon the recognition of your error, God can bring you back.

Ruth recognized that sin removes God's fellowship. Look carefully for the words that signal this lesson. Do you see the words "out" and "home"? She knew that sin had placed her on the outside of God's will for her life. She saw that Bethlehem was home. She knew that by coming back home, her broken fellowship would be restored. Sinful choices that take us to Moab will always break our fellowship with God.

Ruth further recognized that sin robs God's fruitfulness. Consider the words, "full" and "empty." Though Elimelech and she left Bethlehem in a famine, she now saw herself as having left there full. Surely she noticed that the townspeople who had remained to cope during the famine had come through it. They were better off now than she and Ruth. Naomi now declares herself as bankrupt because of her sinful departure from God's will. She learned that Moab never makes you richer, only poorer!

Lastly, Ruth recognized that confessed sin reveals God's faithfulness. Consider the remaining word in this phrase, "again." Do you remember, in verse 5, Naomi had heard how God had visited his people again, and she began her trip home? God allowed Naomi to come home AGAIN, after she learned her lesson in Moab. God revealed his faithfulness in permitting her to come home, again. John would later write in his epistle the lesson Naomi had just learned *"He IS faithful and just to forgive us our sins . . . "* AND to let us come home AGAIN!

Think about it . . . and come home!

Return to sender . . .

Ruth 1:22 *So Naomi returned, and Ruth the Moabitess, her daughter-in-law, with her, which returned out of the country of Moab . . .*

The letter from the post office arrived. On its envelope was marked, "Return to sender – undeliverable as addressed." A long time had passed since its sender had posted it. In fact, the envelope resembled one sent years ago by the sender. Though it has picked up a few markings along the way, it has made its way back home. The postal service had not found a place to deliver the piece, so they just sent it back with one phrase, "Return to sender – undeliverable as addressed." It was the postal service's way of indicating; "This piece does not belong here, so we are sending it back from whence it came."

This simple illustration helps us understand Ruth 1:22. More than 10 years before, Elimelech "sent" his family to Moab. Now after these many years, the Holy Spirit of God stamped Naomi's life with a message, "Return to sender – undeliverable as addressed." There was no place for Naomi in Moab. She and her kin belonged in Bethlehem. God canceled the self-delivery attempts of Elimelech and Naomi in Moab and put

Naomi on the mail route of forgiveness that made deliveries to Bethlehem.

Like the returned letter, Naomi had the markings of her journey. These markings she bore on her brow and in her heart. Yet, upon her return, we can identify the marks of God's grace. She had been "Returned to Sender" not placed in the dead mail pile. She had been received by the home folk, not rejected. The company she had brought with her from Moab had comforted her loneliness and rejection on this journey home. Yes, God had been so good to her. Naomi's trip home began when she came to herself and wanted to get back to Bethlehem.

You may have tried to deliver yourself to a place down in Moab. This is not where you belong. The day you come to yourself, God will place you on the mail route of forgiveness and send you home. Weary travelers come home! There is NO place for you in Moab!

Think about it . . .

Three funerals and a wedding . . .

Ruth 1:22 . . .*and they came to Bethlehem in the beginning of barley harvest.*

So much has happened in the lives of these two women in the past ten years. Travelers who passed these two women might have remarked as to the oddity of seeing two women traveling alone. Others may have queried amongst themselves as to why two widows would be traveling.

No one person could aptly tell their story just from glancing at this traveling couple. The sorrow that was entombed in their hearts, the agony of disappointment that etched their faces, and the defeat that might have affected their posture, all played a role in the journey home.

They completed their 67 miles of reminiscing and replaying the videos from their library of memories. Their arrival in town is marked by the comments of the townspeople and the much-awaited beginning of the barley harvest.

The latter half of this verse is marked by two elements worthy of comment. Note the first element pertains to the words "and they." This is reminiscent of verse two of this same chapter. " . . . And they came into the country of Moab . . ." The 'they' is different this time. It is comprised of a Jewish mother-in-law with her recently converted Moabite daughter-in-law. Naomi did not leave Moab alone; God saved a Moabite girl who would be used to bear a child in the line of her deceased father-in-law. This child would be grandfather to David, King of Israel, and in the earthly line of Jesus Christ. The words "and they" reveal and confirm the promise God made to Abraham back in Genesis 12 and reaffirmed to Jacob's sons. (Genesis 49:10)

The second element is found in the time of their arrival. God is bringing two strangers together and it would be set against the backdrop of the barley harvest. Outside of town, in the barley fields they passed; they did not know that God had the barley, growing in Boaz's field, waving its welcome to Ruth and Naomi. Ruth saw in the barley a potential occupation and provision for immediate needs, but God had a different plan.

You see, their story is more than just a tale of three funerals. This would be the story of three funerals and a wedding. You may be facing difficult days. You may now only see the difficult and the disappointing, but remember God's timing is precise, perfect, and providential.

Think about it . . .

Bounty in Bethlehem . . .

Ruth 2:1 *And Naomi had . . .*

The book of Ruth in its first chapter stands in sharp contrast to chapter two. The disciplined reader of chapter one could recall the many things Naomi did not have. Naomi had no living husband. Naomi had no sons. Naomi no longer had two daughters-in-law with her. Naomi had no grandchildren. Naomi had no future of a family. Naomi had no way to restore the family name.

If you asked Naomi what she had when she was in Moab after ten years, she would reveal that she had nothing! Naomi had no wealth. Naomi had no place to call home. Naomi had no happiness, joy or mirth.

Yet, the verse begins, "And Naomi had . . ." What a precious thought! In Moab, she had nothing. In Bethlehem, she had something. In Moab, she had no-one. In Bethlehem, she had someone. Although Naomi left Moab with empty hands and an empty heart, when Naomi arrived in Bethlehem, the Scriptures show that she possessed some things.

God gave Naomi a kinsman. God gave Naomi a kinsman on her husband's side. God gave Naomi a kinsman who was wealthy. God gave Naomi a kinsman who was powerful. God gave Naomi a daughter-in-law who came with her. God had Naomi to come home at the time of barley harvest. Naomi had God, who cared enough for her well-being that He sought her out to bring her home after ten years of emptiness.

Consider this, my friend, in God's will she had provision, promise, and protection. Outside of God's will, there were things that she lacked. It would be wise if we would all settle on doing God's will in our lives. Doing His will assures us of having exactly what He wants us to have. Are you doing God's will?

Think about it . . .

A widow's portion . . .

Ruth 2:1 *And Naomi had a kinsman of her husband's, a mighty man of wealth, of the family of Elimelech; and his name was Boaz.*

Naomi had spent quite a bit of time in Moab. Life there had been hard and full of hurtful memories. She could not go out to her husband's grave and reminisce over their unfulfilled dreams. Even seeing his name on the tombstone in Moab seemed to be contradictory. "Elimelech," one whose name meant, "My God is King," was buried beneath the sands of Moab amongst a people who cared little for the ways of God or His kingdom.

Naomi would not be able to see the graves of her two boys, for they too were entombed in Moab. Each grave marker stood as a memorial to those who died outside of God's will. Though painful, she believed this would be her portion in life. She had even confessed that she believed the Almighty had dealt bitterly with her.

Yet now, with the dawning of her first days in Bethlehem, we see God has provided the widow a portion of His grace. Elimelech's name would be restored and the line of Christ secured. Naomi's portion from God has a name; his name is Boaz. Boaz is a man of renown, riches, and redemption. He will meet her every need. What Naomi believed was lost, Boaz will redeem.

As God had a portion for Naomi, so God has a portion for you. Jeremiah wrote in the third chapter of Lamentations, "The Lord is my portion." Would to God, we could learn to stay in God's will and fix our wants and have our contentment in Him. God's portion for us is always best.

Think about it . . .

It's in the past . . .

Ruth 2:2 *And Ruth the Moabitess . . .*

Initially, Ruth carried a moniker, "The Moabitess." No, it is neither a fancy title nor a glamorous position; it is nondescript in both its hearing and its reading. Yet, the townspeople carelessly and callously referred to her as "Ruth, the Moabitess."

"You know she is not from around here! She is a Moabite and you know how they are! She is probably here just to get bread and whatever else she can. I have seen these kind come and go. I am just going to stand back and watch this one!"

"Moabitess" – the name seemed to stick for a while; however, in Ruth's heart she knew that she came to Bethlehem for a brand new start. Still, the people referred to her as "the Moabite woman." I wonder if, in Ruth's heart, she pondered,

"I have converted to the Jewish faith. I declared my spiritual intentions on Israel's border. Why must they identify me with my past and not my present?"

In our churches, we show the same tendency as those of Bethlehem. We are so quick to cast a cloud of doubt over a new believer's salvation. I have seen church members struggle with the decision of a lost soul needing salvation, all because they knew that person's past. I have seen church members keep a new convert at arm's length, all because they knew the details of that person's background.

My friends, let us not forget that God was willing to accept our past and our conversion and will NEVER bring it up again. Why don't we apply God's standard to our pride-filled ways and accept every convert in the way God does? *But God commendeth his love toward us, in that, while we were yet sinners, Christ died for us.* Romans 5:8.

Think about it . . .

Seeking what lacked . . .

Ruth 2:2 *And Ruth the Moabitess said unto Naomi, Let me now go to the field, and glean ears of corn after him in whose sight I shall find grace . . .*

As the reality of the moment settled in, Ruth knew she would need to find substance for both Naomi and herself to live. Bethlehem was now their home. Certainly, Naomi had discipled Ruth in the laws of God in order for her to know about the corners of the land being left for the widows, strangers and the poor to glean. By birth, Ruth was a stranger; by marriage, she was a widow; and by financial standards, she was poor. Ruth had full intentions of going to glean in the corners of a field to find the provision that the God of Israel had ordered to be left for people such as herself.

Certainly, this must have been a comfort to her. The gods of Moab had never made provision for her family back in Moab. Ruth knew the gods of Moab were merely lifeless images that left a vacuum in the hearts of their worshippers. Indeed, the knowledge of the living God's provision brought her security, stability, and safety.

Ruth stated that she was going to seek three things in a benefactor's sight. She was seeking permission to glean in his field, she was seeking provision in his field, and Ruth was seeking pardon for once being a Moabite. Ruth knew that only a limited number of widows could glean in a field: she knew that there was only so a small portion to glean in each field. Ruth knew that the days would be long, but she left with the hope of finding pardon, permission, and provision in a benefactor.

Any, who have been saved from sin, will remember when they needed an Eternal Benefactor. Being born in sin and living in their sinful way, like Ruth, they too needed pardon from their past, permission to have access to Him, and provision for their future.

Oh, the grace of our Benefactor, Jesus Christ, Who granted pardon, permission, and provision through His death, burial, and resurrection. Reader, have you converted to Christianity? Have you not found Him to be all of this and more?

Why not pause right now and thank God, our eternal Benefactor for His goodness in making a way for you?

Think about it . . .

Words of comfort . . .

Ruth 2:2 *And she said unto her, Go, my daughter.*

"Go, My Daughter." Oh, how these words must have sounded to Ruth! Naomi spoke words to Ruth's ears, but Ruth heard them with her heart. Naomi had to have been close to Ruth, as well as Ruth to Naomi. When Ruth sought to go find provision, Naomi responded with three words of comfort. Ruth heard these words and they became words of release, reassurance, and relationship.

Naomi began with the word, "Go." Ruth had promised on Moab's border, the border between hope and hopelessness, that she would not leave Naomi. Yet, she must leave her at home while she finds provision in the fields. The promise Ruth made to Naomi was her priority. Ruth would not leave unless she sought Naomi's release. Naomi replied, "Go."

Naomi then spoke a word of reassurance to Ruth, she said, "My." As Ruth went to find provision in the field, she knew that this parting, the first between them since the flight from Moab, would leave them both apprehensive. Ruth was seeking provision and Naomi sent her away with a word that would resonate in her heart. She indicated to Ruth, "You are **MY** daughter."

Naomi's last word in this brief phrase was a word of relationship. She said, "Go, my **daughter**!" Ruth's heart had to have leapt within her bosom. Ruth was leaving Naomi to find provision, and she left with this phrase echoing in her heart. She knew that she was loved and longed for by Naomi. She would be parting for the day; but she would be taking the comfort of having Naomi's release, reassurance, and relationship.

Have you considered the comfort that you could give in any of your relationships? You hold within your power as a parent, spouse, and friend, the ability to encourage and edify those around you. Take a moment today and affirm a relationship with a friend. Offer them the comfort that Naomi offered Ruth.

Think about it . . .

Gone gleaning . . .

Ruth 2:3 *And she went, and came, and gleaned in the field after the reapers . . .*

With the blessing of her mother-in-law, Ruth left the house in search of the provision for their home. Now where would she go? Whose field would she choose? Fields were abundant in Bethlehem. She had to choose a field where they would accept her Moabite birth, and her Israelite widowhood, and her financial poverty.

Certainly, it was with a whispered prayer to the living God of Israel that she began her day. The thought of days gone by in Moab, where whispered prayers to idols brought no hope, relief, or peace, were now replaced by the confidence that God hears the prayers of His people. What a joy it was for

Ruth to pray to a God who heard and delighted in answering the prayers of His people!

Ruth would have never found the field, the fellowship, or the abundance of fruit, if she had never gone to look for God's "field" for her life. She would never have gleaned if she had not left the house to seek God's will. Clearly, Naomi had taught Ruth well. Naomi could explain from experience that if you seek provision, protection, and partnership in the wrong place, you will miss out on so much of what God offers His children. God never intended for your life to be complicated. He has given us His word, which is simple. He has given us His Holy Spirit, Who guides us.

Why should we sit around and fret over life's details when we can simply go to Him and ask, "What would You have me to do today?"

Think about it . . .

Just happened by . . .

Ruth 2:3 . . . *and her hap was to light on a part of the field . . .*

"And her hap . . ." What an interesting phrase! It is a comfort to know that the Lord of Glory Who places queens in palaces, Who softens the landing of sparrows that fall, and Who provides rams in thickets also guided the incidentals of Ruth's life. She was simply looking for a job, and God brought her to the right one.

If Ruth chose the wrong field, she would have missed out on God's handfuls of purpose. If Ruth chose the wrong field, she would have missed God's man for her life. If Ruth chose the wrong field, she would have worked harder for less barley. If

Ruth chose the wrong field, she would have been childless forever. If Ruth chose the wrong field, she would have failed to see the best that God had and would have unknowingly settled for second best.

The Lord directed the steps of Ruth and allowed her to see that the best place to glean was the field of Boaz. How many times have we walked along the paths of our lives and thought we happened to discover something, and never once contemplated that it was a sovereign God Who orchestrated the events of our lives so that we could "happen" upon His will.

When in God's will, the places we will walk today, the people we will meet, and the provisions we will discover are all designed to reveal His goodness. The Lord orders the steps of a good man. Why not purpose in your heart to take each day and look for God's hand at work in your life?

Friend, before you today are choices that may determine if you will be in the place of His handfuls of purpose. It would be disheartening to have lived your life and look back at life's end and see the handfuls of purpose God would have dropped your way, but did not because you made YOUR choices and not HIS choices?

How much do you include God in the decisions of your life? How often do you communicate with Him over the simple things? Since He is interested in the watch care of sparrows, rams, and whales, which have no souls; surely, He is interested in you and your life's decisions. There are no coincidences with God. Seek Him early, often, and humbly for His guidance, and watch for His handfuls of purpose along your way.

Think about it . . .

A field for His use . . .

Ruth 2:3 *. . . the field belonging unto Boaz . . .*

The book of Ruth, in its first chapter, kept Elimelech and Naomi as the principal characters; however, now the attention will switch from them to Boaz. God used Naomi after Elimelech's death to cultivate His Gentile gem, Ruth. Now, He will use a man named Boaz to care for this Gentile gem.

How will God use Boaz to care for her? He will begin by using his possessions. He will later use Boaz's position. Then, He will use Boaz's provisions. All of this will God do to care for His Gentile gem, Ruth.

God's will placed Boaz as a resident of Bethlehem. Boaz was given the Hebrew title that, translated in other verses, would read *a mighty man of valor.* Boaz, in chapter two and verse one, is declared as a man with great wealth and position. He owned fields outside of Bethlehem that would become the place of provision for Ruth. The fields Boaz owned would become the place of Ruth's presentation. Boaz's fields ultimately became the place of Ruth's protection.

At this moment the plan of God centered on Boaz's will. God had much that he would do for Ruth with Boaz's person, position, and possessions. God was going to do great things for Israel because of Boaz's willingness. God was going to do even greater things for His Son, Jesus because of Boaz's surrender. Boaz was willing to allow God to use him and whatever God had given him.

Oftentimes, we are like young children when it comes to our possessions. We like what is ours; we are not prone to share unless forced to by a higher authority. It takes an earnest threat to get most of us to give something beyond what we might not miss.

We scold our children for their refusal to share toys, food, or money; yet, when it comes to our possessions, we end up acting just like our children. We do not share our possessions, position, or paychecks with anyone, including God. We tend to look at something and say; "Now, this is mine. If God wants to use a rich man's things, that's fine; but I am a poor man and I do not care to have Him use MY things."

Oh, the blessings we miss when we hold back on God! There are times that God would like to use what He has given us, but we are slow to respond, and sometimes, even rebellious about what He wants to use of ours. Imagine what poverty Boaz would have come to if he had been stingy with God? Imagine how poor we become when we become stingy with God?

Think about it . . .

Kindred of Elimelech . . .

Ruth 2:3 . . . *Boaz, who was of the kindred of Elimelech.*

Boaz's history is often untold. We marvel at Boaz's compassion toward Ruth. She was a Moabite by birth; yet, in her new birth, she was an Israelite. When Boaz saw her in his field, there was not instant rejection of Ruth because of her birthplace; he simply accepted her status in the faith over her status as a foreigner.

Normally, Israelites would be slow to accept an outsider. What then made Boaz so apt to accept Ruth? Perhaps the answer would become clear, if we paused to look at Boaz's family album. Let's ask him:

"Boaz, do you have a picture of your parents?"

"Oh, yes, let me show you my parents," his reply would be. "Here is my father, Salmon. He was an Israelite prince."

"Oh, I see . . . do you have one of your mother?"

"Yes, let me show you. You may have heard of my mother. Did you ever hear the story of the walls falling down in Jericho except for one woman's apartment?"

"You mean Rahab the . . . Rahab the harlot?"

"Yes, Rahab, the Gentile girl from Jericho, is my mother."

Now, it is quite easy to see why this powerful man would take the time to accept a young, widowed Moabite convert by providing for and protecting her.

This same Boaz was also a man with a heritage. He belonged to the same family line of Elimelech. This was not by happenstance. It was God, in His sovereignty, Who placed Boaz in the family that would be able to redeem the name of Elimelech, and thereby, restore the line of Christ.

Boaz was also a man of honor. Although, this point will later be clearly seen, it is sufficient to say that Boaz was honorable in his integrity toward men, women, and God. No wonder God chose to use him!

Many times people believe that their lives have very little value or importance. They will often discredit their abilities; they will discount their talents and even minimize what God has bestowed upon them. It would be easy to discredit or discount your abilities or heritage, but God has placed you where He needs to use you. Never grumble or gripe about what you do not have. You have what He wants you to have for what He wants to do with you.

Think about it . . .

My hometown . . .

Ruth 2:4 *And, behold, Boaz came from Bethlehem, and said unto the reapers, The LORD be with you. And they answered him, The LORD bless thee.*

Boaz's arrival is marked by the fact that he came from Bethlehem. The city, at 2,350 feet above sea level, overlooks the main highway to Hebron and Egypt. His walk to the fields may have brought him by the burial site of Rachel, Bethlehem's hometown girl, whom they affectionately called, "The Mother of Israel." Rachel, Jacob's wife, would be long remembered in this little town for her marriage, her children, and her life.

Much would happen in this little town, nestled in the hills of Judah. Boaz had no idea that this little town of Bethlehem would be so significant in God's plan. Kings would be anointed here; men of valor would rush here and endanger their own lives for a glass of water for their anointed King David.

Jesus, the Son of David, Bethlehem's greatest inhabitant of all, would choose to be born in Bethlehem. Outside this quiet town, nestled in the hills of Judah, shepherds would receive an angel's message as they kept the night's watch over their sheep. The angel's message would be followed by a multitude of the heavenly host, who were "waiting in the wings" to herald their message right here, outside of Bethlehem.

Celebratory days would not be the only images in Bethlehem's scrapbook of history. There would come a day when there would be great sorrow in her streets over the slaying of the young children in this town. An even sadder day was yet to come when Bethlehem's greatest resident would be hung on a cross in the neighboring town to the north.

For generations it has been a part of our culture to evaluate someone by their hometown. Perhaps there was some people of Boaz's day that would criticize him because of his hometown.

People criticized Jesus and questioned whether good could come from Nazareth, his hometown. They diminished him by saying He was just the carpenter's son. It would be wise to recall Mark 6:4, " . . . *Jesus said unto them, A prophet is not without honour, but in his own country, and among his own kin, and in his own house.*"

The next time you see a guest in church evaluate the needs of their heart instead of evaluating them based on their neighborhood. What could happen in your heart if you would encourage people instead of discouraging them over senseless things? What would happen in your heart if you would cease from being critical and cynical of others and become more Christlike?

Bethlehem would not be the largest town; nor would the religious elite herald it as the "preferred" town. Bethlehem was little and unbecoming enough for God to make it a great hometown.

Remember, it is not in our own merits that greatness is established, but rather by God's mercy that great things are wrought!

Think about it . . .

Boaz from Bethlehem . . .

Ruth 2:4 *And, behold, Boaz came from Bethlehem, and said unto the reapers, The LORD be with you. And they answered him, The LORD bless thee.*

Boaz, our new principal character, breaks across the line of the horizon as he comes from town to see about his business in the fields. It would not be uncommon for the field owner to visit his fields; you see this was the time of harvest. As the field owner, Boaz had every right to check his servants, their service, and the status of the harvest. His arrival is not in judgment, but rather, in an inspection of his expectation for the harvest.

You know, our Eternal Boaz has an interest in His harvest and His harvesters. His harvest is one of souls. He has an expectation of His harvest. He knows when the seed was planted, and He knows when there should be a reaping. He knows what His fields will produce given the conditions they have been experiencing.

Jesus, our Eternal Boaz, also has an expectation of His harvesters. He expects them to be present in the fields and prepared to work in the fields. He will not leave His workers in the field without provision.

When Jesus inspects the section of the harvest upon which you are working for Him, what does He find? Are you present in the fields? Are you reaping the harvest He expected you to receive for the seed He had cast there? Are you producing for Him in the fields?

It is rather easy to spend all of our time checking on everyone else's lack of productivity in the harvest. Often we do this and neglect our own production for Him.

Oh, friend, when He comes determine to be found present, productive, and pleasing to Him in the work of the harvest.

Think about it . . .

Words for the workers . . .

Ruth 2:4 *And, behold, Boaz came from Bethlehem, and said unto the reapers, The LORD be with you. And they answered him, The LORD bless thee.*

Boaz loved his workers, and he knew them very well. He looked after his harvesters, as well as their harvesting. He came to his workers with a greeting. "The LORD *be* with you," he said to them. They enjoyed when Boaz came by and just visited them in their work. They knew his position, power, and prestige; but, oh, how they loved his presence among them!

They would reply to his greeting, "The LORD bless thee." What a response! The field owner has come to the work place. His presence is made known to them, and they tell their boss, "The LORD bless thee." This would be the kind of place anyone would love to work. It was a workplace where harmony ruled and attacking the other workers was unknown. It was a workplace where Boaz's presence was longed for, not loathed. It was a workplace where good words replaced worthless gossip.

Boaz knew his fields were God's fields. He knew his workers were God's workers. He wanted everyone at his workplace to know that God's presence was to be recognized, revered, and rejoiced over, even though they were in the field. They enjoyed the spiritual while they occupied themselves with the servile.

Today, we can draw many lessons as we contemplate the Lord of the harvest, the Lord's harvest, and the Lord's harvesters. Has the work of the harvest become so tedious that you have neglected spiritual fellowship with your co-laborers? Is harmony ruling in your spiritual work for the Lord? Has gossip become the theme of the conversations in your spiritual workplace?

You probably know all the attributes of our Eternal Boaz's great position, power, and prestige; yet, is what you love most about God, His presence? You may say, "I fear His presence." I encourage you to *look* for His presence. Just take pleasure in Him the next time He passes your field.

When last did the Lord come by your harvest field? You may say, "He has never passed by my field!" Friend, does that really sound like our Boaz? He probably has come by your field many times to fellowship with you, and you were too busy griping, gossiping, and grumbling about working so hard. You may know the facts about our Boaz, but do you know His fellowship?

Think about it . . .

The behavior of Boaz . . .

Ruth 2:4 *And, behold, Boaz came from Bethlehem, and said unto the reapers, The LORD be with you. And they answered him, The LORD bless thee.*

This is the fourth time we have come to this verse to draw from its resources to help us in our walk with the Lord. Today, as we draw from the enriching resources in this passage let us reflect on the behavior of Boaz.

An analysis of the verse reveals that Boaz came to them in the field. What a precious comfort it must have been to those who worked for Boaz! Boaz knew where they were working. He was not so busy with his other concerns that he had forgotten where they were. He set aside time in his day to come to their field. He made provision for his other responsibilities so that he could make his presence known to his people.

A close look further reveals that Boaz comforted them in the field. Boaz visited the field that day and did not just stand there; he initiated the conversation with them. He said, "The LORD be with thee." He placed a higher priority on letting them know he was there than he did on their productivity and work schedule. He knew that the hours of the day were passing, but he wanted them to be comforted in their work. He wanted them to know that they were vital to him, so he gave them just what they needed. He gave them the comfort of his presence and words.

We should further note that Boaz communicated with his workers in the field. They were not too far from hearing his voice. Boaz was not too far from hearing their voices, either. Boaz's voice came to them in their place of service. Boaz's message spoke to their hearts and souls.

Note his words of comfort, "The LORD be with thee." It was what his workers needed to hear from him! Boaz's words reminded them that their labor was not in vain. Boaz's words refreshed in their minds that their labor was not without value. They heard Boaz's words and it reminded them that their labor was guaranteed a victory.

Friend, remember our Eternal Boaz knows exactly where we are serving. Our Eternal Boaz will personally come to our "field." Our Eternal Boaz will comfort us in our work for Him. Our Eternal Boaz will communicate with us and listen to us.

Let the words of this spiritual song deliver a message of peace to your soul.

Why should I feel discouraged? Why should the shadows come?
Why should my heart feel lonely and long for Heaven and home?
When Jesus is my portion, my constant friend is He.
His eye is on the sparrow and I know He watches me.

Mrs. Civilla D. Martin

Think about it . . .

A servant to the reapers . . .

Then said Boaz unto his servant that was set over the reapers, Whose damsel is this? Ruth 2:5

Boaz had just come from Bethlehem. Upon his arrival, Boaz has viewed all the harvest activity, he has inspected the condition of the harvest, he has taken time to identify the condition of the harvesters, and he also has taken interest in the conduct of the harvesters.

Boaz specifically chose the servant that he had set over the reapers. This servant would be the one to manage his affairs in the harvest. This servant would be the one who would manage the activities of the harvest. This servant would be the one to whom Boaz would turn for his information. This servant would deliver Boaz's instructions. This servant was expected to handle Boaz's interests in the harvest. Out in the field, this servant was to act on behalf of Boaz in all harvest matters.

What a thrill to be the one selected by Boaz! This servant had many details to maintain for Boaz. He had to see that there were enough harvesters. He looked after the harvester's actions, both on and off the field. As servant set over the reapers, he must be concerned with their well-being in the harvest field. He must see that they would have times of reaping and times of rest. He would provide both refreshment and fellowship as they served in the field. He was a servant to the reapers.

Every church (*a called out assembly of immersed believers, observing the two ordinances, and meeting regularly for worship, work, and witnessing*) must identify and accept its assigned role in the spiritual harvest of souls. Each church is assigned by God to be a servant *"set over the reapers."* It is the job of the church to instill, install, and instruct harvesters in the work of the Lord of the harvest.

The reapers of a church are the missionaries she sends out. Each church is responsible to the Lord of the harvest for their attentiveness toward the reapers. Each church must see that their reapers have both times of reaping and rest. Each church must see that the reapers get the fellowship and refreshment they need.

A church cannot be a church without missionaries. Missionaries cannot be reapers unless they have churches. This understanding defines a clear role for each church; a church is to be a servant to the reapers.

How well are you doing your job as a church member in serving your reapers? The authority in modern missions seems to have been wrongly relegated by churches and given to boards, committees, and councils. It is the church that is to be the servant to the reapers, both in authority over the reapers and in attentiveness toward the reapers.

Think about it . . .

Boaz's heart . . .

Then said Boaz unto his servant that was set over the reapers, Whose damsel is this? Ruth 2:5

Boaz's question to his servant revealed, not only his concern for Ruth, but also his character. Boaz knew that since the Garden of Eden, God has placed every woman under the authority of a man. He knew that Ruth was either under her father's authority or her husband's authority. Boaz did not want to contemplate anything further until he knew under whose authority she lived. Boaz's questioning of his servant reveals that he was a man of spiritual integrity, identity, and insight.

Indeed, Boaz wanted to know about Ruth's authority because he was a man of integrity. During the time in which Boaz lived, every man did what was right in his own eyes. Boaz would not be numbered amongst those who lived, labored, and loved solely for selfish reasons. Boaz's heart remained steeped in the old ways of Israel. Though Israel had no ruler, Jehovah ruled Boaz's heart and home.

Boaz wanted to know about Ruth's authority because he identified more with God's ways than the world's ways. God's ways were immersed in his heart. If Ruth had a man in authority over her, then he wanted to know it. He was determined to be right in his transactions with mankind. Boaz was committed to being identified with the old ways.

Boaz's inquiry of his servant reveals that he was also a man of spiritual insight. Ruth's arrival in his field spawned the question, "Whose damsel is this?" He knew that she was there, but he wanted to know how she got there. He knew that Ruth was there, but he wanted to hear her story. He was not content to think that things just happened that way. Boaz's question revealed his concern AND his character.

God chose Boaz to guide and guard Ruth. God's selection of Boaz was not misplaced. You see, Boaz was a man who had both concern and character. We need men to fill the role of Boaz today in their homes. Men of spiritual integrity, identity, and insight are needed to guide and guard their homes. Every home must have a Boaz and the Boaz of the home must lead his family in a biblical direction.

Modern ways of thinking have infiltrated and seemingly absorbed the biblically defined roles of women. Asking Boaz's question in most Christian homes today would seem out of place. We have allowed our children to select their life's mate with only regard to concern and with little regard to character.

Society has attempted in every generation to outdate Bible ways. Society has "upgraded" the old ways with ways that seem right in their own eyes. Sadly, Christians quickly capitulate to every societal upgrade. What most people do not realize is that an upgrade in society is really a downgrade in spirituality.

Think about it . . .

Boaz looks her way . . .

Ruth 2:5 *Then said Boaz unto his servant that was set over the reapers, Whose damsel is this?*

Boaz had one question on his mind after he surveyed the harvest work. He turned to the servant who was set over the reapers and wanted to know, "Whose damsel is this?"

This question indicates that Boaz inspected his harvest frequently enough to know who was new. Boaz noticed the new lady in the field as he scanned the harvest field and its surroundings. The question he asked should make each reader consider the concern and character of Boaz.

Boaz saw Ruth as she stood and wiped her brow, pushing back the wisps of hair clinging to her brow. He saw this lone figure seeking refreshment in the field house. She held her vessel gently and had a distant look. She seemed to stand in the present, but was able to see both yesterday and tomorrow with her gentle eyes.

God wanted Boaz to notice this Gentile gem that He would soon place and display prominently in the setting of Boaz's life. Ruth would not have to seek Boaz. Boaz would be led by God to seek Ruth.

Boaz had noticed both Ruth's work ethic and her demeanor. Ruth was not the typical gleaner. There was something special about her. Ruth had come to glean in his harvest, and Boaz found that she already had gleaned his heart. Boaz had yet to hear Ruth's voice, but he cared for her as his own.

Was Ruth the sole gleaner in the harvest that day? Certainly not! Why did Boaz notice Ruth? Was it because she was flirtatious and arrayed in a revealing fashion? Boaz's attraction was not drawn to Ruth by her revealing fashion, nor her flirtatious ways. You see, Boaz saw her at a time when most women would not feel that they were at their best. Yet, when Ruth seemed to be at her worst, he noticed her and wanted to know more about her.

God noticed us and was drawn to us when we were at our worst. Our Eternal Boaz loves us more than Boaz loved Ruth. Pause this day and thank Him for His love. *"In that, while we were yet sinners, Christ died for us."*

Think about it . . .

An answer for Boaz . . .

"And the servant that was set over the reapers answered and said, It is the Moabitish damsel that came back with Naomi out of the country of Moab:" Ruth 2:6

"Whose damsel is this?" was the question that began Ruth's love story. The question will cause the servant now to give a full answer to Boaz. The servant now had opportunity to explain to Boaz how his heart had been drawn to Ruth's cause.

The servant had given Ruth permission to glean in Boaz's field. As the servant set over the reapers he held responsibility for her presence in the field. Ruth's procurement from the field was under his direct control. The servant held the key to any prosperity she would gain from the field.

Boaz's question was not to set the servant on the defensive with his master. After all, the servant had acted in light of God's law pertaining to the poor and the stranger being allowed to harvest in the corners of the fields and to glean after the reapers.

> "And when ye reap the harvest of your land, thou shalt not make clean riddance of the corners of thy field when thou reapest, neither shalt thou gather any gleaning of thy harvest: thou shalt leave them unto the poor, and to the stranger: I am the LORD your God." Leviticus 23:22

The servant set over the reapers was responsible for who came and gleaned in Boaz's field. He now had to give an account to Boaz for Ruth's presence. He would now give account for his attitude, activity, and ability in managing the harvest work for his lord.

As a servant-church member set over harvest reapers, what is your attitude toward the harvest? Do you grumble when missionaries come to your church? Do you resent the purpose of their visit? Do you display the right spirit when the harvesters are seeking financial support to do the Lord of the harvest's reaping?

As a servant-church member set over harvest reapers, what has been your activity in the harvest? Have you encouraged the laborers? Have you enlisted more laborers? Have you equipped more laborers? When listening to a missionary as he shares his calling and concerns, do you seek to involve yourself or distance yourself?

As a servant-church member set over harvest reapers, have you used all of your ability for the harvest? Do you, from time to time, respond with excuses of disability? When faced with responsibility, do you respond with all of your ability?

There is a day in God's timetable where believers will give an account to God for their harvest attitude, activity, and ability. We will give an account to God before His Bema Seat after the Rapture of the saints. This accounting must then endure God's gold, silver, and precious stone or wood, hay, and stubble test.

Think about it . . .

That's her . . .

Ruth 2:6 *And the servant that was set over the reapers answered and said, It is the Moabitish damsel that came back with Naomi out of the country of Moab:*

The servant set over the reapers made a decision to help Ruth by permitting her to glean in Boaz's fields; yet, now he gives account for her presence. Boaz wants to know to whom the damsel belongs. The servant replies with how his heart had been touched as she told her story to him. In verse six, the servant tells Boaz of Ruth's history, her holiness, and her happiness. He began, "It is the Moabitish damsel." The servant must have been impressed with her courage, character, and compassion.

Ruth may have shared her story with Boaz's servant this way:

If it pleases the servant of the lord of this harvest, I would love to tell you how I came to your field this day. I was born to parents in Moab. Growing up, I knew only of Moab's iniquity, idols, and immorality. Then, during my late adolescent years, I met a family from a town called Bethlehem. This was the family of Elimelech.

The providence of Jehovah allowed me to meet their son, Mahlon. My heart was taken with this young man. Though it was peculiar to have pure Israelites living in our land, his family's faith attracted me. Disaster struck his home when his father, Elimelech, died. We later determined to marry and make a home in Moab for ourselves. We never had children, though we had a happy home. It was during my married days, that I got to know Naomi better. What a delightful woman! Neither death nor disappointment seemed to sway her faith in El-Shaddai.

Death then took my husband, Mahlon. My sister-in-law, Orpah, lost her husband, Chilion, at the same time. There we were, three widows in Moab. My cultural upbringing caused me to escort Naomi back to Bethlehem. However, what brought me here was the conviction I felt in my heart somewhere between Moab and Bethlehem.

It was there that I confessed my faith and desire to follow Elohim and to identify with the people of Israel. I came back with Naomi with no real possessions to hold in my hand; yet, I had in my heart a possession that was greater than could be valued in the marketplace. I had a new faith, a new family, and a new forever. Sir, I stand before you today, Moabite by birth and Israelite by faith. I come seeking permission to claim the divine right of provision for the poor set out by God for His people and for strangers. Sir, may I have access to your favor and this field?

"My lord, Boaz," the servant over the reapers explained, "When she concluded this story my heart was full of admiration. My eyes were like your eyes are now – filled with tears. So I replied, "Please glean in my master's harvest."

Friend, witnessing is no more than telling what God did for you. When last did you tell the story of your conversion to a total stranger? If you believe that no one will want to hear it, ask God to place a stranger before you today to tell how His grace reached you, then you will see.

Think about it . . .

Ruth's devotion . . .

Ruth 2:7 *And she said, I pray you, let me glean and gather after the reapers among the sheaves: so she came, and hath continued even from the morning until now, that she tarried a little in the house.*

The servant continues his story to Boaz as to how "this damsel" got to his field. It is touching to see in this one phrase: the interest of Boaz, the impression on his servant, and the imploring of Ruth. The servant set over the reapers was touched by Ruth's plight and present need. He had permitted her to glean, and now Boaz was interested in the particulars of how it happened.

In the servant's explanation to Boaz, he quotes Ruth's words, "*I pray you, let me glean and gather after the reapers among the sheaves . . .*" The diligent reader will not be able to escape noting the devotion, desire, determination and dedication in her words.

Ruth implored the servant set over the reapers by saying, "I pray you." Her devotion was to work for provision for Naomi and herself. Ruth was seeking for an answer in her request. She prayed him that he would let her work. She did not come up and say, "You don't have anything for me to do here, do you?" She never said, "It looks like you don't need me here." She prayed to be involved in the harvest of Boaz. She did not mind if she looked as if she was begging; she just wanted to be involved in this harvest.

Is this how you contemplate the work of the Lord's harvest in your church? Is local harvesting in your church merely a night where people go out for an hour? Our local harvest work must not be a weekly event we attend for an hour. It must be an everyday part of our lives. Ruth prayed to be involved in Boaz's harvest. Do you pray to be involved in the Lord's harvest?

When you consider the Lord's harvest outside of your locale, do you pray to be involved? Again, consider Ruth's words, "I pray you!" She wanted to have a part in Boaz's harvest work. Wherever the sheaves were, that's where she wanted to be involved.

God has sheaves all over the world. Are you confident that He does not want you to go and glean amongst them? Do you faithfully finance the efforts of the reapers (missionaries) sent out by your church?

Friend, God wants us involved in His harvest. Are you devoted to the right cause?

Think about it . . .

Ruth's desire . . .

Ruth 2:7 *And she said, I pray you, let me glean and gather after the reapers among the sheaves: so she came, and hath continued even from the morning until now, that she tarried a little in the house.*

Previously, we considered how Boaz's servant had been touched by Ruth's request for involvement in the harvest. Boaz was interested in this one who came to work in his field. The servant had been impressed by her request and her work ethic. Ruth's words are simple and convicting to the heart of a believer yielded to God. She said, "*I pray you, let me glean and gather after the reapers among the sheaves . . .*"

Focus with me on the facet of her request that reveals her desire for involvement in Boaz's harvest. Her desire is evident in the phrase, "Let me glean and gather." Her desire was to WORK in the harvest of the servant's master. She pleaded with him for access to the harvest, an activity in the harvest, and an area to work in the harvest.

Oh, there are lessons, dear reader, for our church's global and local evangelistic outreach in this passage. Ruth was not seeking to be lord of the harvest, nor was she aspiring to lead the group of laborers. Ruth was not looking to implement a program of harvesting that she was familiar with in other fields. She was not looking to re-train the workers in the Moabite way of reaping. Ruth simply had her heart's desire set on gleaning and gathering.

When it comes to harvest work, what is your desire? Do you see yourself in management or are you content to just be a common laborer for the Lord? It seems we have many who want to manage and maintain the harvest, but few who will get out and do the work of the harvest.

How much more could be done for the Lord if we would have the desire of Ruth in the fields of our Eternal Boaz? Would you say today, "God, let me glean and gather for you?" How much more would be done for our Lord if we would have the right desire when it came to His fields?

May God help us to have Ruth's desire when it comes to His harvest work in our churches, both at home and around the world.

Think about it . . .

Ruth's determination . . .

Ruth 2:7 *And she said, I pray you, let me glean and gather after the reapers among the sheaves: so she came, and hath continued even from the morning until now, that she tarried a little in the house.*

Boaz's servant is in the midst of relating Ruth's conversation with him to Boaz. Boaz's interest has been stirred by this gentle soul who came to glean in his field. He inquired of this servant that he had set over his reapers about the new gleaner.

Previously, we considered how the servant was uniquely impressed by her devotion and desire: however, this phrase *"after the reapers among the sheaves"* helps us to discover Ruth's determination.

The phrase from verse seven indicates to me the level of Ruth's determination for Boaz's harvest fields. Ruth is determined not to seek a lofty position in Boaz's harvest. She wants to be in a place *"after the reapers."* She is not seeking to be elevated to reaper status; she only wants to be behind the ones doing the reaping. She was determined to be involved in the shadows of the harvest work. She did not want the spotlight for herself.

Furthermore, Ruth is not looking for the easiest place to labor; she merely wants to pick up the droppings around the sheaves. Ruth only cared that she got to be involved in the harvest, not whether she was noticed in the harvest. Her mind was set on harvest work, not her own worth.

Ruth's level of determination is quite convicting in light of the present situations in our churches concerning the Lord's harvest of souls at home and abroad. Today, many Christians have only a casual interest in our Eternal Boaz's fields. They want to hear the unique stories from the harvest field, but never care to do anything themselves. They love the missionary stories, but they will not exert an ounce of determination toward being involved in giving or going to the mission field.

Our Eternal Boaz is aware of your participation in His harvest. Your Pastor is concerned for your involvement in the harvest. Remember your pastor is God's servant set over you as a reaper. Hebrews 13:17 commands believers to, *"Obey them that have the rule over you, and submit yourselves: for they watch for your souls, as they that must give account, that they may do it with joy, and not with grief: for that is unprofitable for you."*

When it comes to doing God's work in your church, contemplate and then answer these three questions.

Does my devotion to the harvest meet the approval of my Eternal Boaz and my Pastor?

Does my desire for the harvest meet the approval of my Eternal Boaz and my Pastor?

Does my determination for the harvest meet the approval of my Eternal Boaz and my Pastor?

Think about it . . .

Ruth's dedication . . .

Ruth 2:7 *And she said, I pray you, let me glean and gather after the reapers among the sheaves: so she came, and hath continued even from the morning until now, that she tarried a little in the house.*

As the sun rose to meet the hills of Judah, Ruth was seen walking toward the terraced hillside belonging to Boaz. Ruth's heart was clear when she left the house that morning. Ruth left seeking provision from a benefactor. Ruth found all that she needed in Boaz's field. Boaz looked Ruth's way. Ruth, a simple Moabite girl, had gleaned more than his harvest. Ruth had gleaned Boaz's heart. Ruth had not even spoken a word to Boaz; yet, God brought their hearts together.

Boaz both saw and heard the servant's testimony of the dedication of Ruth's heart. Clearly, Ruth's devotion, desire, and determination in the harvest were not forced. She did not have to fake her level of commitment to the harvest. Her participation in the harvest came from within her heart. Ruth's heart contained the overwhelming appreciation for the opportunity to glean for Naomi's sustenance.

Ruth's commitment to Naomi raised the level of intensity she felt inwardly. Ruth had to find a place to glean. When she arrived and met the approval of the servant set over the reapers, she set out in her heart to stay and work in earnest. This decision revealed Ruth's dedication to the harvest of Boaz.

Ruth's dedication to the harvest made an impression on the servant. "*From morning till now,*" said the servant to Boaz. These words declared Ruth's dedication to the harvest. The servant had seen many gleaners come to the field, but something about Ruth was different. Ruth's heart maintained a level of dedication to the harvest that was noteworthy.

Other gleaners may have come and discussed with Ruth about the quality and quantity in the corners of other fields. These statements could easily have been unintentional attempts to sway Ruth's dedication. Yet, Ruth's dedication of heart was not affected by the comments of her co-workers or conditions in other fields.

The servant's testimony to Boaz of Ruth's participation in the harvest should reveal to believers a spiritual checklist of the heart. Our Eternal Boaz knows the content of our hearts. He sees when our dedication wavers and wanders.

What would our Eternal Boaz say of you? "*From the morning of our relationship until now, you have been in the harvest.*" May Ruth's dedication be our dedication until our Eternal Boaz calls us home!

Think about it . . .

She came to continue . . .

Ruth 2:7 *And she said, I pray you, let me glean and gather after the reapers among the sheaves: so she came, and hath continued even from the morning until now, that she tarried a little in the house.*

Boaz's servant has been explaining the events surrounding the arrival of Ruth to Boaz. When Boaz came from Bethlehem, he found this woman who had come to glean in his fields. However, it seems that, since his arrival, she had gleaned much more than his harvest; she had gleaned his heart. Boaz is taken with Ruth's presence in the field. The servant told Boaz about Ruth's devotion, her desire, her determination, and her dedication concerning working in the harvest.

The first element of the phrase reads, "So she came . . ." Yes, Ruth was given access to the fields of Boaz. She could come and go in the fields that day with the authority of the servant. She did not have to sneak into the fields or operate in a covert manner. She had full access to Boaz's fields.

Ruth was even given an area where she was to work for Boaz. She was to glean among the sheaves for Boaz. She had an area with which to concern herself. She did not have to look after another's work, just her own.

Ruth had a specific activity to carry out for Boaz. She was to gather anything that was dropped. Not a grain of barley was to be left in the field. Every grain was important to Boaz, so what was important to Boaz became important to her. Boaz's assignment became her chief activity.

Yet, we cannot look lightly upon the next phrase in verse seven, "And hath continued . . ." Ruth came early and stayed late to get the job finished for Boaz. Ruth knew that harvesting was daylight work. She had to be in her area, fulfilling her assignment for Boaz in order to complete the harvest work. Ruth determined that she had come to Boaz's fields to stay.

Have you come to stay in the fields of our Eternal Boaz? Have you determined to stay and complete your assignment? Have you decided that you are going to step back and let others take care of things? Did you get to the harvest field, see the workload and just quit?

Harvesting souls, both locally and globally, is daylight work. You know, the night is coming when no man can work. Make up your mind that you have come to our Eternal Boaz's harvest to continue.

Think about it . . .

A time for resting . . .

Ruth 2:7 *And she said, I pray you, let me glean and gather after the reapers among the sheaves: so she came, and hath continued even from the morning until now, that she tarried a little in the house.*

The servant related to Boaz about Ruth's devotion to the harvest, Ruth's desire to harvest, Ruth's determination in the harvest, and Ruth's dedication to the harvest. The servant was impressed with her declarations to him and her duty to his boss. At the end of his testimony of Ruth's demeanor, the servant mentions an interesting point for the believer to ponder.

The servant set over the reapers said Ruth had "*continued even from the morning until now, that she tarried a little in the house.*" Notice with me his last eight words. "*That she tarried a little in the house.*" It is apparent that Ruth was a good harvester for Boaz. The servant pointed out to Boaz that Ruth had tarried only a "little" in the house.

The servant set over the reapers had a place where all in his charge could come and seek refreshment and rest. Service in the field requires rest and refreshing. The reapers would, after a period of work, come to the house and gather for fellowship. The resting house was also a place of rejoicing when the harvest was completed.

The thought of a house in which to rest to rest in from our labors bring two concerns to mind in light of this present generation. The first concern is that of God's laborers ignoring times of needed rest. Many times, in the service of our Eternal Boaz, we pride ourselves in our work and brag that we never take a break or a time to rest. Ruth was a diligent worker, both in her reaping AND her resting.

The second concern is one that is far too common among 21st century believers. This is the danger of all rest and no labor. Many today have made a ministry of staying in the house and never going to the fields.

It is clear that it could be said of many, "They have tarried too long and labored too little for our Eternal Boaz." You can always spot those in this way; they are the spiritual hogs of the church. They linger long at the trough and do little but grunt if they cannot feed their bellies.

Friend, it should be overwhelmingly apparent that the believer working in the field should make regular trips to the house of God. We should go to the house of our Eternal Boaz for rest from the noonday sun AFTER we have labored for Him.

We should get to the house of our Eternal Boaz; it is there we will meet other harvesters, and we can fellowship over our labors. We should get to the house of our Eternal Boaz for needed refreshment and to listen for words of encouragement from Boaz. We should get to the house of our Eternal Boaz for times of rejoicing over the harvest.

Temporary rest is vital; full-time rest will come when we leave this earth for the eternal house of our Boaz. *"Let us labor to enter into that rest."* Hebrews 4:11

Think about it . . .

"He speaks and the sound of His voice . . ."

Ruth 2:8 *Then said Boaz unto Ruth, Hearest thou not, my daughter? Go not to glean in another field, neither go from hence, but abide here fast by my maidens:*

While God was at work in Moab bringing out Ruth for Himself, He was also working in Bethlehem on Boaz. Boaz's background prepared him for this moment of conversation. His mother was Rahab from Jericho. His father was an Israelite prince. He was an original inhabitant of Ephratah. God had given him good relationships in his community, great resources at his control, and the desire to be a gracious kinsman-redeemer.

Boaz inquired of his servant the details of Ruth's arrival, her activity, her associations, and her abilities. Boaz, a seeker of God's way and a steward in God's work, has heard and observed all the transactions related to Ruth. Boaz will not be without comment.

In a few moments, Boaz will offer Ruth his protection, provision, and handfuls of purpose. Boaz and Ruth, as a couple, will be long remembered in Israel's history. In a single moment in time, God's plan takes shape and the rest is His story.

Let us not lightly consider that our Eternal Boaz is observing our harvest work. He has invested much in this harvest and expects our best. God watched our arrival into His harvest field. He evaluates our activities, associations, and the use of our abilities in His field. Our Eternal Boaz even sent us His Servant, the Holy Spirit, to comfort us until the day He comes to get His gleaners for Himself.

Though we have not heard with our ears the actual, audible voice of our Eternal Boaz, there is coming a day when we will hear him speak. The dictionary cannot contain enough words to describe our joy when we hear His voice for the first time on the other side.

C. Austin Miles, the song writer, wrote in his song, "In the Garden," these words that could describe our coming joy and Ruth's present joy in hearing Boaz's voice.

> He speaks and the sound of His voice,
> Is so sweet the birds hush their singing,
> And the melody that He gave to me,
> Within my heart is ringing.

The sense of anticipation in hearing the voice of our Boaz should be enough to carry us through the harvest from this day until we actually hear His voice.

Think about it . . .

Swift to hear . . .

Ruth 2:8 *Then said Boaz unto Ruth, Hearest thou not, my daughter? Go not to glean in another field, neither go from hence, but abide here fast by my maidens:*

Until this moment we have no recorded words between Boaz and Ruth. Ruth had noticed Boaz's interest in her. Since Boaz's arrival, both the servant and Boaz would look her way, and then they would speak earnestly with each other. They were gesturing with their hands, and then both would glance her way.

What could they be saying? What could she have done that would have garnered this kind of attention? Ruth reviewed the morning hours in her mind. What thoughts those must have been! Listen to what she could have been thinking.

I know when I came to the field this morning that I first spoke to that servant. Oh, the compassion I sensed in his ability to listen; it seemed he hung on my every word. It was a bit unusual that a stranger would show this kind of concern and compassion on behalf of his master.

It seemed his heart was prepared for my arrival. What was that word Naomi said when she told me one of the stories of our Father Abraham? Yes, I remember now, Jehovah-jireh. Yes, God had provided a ram in the thicket for Abraham and a servant in the field for me. I really wanted to thank the servant more, but I sensed that the praise for that servant belonged to God. Yes, God loves me!

He told me I could glean among the sheaves. I have so much enjoyed working here amongst the servants of Boaz. I have attempted to do the best I could. I have only taken one break. I hope they do not want me to leave. I know I am just a Moabitish damsel; I am unwanted by most, but I felt like I belonged again. "Please God, make it so I can stay and work here!"

There was no more time for reviewing the morning's events in the journal of her heart. Boaz was headed her way. Her heart began to beat faster; her palms became sweaty and her mouth dried in an instant.

What would he say to her? Each step seemed to take an eternity; she just had to hear what he was going to tell her. If Boaz's servant could listen to her with compassion, what must Boaz be like?

Reader, many times we lose our sense of anticipation of hearing from our Eternal Boaz. It is as if we think we know what He is going to say, so we lose our eagerness to listen to God through His Word. Thankfully, Ruth did not listen to Boaz like most believers today listen to God.

There is a sense of half-heartedness and complacency in many believers when it comes to their personal time of listening to the Lord in His Word.

Dear reader, when last did you become stirred over what God would say to you when you read His Word? When last did you sense He was speaking to your heart in a church service? How long has it been since you heard God speak to your heart? Ruth yearned to hear from Boaz. Do you?

Think about it . . .

From damsel to daughter . . .

Ruth 2:8 *Then said Boaz unto Ruth, Hearest thou not, my daughter? Go not to glean in another field, neither go from hence, but abide here fast by my maidens:*

Boaz looked intently at this gentle soul that had come to glean in his fields. Ruth had gleaned far more than Boaz's harvest; you see, Ruth had gleaned his heart. He gazed at this damsel who had recently come from Moab. Boaz saw Ruth as he had seen no other gleaner.

Ruth, who had turned to Jehovah by faith, now stands before him vulnerable and transparent. Boaz sensed within his bosom a divine responsibility. God had placed upon him the responsibility of offering his protection and provision to Ruth. Boaz sensed that she was God's valuable vessel.

Ruth's heart continued to pound furiously. What would he say to her? She wanted to hear his soothing voice and personal message. Would she have to leave his fields? Would she find that she was unwanted because she was a widow? Inwardly, she might have even convinced herself she would have to leave because she was, by birth, a Moabite.

Ruth's thoughts were coming fast. Apparently, Ruth's thoughts were so loud; she might not have heard Boaz's voice when he first spoke. Notice what Boaz said, "*Hearest thou not, my daughter?*"

In one statement, Ruth went from a damsel to a daughter. "My daughter." These two words were heard in her heart. What she lacked in protection and provision had been met in Boaz. Boaz, in one phrase, brought Ruth into his harvest field and into his heart. The ache of loneliness dissipated in an instant. Security and stability were now ushered into her heart where loneliness once reigned.

Often, my wife, Kimberly, will ask the story of a couple's first meeting. She revels in the details of what attracted the one to the other. She loves to hear the occasion of how the man asked the woman to be his wife. My wife has found everyone tells their story with a twinkle in their eye and with joy in their voice.

For the believer, there was a day in eternity past where our Boaz was attracted to us, and He saw our greatest need. We, who had been orphaned, widowed, and even marooned by sin, now were offered the provision of his resources (*my*) and the protection of his righteousness (*daughter*).

Reader, we too have a story to tell. It is a story of when we met Boaz. Remember to tell it with a twinkle in your eye and joy in your voice. We must tell others how He brought us from a damsel to a daughter, from a sinner to a saint.

Think about it . . .

Your search is over . . .

Ruth 2:8 *Then said Boaz unto Ruth, Hearest thou not, my daughter? Go not to glean in another field, neither go from hence, but abide here fast by my maidens:*

Boaz's offer of his provision and protection was not lost on Ruth. Boaz brought Ruth under the umbrella of his authority when he called her daughter. Though his servant had given Ruth access, an area to work, and an assignment; Boaz gave her something his servant could not give. He gave her adoption.

Her adoption signaled to the community that she was not without a kinsman. This adoption prevented her from having to find provision somewhere else. Boaz's adoption of Ruth exempted her from seeking protection from someone else. Ruth's adoption indicated that she would no longer need to ponder the future; Boaz had embraced her into the family. Boaz's adoption sent one resounding message, "Your search for a place is over; you are at home now."

The message of Boaz's invitation to Ruth must not be lost in our cultural ignorance. Boaz's inclusion of Ruth in his harvest work assured her that she did not need to go anywhere else to glean. It was as if he was saying, "I will take care of all your tomorrows. Your future is secure. You have everything you need right here. I will take care of you from here on out. Your search is over."

When reading these words of Boaz it is easy to sense his comfort and concern; yet, there exists a greater meaning for the believer. Boaz's words should reveal a command for every believer to heed. We are not to seek our own provision, protection, or promise from anywhere, anyone, or anything else. Our Eternal Boaz has placed everything we need right here in the field of His will.

"Go not to glean in another field," is a command worth heeding. Why on earth would you run from job to job, church to church, and spouse to spouse, seeking personal satisfaction? Boaz has placed everything we need in the field of His will. Determine this day to seek provision, protection, and promises only from our Boaz.

Think about it . . .

Abide here . . .

Ruth 2:8 *Then said Boaz unto Ruth, Hearest thou not, my daughter? Go not to glean in another field, neither go from hence, but abide here fast by my maidens:*

The words *"But abide here fast by my maidens,"* must have made Ruth's heart leap. Ruth, the immigrant and convert from Moab had found a home. Ruth, whose conversion to Jehovah had caused no small stir in Bethlehem, had found a home in the fields of Boaz. Boaz told Ruth to go nowhere else.

Boaz's words were clear; they spoke directly to her heart. Boaz's harvest field would provide Ruth food for her body, fellowship for her soul, and friends for her heart. Ruth would not need to fret any more about her future prosperity. Ruth would not need to ponder over tomorrow's provision. She would no longer need to wonder whether she would ever find a kindred spirit to share her heart's dreams and delights.

Boaz had told Ruth, "Abide here fast." She was not to wander away from his field. Ruth would not have to wonder whether provision were better anywhere else. Ruth would not have to wither away, starved for friendship. Everything she needed was here with Boaz and his gleaners.

Beware - the world will offer cheap imitations of everything Boaz provides. Would to God we would repeat this message to ourselves and to this generation.

"*Abide here fast*" - everything we need as reapers and gleaners can be found in our Eternal Boaz's field."

"*Abide here fast*" - seek your friends and fellowship here in our Eternal Boaz's field."

"*Abide here fast*" - find comfort and satisfaction here in our Eternal Boaz's field.

Ruth found that Boaz's promises were sure and reliable. Ruth would prove Boaz's word steadfast. Ruth would test his word in the field. Soon, Ruth would test Boaz's word in the threshingfloor. Later, Ruth would test his word while she waited at home for him to come from the city's gate as Boaz obtained her redemption. Ruth would know from this moment forward that Boaz would keep his word.

What about you, dear reader? Upon our salvation, our Eternal Boaz told us "Abide here fast." Have you? Or have you been of the sort to abide only when it is convenient and comfortable? In your church attendance, in your ministry service, in your marriage, in everything you do, heed our Eternal Boaz's call, "*Abide here fast.*"

Think about it . . .

Sinner saved by grace . . .

Ruth 2:8-9 *Then said Boaz unto Ruth . . . Let thine eyes be on the field that they do reap, and go thou after them: have I not charged the young men that they shall not touch thee? and when thou art athirst, go unto the vessels, and drink of that which the young men have drawn.*

Ruth listened with delight, as Boaz's words seemed to go from his heart straight to her heart. She knew this was unusual; the lord of the harvest, himself, had taken interest in her.

Ruth knew there was nothing comely about her heritage, her homeland, or her history. She wondered, "*What could he see in me? I am just a Moabite by birth and an Israelite by grace.*" She knew her own background. It took no effort for her to revisit that hopeless feeling that was buried six feet deep in her heart. The day her husband died, many things died within her heart as he was buried in the sands of Moab.

Hope had been dormant for what seemed like an eternity; yet, Boaz's words seemed to kindle hope's fire in her bosom. She considered and contemplated Boaz's words. This was more than just an employer speaking with an employee. Boaz had taken special interest in Ruth and she reacquainted herself with hope once again.

Ruth pushed back the hair from her brow and looked at Boaz's heart through his eyes. She could see Boaz cared for her. Though she could not understand why Boaz would care so much for her, she graciously nodded her head to signal to him that she understood. Inwardly, her heart was about to burst with thanksgiving to God for His gracious provision of her needs.

Those who have tasted of the heavenly gift know well the feelings Ruth experienced at that moment. We look at ourselves and ponder why our Eternal Boaz would love us so much. Like Ruth, we look at our heritage, and we are ruined. We look at our homeland, and we are scarred. We look at our history, and we have nothing to offer.

Though we are unworthy, our Eternal Boaz still speaks words of grace that reach our hearts from just outside the city's gate on Calvary's cross. His words kindle eternal hope in our hearts. Our unworthiness of receiving His grace is aptly described in the song, "Sinner, Saved by Grace."

"If you could see what I once was, if you could go with me.
Back to where I started from, then I know you would see.

A miracle of love that brought me to His warm embrace,
He made me what I am today, a sinner saved by grace.
I'm just a sinner saved by grace!"

Gaither/Humphries

Never forget that it was His grace that brought you from Moab to His fields. It will be His grace that keeps you in His fields. Rest assured, at life's end, it will be His grace that will escort you home.

Think about it . . .

Follow the directions . . .

Ruth 2:8-9 *Then said Boaz unto Ruth, Hearest thou not, my daughter?*

Ruth listened intently, and she fully understood Boaz's instructions. Boaz wanted her to be aware of three priorities pertaining to his harvest. In essence Boaz said "Stay with my fields, stay in fellowship with my maidens, and keep your eyes on my harvest.

There was no need for Boaz to say it twice. Ruth would need no further reminders about those instructions. She did not have to be told to stay, because she wanted to stay and serve. There was nothing any other Boaz could offer that could be better. She resolved in her heart that she had come to stay.

Ruth knew that, in order to have Boaz's fullest blessings, she would have to stay in his fields. She could not expect the protection, provision, and promises of Boaz if she was in the field of another. Ruth determined that if he cared so much for her, why would she want to leave his fields?

Boaz told her to stay with his maidens and follow them wherever they went. Ruth already had met some of his gleaners and his reapers. This would not be hard, for there was a kindred spirit amongst them. She enjoyed the harvest fellowship they were having. She could not imagine what would draw her attention from this fellowship of harvesters to anyone else's fellowship.

Ruth heard Boaz's words, "Let thine eyes be on the field." Though this seemed so basic, there must be a reason he told her. She pondered, "I wonder what could take my eyes off of the harvest? How could I be in the harvest fields and still not see the harvest?" She determined she would keep these things close to her heart. She knew she would not want to disappoint Boaz in any way. Since these were Boaz's directions, she would follow them.

Far too often, believers today tend to wander from their Eternal Boaz's fields seeking their own provisions and promise of fulfillment. So many times we miss the blessing of His handfuls of purpose. Many seem to have lost the joy of fellowshipping with other harvesters. It is easy to be in the harvest fields and miss the harvest around us as we become absorbed in "busy-ness."

Friend, our Eternal Boaz has given us similar directions to follow. Determine today that you will keep your feet in His fields, your eyes on His harvest, and your heart with His harvesters.

Think about it . . .

Boaz quenches my thirst . . .

Ruth 2:9 *And when thou art athirst, go unto the vessels, and drink of that which the young men have drawn.*

Boaz had thought of every need Ruth could contemplate and met them in advance. Ruth felt special to be cared for in this manner. Though Moabitish by birth, she was finding that Jehovah provides for His children. As a girl growing up, all she had known were the gods of Moab. She knew those gods to be lifeless and uncaring; but in Bethlehem, things were different for Jehovah's children.

Ruth discovered quickly that Boaz had provided for her protection in his fields from the young men who might make her feel uncomfortable. Boaz had given her his promise that she could come to his fields and glean with his regular gleaners and reapers. As if that were not enough, Boaz now tells her that if you thirst, I have made provision for you.

Certainly, Ruth would get thirsty in the days ahead as she labored in the fields of Boaz. Typically, gleaners of Ruth's status would bring their own refreshment and provisions to the field; however, Boaz informed her that she would not need to bring her own vessel, because he would have one for her. Ruth would not have to draw water for herself; Boaz would have the young men to draw out the water for her refreshment as she labored.

The two shared this moment of tenderness together, not as employer and an employee, but rather as two souls brought together, fulfilling a divine purpose and embracing God's destiny. Her heart was full. The thirst of her body would be satisfied with water from Boaz. Boaz would quench the thirst of her heart, and Jehovah had quenched the thirst of her soul. Ruth knew the truth; God is good to His people!

When last did our Eternal Boaz quench your thirst? Does your heart recall the day when the Eternal Boaz offered the water of life freely to you? Do you well remember when the thirst of your soul was satiated in Him?

Our Eternal Boaz offers water for the soul's salvation. He offers in His Word, living water for our spirit's thirst. He offers water to both the weary and the worn. Have you a thirsting for His water this day? "*O taste and see that the Lord is good!*"

Think about it . . .

A servant to draw . . .

Ruth 2:8-9 *Then said Boaz unto Ruth . . . drink of that which the young men have drawn.*

Boaz's heartfelt explanation to Ruth conveyed he cared deeply for her. His instructions to his servants revealed that he was concerned for Ruth's safety, security, sustenance, and satisfaction. He told them not to harm or hinder this gentle soul, but to help her.

He instructed the young men to draw water when she was thirsty. His helpers knew from these instructions that she was dear to the heart of Boaz. A weary Ruth could make her way to the vessels, ordinarily assigned to the workers, and get refreshment from the young men assigned to draw water. She would not have to explain to them why she had a right to the water of the reapers. Boaz's orders required them just to draw it out.

The picture of a meek Ruth coming over to the well is a vivid image in my mind's eye. The young servants have been given the responsibility to draw out water for Ruth. In order for Ruth to receive her promised water, the servants would have to know the words of Boaz. These servants drawing the water for Ruth will also need to yield to the words and will of Boaz.

Believers today are in a similar situation with Boaz's servants. Our Eternal Boaz has also given us commands to fulfill on His behalf. We are to love the brethren. We are not to forsake our assembling together as believers in church. We are to evangelize the world with the Gospel. Our Eternal Boaz's commands are non-negotiable. We are simply servants assigned to a task.

How well are you doing in obeying our Eternal Boaz? Are you aware of the words of Boaz? Are you yielded to the will of Boaz? Are you doing the work of Boaz?

Think about it . . .

Water for the weary . . .

Ruth 2:8-9 *Then said Boaz unto Ruth . . . drink of that which the young men have drawn.*

The servants of Boaz had a new assignment from him. The assignment involved Boaz's newest gleaner, Ruth. The servants were to draw out water and permit Ruth to have it for her refreshing.

Though this would not be the usual and customary method for gleaners to have refreshment, Boaz delighted in meeting Ruth's needs exceedingly and abundantly above all she could even ask or think.

The obedient act of his servants in drawing water for this weary worker must not be overlooked. Ruth, though weary from the fields, would have full access to the vessels, water, and servants assigned to this task. Caring servants, responsible for the water, would be able to spot the weary one on her way to the water and could have it ready for her refreshing upon her arrival.

Servants of Boaz, look around you today. Nearby, there may be a weary Ruth that needs refreshing. You may say, "I have not been given that command." Or you may say, "I am too busy today to even take the time to think of refreshing a believer."

Please take this then as a gentle reminder from God's word. Jesus said, "We ought to wash one another's feet." Are we too busy to provide refreshing for weary workers? Our Lord lived 33 years upon this earth, and He took the time to refresh His fellow workers. Shouldn't we?

Foot washing is not a literal duty today, nor is it to be viewed as a third church ordinance. It is a command for the servants of the Eternal Boaz to refresh workers and to not neglect the needs of a weary Ruth around us.

Have you ever encountered a weary worker of God? You may see them in church or out in public. You may have noticed that they look a little weary in their well doing. Do not forget to look to the mission field where your missionaries serve our Eternal Boaz. Do their shoulders look drooped? Is their head hanging just a little?

You are a servant of the Eternal Boaz; rise up, get the refreshing water of the Word of God and find a way to bring them this water. A letter, phone call, or even a visit will refresh a weary worker and will renew his soul.

As servants of Boaz, let us be mindful of His servants and their needs. Determine today to find a weary worker and encourage them!

Think about it . . .

Protected by Boaz . . .

Ruth 2:9 *Let thine eyes be on the field that they do reap, and go thou after them: have I not charged the young men that they shall not touch thee? and when thou art athirst, go unto the vessels, and drink of that which the young men have drawn.*

Boaz took the time, before his conversation with Ruth, to seek out the young men in his field that had selfish interests and ill motives. He informed them that Ruth, the beautiful Moabite, was off limits to them. Boaz wanted no one to harm, hurt, or hinder the Gentile gem God had placed in his care.

Ruth, a poor, widowed stranger in the land, has no husband to protect her. She has no father to stand for her cause in matters of the heart and home. Her arrival in Boaz's field during such a tumultuous time in Israel had brought this reality to the forefront. The words *"have I not charged the young men that they shall not touch thee?"* spoke volumes to her heart.

Ruth's heart filled with joy as she realized the efforts Boaz had made, even before he had spoken with her, for her protection. Ruth listened intently to Boaz. She recognized that Boaz met everything she needed at this moment in her life.

Ruth needed a place to glean; Boaz met the need. She needed provision for her future; Boaz met the need. She needed protection from the self-gratifying men of the day; Boaz met the need. She reckoned with certainty that Boaz was sufficient for her.

We need to remember that as the days grow dark and gloomy, and as Satan roams about with his selfish interests and ill motives, our Eternal Boaz is protecting us. When Satan seeks to rob us of the confidence of His provision, rest assured that our Eternal Boaz is providing for us.

When our hearts feel empty and hurting, our Eternal Boaz has left a handful of purpose for us. Reader, we would do well to recognize that our Eternal Boaz is all-sufficient for all our needs. Our needs for provision and protection are met fully, and only, in Him. Keep looking up; our Eternal Boaz is near!

Think about it . . .

Revealing her heart and humility ...

Ruth 2:10 *Then she fell on her face, and bowed herself to the ground...*

Ruth had been listening with her heart to the words Boaz spoke. He told her everything that he had prepared for her. Ruth saw in his eyes and heard from his heart the genuine compassion of Jehovah. This God-sent man had just settled every concern of her heart. Her fears of the future were met in Boaz's promise. Her concerns for provision were met in Boaz. Her concerns for Naomi's quality of life were met in Boaz.

She was looking into the eyes of one who cared deeply for her. What words could she say in response to such an outpouring? Her heart responded before her lips could form words. Instantly, she dropped to the ground and hid her face from Boaz.

Ruth fell on her face as an unworthy servant. Ruth knew there was nothing of value or merit that she could offer Boaz. Knowing she was the recipient of his power, provision, and promise, this was not a moment for trying to find fitting words to express her inward gratitude. This was a moment reserved for appreciating the kindness of Boaz. Ruth knew she could never repay Boaz for his generosity, goodness, and grace. Ruth knew that she did not deserve his attention or his affection.

Ruth's first response was from within. When she fell on her face, she revealed her humility. When she bowed herself to the ground, she revealed her heart. She cared not about those standing around who were peering in her direction. Her response came from within as she pondered the goodness of Boaz.

We would do well to remember that we live our lives in the presence of our Eternal Boaz. Often, we are too casual in our approach to Him. We neglect to reflect on our first meeting, when He saved us from a life of misery. It seems most believers have become comfortable with His grace, casual in His presence, and calloused in their hearts.

Today, will those around you see your heart and humility?

Think about it...

Unwrapped presents of grace...

Ruth 2:10 ... *And said unto him, Why have I found grace in thine eyes, that thou shouldest take knowledge of me, seeing I am a stranger?*

Although Ruth had responded from her heart and with humility, her first recorded words to Boaz in the Inspired Text are in the form of a question. She could not understand how she had garnered this kind of interest from such a gracious and powerful man. She asks, *"Why have I found grace in thine eyes?"*

Ruth, from a prostrate position, spoke softly to Boaz. She inquired why *she* found grace in his eyes. She felt unworthy to even speak with him. Before uttering her question Ruth reflected in her heart the packages of grace that Boaz had presented to her since his arrival from Bethlehem. In a single moment of time, she reviewed her unwrapped presents of Boaz's grace. Listen to what might have been her thoughts:

> *"Look at all the presents of grace that have been unwrapped! Boaz spoke to me when he could have ignored me. He called me 'Daughter' when everyone else called me 'Damsel'. He recognized me as an Israelite and not as a Moabite. Boaz granted me full and unhindered access to his fields. He arranged for me to stay by his maidens when he could have easily left me to fend for myself. Boaz sought to protect me from the young men that might have caused me harm. He gave me his vessels from which to drink. He even gave me someone to draw it out for me."*

In just two verses, Boaz unwrapped seven presents of his grace. Boaz gave Ruth acknowledgement, adoption, acceptance, access, assurance, asylum, and affection. Ruth does not know what is about to happen in her life. Boaz has not exhausted his supply of grace for Ruth, God's Gentile gem. Ruth will find in the days ahead that there is grace yet uncovered for both her home and her heart.

Perhaps your heart has already considered that our Eternal
Boaz presented you the same seven presents of His grace when
you accepted Him as Savior. Our Boaz acknowledged us when
we were yet sinners. Our Boaz adopted us as His own when no
one else could help us. He called us sons, when we were sinners.
He accepted us and acquired acceptance for us with the Father
through His blood. Like Ruth, we were Moabite by birth; and
now, by grace through faith, we are His children.

Our Boaz gives us full access to His power, promises, and
provision. Our Boaz gives us the assurance of His presence
wherever we go. Our Boaz provides asylum from those who
would harm and hinder us. Our Eternal Boaz reveals His
affection for us by leaving us vessels for my supply and servants
to help me in my hour of need. Friend, although Ruth may
have thought she had unwrapped all of Boaz's presents of
grace, she would find there were yet presents of His grace to
be unwrapped tomorrow.

Jesus, our Eternal Boaz, has not exhausted His presents of
grace for His children. The longer you walk with Him the
sooner you will discover that for each day He has presents of
grace to be unwrapped.

Think about it...

Boaz overlooks my past ...

Ruth 2:10 ... *That thou shouldest take knowledge of me, seeing I
am a stranger?*

Ruth's words, punctuated by humility, give us a window to
her heart. Ruth demurely inquired about Boaz's grace. She
could not quite grasp why Boaz cared so much for her. Ruth,
in her meek and modest way, had come solely to glean in the
harvest, but, in turn, had also gleaned Boaz's heart. Boaz's
grace was the response to Ruth's gleaning of his heart.

Boaz had taken knowledge of Ruth. Boaz saw Ruth's past, her problems, and her poverty; yet, he still cared deeply for Ruth. Although Ruth had a past that was unmistakably marred by her Moabite birth, Boaz still loved her. Ruth had problems abundant; still, Boaz was unmovable in his commitment to Ruth. Ruth's poverty was at an all-time low; yet, Boaz still cared for her.

Ruth had not intended to draw attention to herself. She simply came to Boaz's field as a needy woman seeking a potential place of provision. She realized with amazement that Boaz was interested in her. She asked why he had taken knowledge of her.

Dear friend, you should know our Eternal Boaz also saw our past, our problems, and our poverty. Yet, even then, He still loved us. Our Eternal Boaz's love reaches far and will touch all that come to Him.

Think about it...

O how I love Boaz ...

Ruth 2:10 ...*That thou shouldest take knowledge of me, seeing I am a stranger?*

Ruth's past hung around her neck like a medallion. Her speech declared she was Moabite. Her clothing may have revealed she was a Moabite. Ruth's reputation indicated she was a Moabite.

Her words and their message were clear. "*I am a stranger in this land.*" In Ruth's thinking, her past affected her present. Yet, just spending a few moments with Boaz made her past fade away and her future look bright. This sense of assurance bred adoration in Ruth's heart for Boaz.

Mankind's past is marked by God's separation. Our father, Adam, incurred the wrath of God. Because of God's wrath, we were expelled from the place and presence of His fellowship. Yet, even then, we were never expelled from the promise of His fellowship if we would just return to Him in faith.

Man's problems could not deter the love of our Eternal Boaz. Mankind stood before God with the problem of unforgiven sin. It was an unmistakable scar from his sin. Mankind is left in an unfortunate situation because of his inability to settle his sin. Jesus Christ died on the cross to forgive mankind's sins, take his scars, and with His blood He settled his debt with God.

The family of man stood in poverty before our Eternal Boaz. We saw the debt, but we could not pay. We knew the payment, but had nothing to pay. Like a man trying to use a handkerchief as a blanket to keep warm on a cold night, we could not cover our spiritual indebtedness. Mankind stood before God shameful and bankrupt of righteousness.

Our sinful marring did not deter the grace of our Eternal Boaz. He loved us when we were unlovable. He took knowledge of us and loved us in spite of ourselves.

How is it *"That thou shouldest take knowledge of me, seeing I am a stranger?"* May we never wander from this truth! I was a stranger. My Eternal Boaz took me and loved me, though poor and with a troubled past. How great is His love for this impoverished and problematic Moabite! Consider the hymn, "O How I Love Jesus!" Today, as you ponder the goodness of our Eternal Boaz, sing these words:

"There is a name I love to hear, I love to sing its worth;
It sounds like music in mine ear, The sweetest name on earth."
                                                    Fredrick Whitfield
Think about it...

A stranger in Bethlehem ...

Ruth 2:10 *Then she fell on her face, and bowed herself to the ground, and said unto him, Why have I found grace in thine eyes, that thou shouldest take knowledge of me, seeing I am a stranger?*

Ruth struggled as she reconciled her unworthiness as a recipient of Boaz's grace. Ruth's deportment and disposition indicated this to Boaz and to any onlooker. Boaz had spoken so tenderly to her. She felt overwhelmed with a myriad of emotions. She wilted to the ground in humility. She had found grace in Boaz's eyes. The inexplicable mystery in receiving Boaz's grace left her baffled.

The unresolved matter in her heart was the core issue of her Moabite birth. The very point possessed her heart. It is quite evident in her statement when she confessed, *"I am a stranger."* Blushing shame and broken sorrow punctuated her statement to Boaz.

Ruth's perception of being a stranger seemed to have distressed her more than it did Boaz. Ruth seemed to be heavily influenced by her identity with Moab and her widowhood. Boaz focused more on her heart's confession en-route to Israel, her heart's conversion to Jehovah, and her heart's compassion toward Naomi, his relative.

"I am a stranger," Ruth reminded Boaz. Yes, Ruth's heritage made her a stranger, but her confession made her family to Boaz. Ruth's homeland made her a stranger, but her conversion made her family to Boaz. Ruth's hurts made her a stranger, but her compassion for Naomi made her family to Boaz. Boaz would see that Ruth would not be a stranger in Bethlehem, nor in his fields.

Although in this world believers are pilgrims and strangers, in the family of God no one should be a stranger. Consider what happens in our churches. We permit many unsaved guests to come and go in our services and never attempt to make them feel welcome and wanted. There are also occasions in our churches where unresolved conflicts with a fellow believer extend for years, and we treat that fellow believer as a stranger.

Let us take Boaz's approach with sinners and believers alike and make sure no one is treated as a stranger. Perhaps today you feel estranged from the family of God. If a brother has offended you, go to them; seek reconciliation and pursue the path of restoration with them today.

Think about it...

Boaz listens to me ...

Ruth 2:11 *And Boaz answered and said unto her ...*

Boaz listened to Ruth with delight. She was so taken with his grace that he could not help but smile. He listened to her inquiries of his grace and the insistence of her great hindrances. Boaz took the time to listen with patience to all of Ruth's concerns. Boaz had the answers already prepared for Ruth's questions. Scripture indicates, *"it had been shown fully to him."* Yet, he still listened.

Boaz did not quickly silence Ruth from speaking. He did not ignore Ruth's concerns about her past, her problems, and her poverty. He listened to her as a father would listen to his own daughter. It is apparent that Boaz listened attentively and lovingly answered Ruth's questions.

Boaz was not without an answer to Ruth's questions. Ruth was burdened about her heritage, and Boaz listened attentively and offered a loving answer. Ruth felt the weight of her need to provide for Naomi and herself, and Boaz listened attentively and offered a loving answer. Ruth was keenly aware of her vulnerability as a widow, and Boaz listened attentively and offered a loving answer.

It is important to recognize that Boaz listened to Ruth before he answered her. Boaz had his answers ready before she questioned him. Boaz treated Ruth in a tender and special way. Ruth knew from Boaz's response that she was loved.

Every believer should be mindful that we are treated in a tender and special way. This treatment is to an even greater degree than Ruth received from Boaz. Our Eternal Boaz listens attentively and offers loving answers for all of our concerns. Have you noticed in your prayer time how attentively He listens to you? God attentively listens to your prayers whether you are driving down the road or drifting off to sleep.

God not only attentively listens to our needs, but also offers to us His loving answers. Our Eternal Boaz's loving answers are found in His Word. Our Eternal Boaz greatly magnifies the simplicity of Boaz's actions toward Ruth.

Although our Eternal Boaz already has given His answer in His Word, He always attentively listens before He lovingly answers.

> *"What a friend we have in Jesus, all our sins and griefs to bear!*
> *What a privilege to carry everything to God in prayer!*
> *O what peace we often forfeit, O what needless pain we bear,*
> *All because we do not carry, everything to God in prayer!"*
> Joseph Scriven

Think about it...

Shown fully ...

Ruth 2:11 *And Boaz answered and said unto her, It hath fully been showed me.*

Boaz stood before a prostrate Ruth. Her words of amazement brought delight to his heart. He explained, in part, about how he came to this decision to care for her. The preamble to his explanation, "It hath fully been showed me," is worthy of notice.

The servant set over the reapers played a vital role in Boaz's comprehension of Ruth's situation. He had explained to Boaz about Ruth's arrival in the field. The servant spoke of her request to glean and of her knowledge of the laws of Jehovah. His servant related much about Ruth to Boaz.

Yet, Boaz stated that it had been "fully shown" to him about Ruth's condition, conversion, conduct, and communication. Boaz knew far more about Ruth than what the servant had said. Boaz, a resident of Bethlehem, would have heard about Naomi's arrival with the Gentile convert from Moab.

The diligent reader of the Inspired Text would recall the whole town of Bethlehem was aware of Naomi's return. The townspeople inquired not just of Naomi's return, but also of Naomi's rescue of a Moabite. The supper tables of Bethlehem were probably filled with conversations of the testimony of Ruth. The city gate also had its share of information about Ruth, as the people there were the first to notice Naomi's return.

We must not easily abandon the message in Boaz's statement. God's involvement with Boaz's knowledge must not be overlooked. Man could only know in part of Ruth's coming, her conviction, her conversion, and her conversation. Yet, Boaz said, *"It hath fully been showed me."* God saw to it that

Boaz's heart, spirit, and soul were prepared for this special moment in the line of Christ.

There is another special moment in God's eternal plan. It has been shown fully to us in His Word. God's Word is the primary method to "fully show" His truth to people today. The Word of God fully shows the truth of man's rebellion, ruin, and rejection. The Bible fully shows God's redemption, restoration, and return for men converted by grace through faith.

Do you need to understand what God is doing around your heart and home? Remember, "*It hath fully been showed*" you in the Word of God.

Think about it...

A lesson in compassion ...

Ruth 2:11 *And Boaz answered and said unto her, It hath fully been showed me, all that thou hast done unto thy mother in law since the death of thine husband ...*

Boaz's response to Ruth indicated that he was deeply affected. He commended Ruth for her compassion toward Naomi. He used terms of admiration when speaking of her heartfelt conviction to depart from Moab. He concludes this statement with speaking of her conversion to the God of Abraham, Isaac, and Jacob.

Consider with me Boaz's commendation of Ruth for her compassion toward Naomi. Ruth, a young bride in Moab, married outside of her people and into the Israelite family of Elimelech. Much had happened since she and her husband Mahlon had said, "I do." She first lost her father-in-law, and then, in an unexplained situation, both her husband and brother-in-law died. Ruth was left with Naomi and Orpah, her sister-in-law. The three widows only had their memories and each other.

Ruth shared Naomi's pain in a different way than Orpah had. The three left Moab, but only two made the journey to Bethlehem. Ruth determined that there would be nothing that would separate her from Naomi. She felt a sense of responsibility in caring for her husband's mother since Mahlon was Naomi's first born.

Ruth chose a role that was not dictated by laws of country, culture, or creed. She accepted this role because of the laws of compassion. Compassion's rules are not written, but they are known. The rules of compassion while not commanded are compelling.

Ruth heard compassion's call from within her bosom and responded. She spoke from her heart to Naomi's heart. Her words told the story that affected Boaz. *"Entreat me not to leave thee, or to return from following after thee: for whither thou goest, I will go; and where thou lodgest, I will lodge: thy people shall be my people, and thy God my God: Where thou diest, will I die, and there will I be buried: the LORD do so to me, and more also, if ought but death part thee and me."*

Boaz was aware of the compassion of Ruth, the Moabite, to Naomi, the Israelite. He knew Ruth's compassion was more than just a daughter-in-law's care for a mother-in-law. Boaz recognized that within the heart of Ruth was a well of compassion. Ruth set an example for Israel. Boaz determined to reward Ruth's compassion with compassion in the pattern of Jehovah-jireh.

Ruth's compassion must serve as a lesson to our hearts. Often, we use a filter of pride to determine how and when we exhibit compassion. Our self-determined filters of pride generally will exclude the unlovely, unfamiliar, and untoward. Yet, Ruth did not use any of these filters. She merely indicated, "My heart is drawn to your heart."

When compassion like Ruth's is displayed in our lives, it too captures the attention of our Eternal Boaz. Compassion declares, defines, and determines our "sonship" as seen in John 13:35. Have you the compassion of Ruth? If yes, display it; if no, determine to obtain it today!

Think about it...

Lessons in conviction ...

Ruth 2:11 *And Boaz answered and said unto her, ... and how thou hast left thy father and thy mother, and the land of thy nativity...*

Boaz's heart has been drawn to Ruth's cause. This precious Gentile gem from Moab's plains has made quite an impression on him. Boaz first took note of Ruth's compassion for Naomi. Naomi was both his relative, and Ruth's mother-in-law. Boaz then indicated to Ruth that his graciousness to her came also because of her heart's conviction. Boaz knew that Ruth to be a woman who would wholly follow what she believed in her heart to be right, despite any ties that would need to be severed.

It was unusual to find people who demonstrated their convictions, considering the days in which Boaz and Ruth lived. They lived in the days when the judges ruled. Those were days when "...*every man did that which was right in their own eyes.*" When people do what they think is right, and live in this selfish way, they indicate that they have a lack of righteous conviction.

Boaz stated, "*Thou hast left thy father and thy mother, and the land of thy nativity.*" Ruth's behavior revealed her heart's conviction when she stood on Moab's soil and determined to leave. Boaz knew when Ruth left both her family and the familiar to come to the foreign, she was showing that she was a woman who possessed conviction. Ruth's behavior indicates a simple definition of the word, "conviction." Ruth believed in righteous living so strongly that it altered her actions, her associations, and her attitude.

Ruth's convictions altered her actions. She left Moab for Bethlehem. She did not remain in Moab with righteous convictions. She did not attempt to change Moab from the inside. Ruth left Moab when her convictions came.

Ruth's convictions altered her associations. She left her family and the familiar for the unknown and unfamiliar. She did not allow her convictions to be thwarted because of relationships. She simply left everyone behind because of convictions.

Ruth's convictions also altered her attitude. No longer would she be among those who lived by the rules of pride and selfishness. She began to think differently as she left her hometown's ways of living for self. Ruth could not maintain her old attitude with her new convictions. Ruth's convictions changed her way of thinking.

We live in a day when people of righteous conviction are in the minority. We need people today who will alter their actions, their associations, and their attitudes for the cause of righteousness. People with righteous convictions do not stay in Moab; they seek to get out of Moab. Christians with righteous convictions will sever the ties with those that would deter them in their walk with the Lord. Believers with righteous convictions have a Christ-like disposition as they stand for truth. Godly people with righteous convictions alter their actions, associations, and attitudes. Are you a believer with righteous convictions?

Think about it...

Lessons in conversion

Ruth 2:11 *And Boaz answered and said unto her, ... and art come unto a people which thou knewest not heretofore.*

The tenderness of Boaz's conversation moved Ruth's heart. She inquired why Boaz sought her out and loved her so much. He spoke compassionately of how his heart had been touched with her move from Moab to Bethlehem. Boaz had been affected by Ruth's decision to identify with the people of God. Boaz saw Ruth and cared deeply for her pitiful condition. Boaz saw Ruth's compassion for her mother-in-law. He noticed Ruth's conviction to leave her people, and her conversion to his God. Boaz responded to Ruth with a measure of grace sufficient for her need.

Ruth knew well the Moabite's ways of family, friendships, and faith. The Moabites were a people scarred by the sin of Lot's daughters. Lot's daughters had gone in to Lot, fearing they would never marry and bear children to carry on the family name. (*You see, Lot's family had lived in Sodom so long that an incestuous rationale made complete sense to them.*) The fruits of Lot's union with his daughters were the Moabites and the Ammonites.

By birth, Ruth belonged by birth to a people who were among the antagonists of the Israelites. Yet, her arrival to Boaz's field was met with grace and goodness. The Moabites shared the Hebrew's language, but maintained their friendships with the Ammonites. These two groups were an "anathema" to God's people. Yet, when Ruth arrived, Boaz, God's ambassador to Bethlehem, met her with grace and goodness.

The Moabites and Ammonites had their faith founded in the gods of Chemosh, Molech, and Baal. Ruth's people placed their faith in gods whom they could only appease by human sacrifice and vain rituals. Yet, her arrival to Boaz's field was met with grace and goodness.

Perhaps now you see why Ruth was so puzzled at the measure of grace poured into the empty vessel of her heart. She, who had only known the vile ways of Moab's people and gods, now stood in Israel, a convert to the God of Israel. Ruth came to Bethlehem, not seeking asylum, but rather, adoption. She arrived in Bethlehem scarred by her past and her losses. She could not even bring her own merit to the town of Bethlehem or to the fields of Boaz. Ruth came to Israel with only her conversion to Israel's God settled in her heart.

What a wonderful reminder as you go about this day. You and I once belonged to a people who were estranged from God. We served with fervor the god of this world, Satan. We were friends with everyone that stood in opposition to God. Yet, in our scarred and tainted state, while we were yet sinners, God saw us and had compassion upon us.

Our Eternal Boaz pours out measures of His grace. His measures of grace are always sufficient to our every need. May we never grow accustomed to His grace and goodness, as some in our faith have done. Let us determine to praise and proclaim the goodness of His grace.

Think about it...

Recompensed by Boaz...

Ruth 2:11-12 *And Boaz answered and said unto her, ...The LORD recompense thy work ...*

Boaz's attentiveness warmed Ruth's widowed heart. Boaz was not an ordinary man whom she might have met in Moab. Boaz was unique because God had hand-selected him to fulfill His purpose.

Boaz's words, to Ruth's ears, were more melodious than an orchestra and clearer than the robin's chirps before the arrival of spring. Boaz's words penetrated Ruth's soul as she listened to his caring message and perceived his compassionate manner. Boaz's words revealed his discernment of the Lord's will and Word.

Boaz's words indicated God's awareness and attention to Ruth's work. Boaz spoke with confidence. He knew Ruth's service to Naomi had garnered God's favor. Boaz related to Ruth the recompense God offers to those who sacrifice for Him. Boaz knew that God not only had the ability to compensate for any deed, sacrifice, or effort made for His cause; but also that He WOULD recompense this widow from Moab.

Ruth recognized that Boaz spoke of a recompensing far beyond these fields of grain. Boaz's words transported the two of them into the realm of the Eternal Boaz. God Himself, the Guardian of Israel and Protector of the line of Christ, saw Ruth's heart as she cared for Naomi. Ruth had sacrificially given herself to Naomi first in Moab and now in Bethlehem. Ruth's work were of more consequence than just the emotional relief it provided Naomi. Ruth was to be recompensed by our Eternal Boaz.

Dear Laborer for God, your labors for Him on this sod have not escaped His awareness. Our Eternal Boaz has the ability to compensate for any deed, sacrifice, or effort made for Him. Our Eternal Boaz does recompense His workers, both on this field and at life's end when we complete our labors for Him. Have you grown weary in your well doing? God is aware of your labors. He pays attention to what you have done for His cause. His recompensing exceeds our imaginations. Keep your mind on your laboring, and He will take care of your recompensing.

Think about it...

Rewarded by Boaz...

Ruth 2:11-12 And Boaz answered and said unto her...a full reward be given thee of the LORD God of Israel...

Ruth listened intently as Boaz continued to deliver God's message to her. Boaz commented on Ruth's compassion for Naomi. He spoke of her conversion to Jehovah. He referred to her conviction as she chose to separate from Moab.

In our previous reading, Boaz told Ruth that the Lord would recompense her for her work. Surely, Ruth became overwhelmed that God would take notice of her kindness. If that were not enough, she was blessed richly because Boaz said God would recompense her for these labors of love to Naomi. Naomi had been so kind to her. Naomi had taken Ruth as a daughter. Boaz's statements of God's awareness, attention, and awards were more than Ruth could assimilate.

Ruth held her breath as she heard Boaz continue to speak. *"What more could he say?* What Boaz would tell Ruth would exceed all she, a Moabite convert, could ever ask or think. Boaz told her that the Lord God of Israel would give *"a full reward"* to her. *"Full reward"* and that by *"the LORD God of Israel?"* Boaz had filled her heart to overflowing with his words of God's grace and goodness.

Ruth heard it with her own ears. She was to be rewarded with *"a full reward"* by God. Ruth was aware that a reward given to someone is restricted to the bounty of the benefactor. Then, when Ruth heard Who the Benefactor was, she thrilled within. Ruth reflected on the limitlessness of God's bounty, which was now promised to her.

"A full reward" for Ruth meant rewards that were "out of this world!" A full reward for Ruth presented blessings beyond compare. Her reward was declared to be full and not partial. Her heart seemingly could not stand anymore.

The ending phrase that Boaz used echoed in the chambers of her heart. It left her with a fearful admiration of God. Boaz stated that "*the LORD God of Israel*" would be carrying out this promise. The very phrase used just over 100 times in Scripture sent a clear message to its hearers each time it was used. This one phrase proclaimed the authority, ability, and association of God. It resonated in her heart, and it left her in awe of God's grace. Her whole life was changed instantly as she encountered the grace of God.

Friend, our Eternal Boaz offers full rewards to His children today. He has not exhausted His supply of goodness nor grace. Your labors here on this earth are noticed and appreciated by God. He recompenses us in this life for sacrifices made for Him. Rest assured, He will reward us in a day yet to come when we stand before His Bema Seat. May your reward and mine be full!

Think about it...

Under His wings ...

Ruth 2:11-12 *And Boaz answered and said unto her, ... under whose wings thou art come to trust...*

Boaz's words of comfort ushered Ruth to a level of serenity she had not known. Boaz spoke of a divine recompensing, and Ruth was thankful. Boaz told of a divine reward, and Ruth was thrilled. Boaz now speaks of a divine relationship, and Ruth is thoughtful.

Two things were evident to Boaz; God had taken Ruth under His wings, and Ruth had come to trust God's power. Like an eagle guides and guards its young, God had guided Ruth through the deepest valleys of her heart. God had led her through the arid emotional deserts of her soul. God had given her the oversight and overshadowing she needed to get to the handfuls of purpose He had lain in store. God had been Ruth's Faithful Guide and Fatherly Guardian. Boaz recognized how Ruth had grown in her faith relationship.

The conclusion of Boaz's trilogy of comfort revealed that he recognized God's hand guiding Ruth's heart. Boaz and Ruth had been guided to the intersection of their divine destiny. Here Ruth would meet God's man for the rest of her life. Here Boaz would find his wife. Mahlon's death had not severed Ruth's ability to love again. Loneliness would not be Boaz's life-mate. God brought these two together for a divine purpose. Images splashed across the screen of Ruth's mind as the cinema of remembrance played the story of her life, with God's goodness having played the lead role.

First, she saw the day when the family of Elimelech moved to town. Seeing now what she could not see then she can identify the shadow of God's wings of provision. Looking back to the grave of her husband, God's wings overshadowed her. Leaving Moab and trekking 67 miles to Bethlehem, she now knows it was the wings of God protecting her. Just this morning, she left seeking provision for an unknown tomorrow. It was that same familiar shadow of His wings which prompted her to Boaz's field .

Looking back over the course of her life, and especially these last 10 years, Ruth saw clearly God's wings of protection, power, presence, and provision. It was the wings of God that prompted her to encounter the best people, places, and promises. Boaz's words spoke peace to her heart as she recognized the relationship between the wings of God and the supply of her emotional and everyday needs.

Dear friend, it is time for us to look back at the milestones of our lives. At each stop, look around you to see the wings of God which have overshadowed you along life's way. Salvation will be the first place you should look. It is here that the shadow of God's wings brought you to the place of conviction, confession, and conversion. From that point in your life until now, reminisce with our Eternal Boaz and thank Him for the shadow of His wings.

Think about it...

Watch for His wings ...

(Ruth 2:11) *And Boaz answered and said unto her, It hath fully been showed me, all that thou hast done unto thy mother in law since the death of thine husband: and how thou hast left thy father and thy mother, and the land of thy nativity, and art come unto a people which thou knewest not heretofore. The LORD recompense thy work, and a full reward be given thee of the LORD God of Israel, under whose wings thou art come to trust.*

Boaz's words were carefully selected. His words lost no impact on Ruth. In one phrase, Boaz accurately verbalized Ruth's feelings and thoughts. Boaz spoke with calming assurance to Ruth, and she listened intently and hung on his every word. Boaz's words draped a mantle of security across Ruth shoulders as she contemplated his ability to understand her needs and her nature. Ruth stood in the field of Boaz and listened in amazement to his words.

Boaz spoke the words that would send her on a journey of discovery in the kingdom of God's goodness and grace. Ruth knew that God, and this treasure of a man named Boaz, cared deeply for her. When Boaz learned of Ruth's compassion, conversion, commitment, and conviction he opened his heart to God's plan and purpose. When Boaz spoke of the "*wings of God*", his message came through to Ruth with clarity. She HAD come to trust the wings of God.

Boaz's statement revealed God's adoption of Ruth, God's acceptance of Ruth, and God's association with Ruth. God adopted Ruth upon her confession of faith in Him; therefore, she could trust in the wings of God. God accepted Ruth, despite her heritage and homeland; therefore, she could trust in the wings of God. God associated with Ruth before all of Israel. Therefore, she could trust in the wings of God.

Ruth knew within her bosom that she HAD come to trust the wings of God. It thrilled her heart to know that the God of Israel had adopted her when she confessed her faith in Him. The same God who had flown as an eagle above the nation of Israel now soared over her heart and hopes. The days of living with a Moabitish heart had been erased by the grace of God. Certainly, it was easy for Ruth to follow God, for He accepted her fully.

Ruth's persuasion was increased as she considered God's acceptance. Despite her marred heritage and homeland. When one is accepted by a group of people, he has a sense of connection. However, acceptance by God generates more than a sense of connection; it brings a secure confidence. What a joy to know that you are accepted, despite being marred and despite past mistakes. While others may not accept you, the God of all comfort, *"under whose wings thou art come to trust,"* enables you to look overhead and see His everlasting wings.

All of Israel knew that Ruth's confession of faith had associated her with God. As she heard Boaz speak Ruth became keenly aware that God had associated with her. The God of creation; The Lord of Glory; the Lifter of her head, heart, and hopes had associated with her. Soaring above her head were the wings of God. Ruth did not have to point it out to Boaz; he saw it for himself. God associated Himself with Ruth.

Friend, look overhead this day for His wings. Seeing His wings over you should indicate to you what it indicated to Ruth.

Your confession of faith in God secures your adoption, signifies your acceptance, and signals that God's association with you.

What greater message of hope could you desire?

Think about it...

Trusting Him ...

Ruth 2:11-12 *And Boaz answered and said unto her, ... under whose wings thou art come to trust...*

Boaz stood in his fields surveying the work being done by the workers. Ruth stood before Boaz as a younger woman who had proven herself in matters of work and worship

Boaz's comment about God's certain recompensing and reward for Ruth settled in her heart. The conclusion of Boaz's comments definitely stirs the intellect and offers inspiration to today's reader of the Word of God. Boaz's words highlight God's relationship with Ruth and Ruth's relationship to God.

Ruth's relationship with God allowed a level of reflection she could not have previously attained. She was able to spiritually reflect upon the graciousness and goodness of God in her life to this point. Ruth had not enjoyed a life of ease. She had seen her share of trouble and trials, but none of those elements were enough to unsettle her faith. Ruth's life revealed a contentment that the world could not rival.

Boaz saw this quality of faith in Ruth. He noticed that she had come under the wings of God and trusted Him. This phrase reveals the determination of Ruth's faith, the development of Ruth's faith, and the decision of Ruth's faith. Ruth's determination in her walk with the Lord is apparent when Boaz said, "*under whose wings.*" Ruth determined that she had lived outside the protection of His wings too long. Her confession of faith indicated that she wanted to be UNDER His wings.

Ruth wanted God's Word to reveal God's way so she could do God's work. She would be under God's wings and not her own. While under God's wings, she would find protection and provision. Under God's wings, she would find shelter and shade. Under God's wings, she would find contentment and confidence.

Ruth's decision is seen in the two words, "*whose wings.*" Ruth made the decision in her heart and chose God's wings for direction and protection. Ruth would not seek the wings of any other. Ruth would not be returning to Moab and seeking the wings of idols. Ruth's decision was clear in her heart and was now becoming clear to the hearts of those around her.

Ruth's development in the faith is evident from Boaz's words as he said, "*thou art come to trust.*" Ruth had come to trust the Lord God of Israel. She had come to trust Him by burial grounds and border crossings. She had come to trust Him in barley fields and Bethlehem. She had come to trust Him in matters of the harvest and matters of the heart. Ruth trusted God; she would not fear the outlook, the outcome, and the outside elements that would seek to dissuade her. Ruth trusted God with the details, direction, and the discomforts of life.

Under whose wings have you come to trust? Have you made the determination Ruth did? Have you made the decision Ruth made? Have you developed in the faith to just trust Him?

Think about it...

Ruth's request ...

Ruth 2:13 *Then she said, Let me find favour in thy sight, my lord; for that thou hast comforted me, and for that thou hast spoken friendly unto thine handmaid, though I be not like unto one of thine handmaidens.*

Ruth knew in her heart that she had found not only a place of bounty, but also a benefactor. She left that morning from Naomi's place and desired a field to glean and a benefactor that would be gracious. Certainly, the Lord God of Israel, under whose wings she had come to trust, had led her to this place of provision and protection.

Previously, she could not understand how she had come to find grace in Boaz's eyes. Boaz made her aware of the reason she had found grace in his eyes. You may recall, Boaz was touched by her compassion, conviction, and conversion.

Ruth's response was a request. She replied, "*Let me find favour in thy sight, my lord.*" Tenderness and humility were woven into her statement. Ruth had received Boaz's grace. Yet, now she is requesting to find favor in his sight.

Initially, the careful reader of God's Word would wonder why Ruth's reply to Boaz came in the form of a request. Ruth's request was not an indication of her failure to grasp the meaning of Boaz's reply. Ruth **did** understand the essence of what Boaz said.

Ruth's words were merely an indication of her heart's desire and her soul's devotion. Ruth desired to find favor in Boaz's eyes every time their eyes would meet. She never wanted to fall out of favor with Boaz. Having favor in Boaz's sight became Ruth's chief priority. Her request for favor in Boaz's eyes was not of greed, but rather of graciousness.

The prayer of Ruth's heart declared her wish to find favor in his sight all the time. Ruth's heart was certainly devoted to the cause of Boaz's fields. She merely wanted Boaz to be pleased with her forever. Boaz had promised Ruth that she could anticipate the blessings of the Lord in her heart and in this harvest field.

Ruth's request, robed in meekness, reveals a wonderful example for believers today. Our heart should be stirred by Ruth's simple request. Certainly, we have found grace in God's eyes for our salvation. We know He has redeemed us and given us His protection and promise.

Do all of your activities and attitudes meet with His favor? Do all of your labors and your earnest efforts in accomplishing your tasks meet with favor in His sight? Is our Eternal Boaz pleased with all you do for Him? May every Divine glance toward our work in the harvest fields be pleasing to our Eternal Boaz.

Think about it...

Ruth's response ...

Ruth 2:13 *Then she said, Let me find favour in thy sight, my lord; for that thou hast comforted me, and for that thou hast spoken friendly unto thine handmaid, though I be not like unto one of thine handmaidens.*

The words seemed to flow naturally as Ruth not only placed her request before Boaz, but also offered her response in the two-word phrase, "my lord." Ruth knew that Boaz's offer was generous and gracious. She knew she was special in his eyes. She was fully aware of his plans to protect her and to provide the help that she needed.

Ruth's request to find favor in Boaz's sight is punctuated by the two words, "my lord." This response placed her heart on display before Boaz. Ruth's two words, "my lord," indicated her pledge to Boaz and her possession of his promise.

When she said, "My, lord," she revealed her possession of his commitment to her. Ruth did not ignore his offers of help. She took possession of his outreach, his offers, and his openness. He offered to her the gift of his adoption, and she accepted. Boaz offered Ruth the gift of his acceptance, and she received it. Boaz offered to Ruth his association, and she accepted it. Ruth did not turn away his offers, but rather took possession of them.

Ruth not only took possession of his promises, but also made a pledge to him when she said, "my **lord**." In one phrase, she surrenders and submits to the lord of the harvest. She also pledges herself to his calling, commands, and commissioning. Ruth pledged her heart to Boaz's will. Ruth also pledged her hands to Boaz's work. In this two-word phrase, Ruth pledged her mind to Boaz's words.

Believer, many today have taken possession of our Eternal Boaz's promises of help for today and a home forever. We bask in His showers of blessing and possess those blessings steadfastly in our hearts. Yet, many who possess the blessings fail to pledge their love and loyalty to Him.

Many say "my," but never complete Ruth's phrase and say "lord." We enjoy possessing His promises, but never pledge our heart to His will. We never pledge our hands to His work. We never pledge our minds to His Word. May it never be said of you, dear friend, that you possessed His promises, but never pledged your heart in submission to His service.

Think about it...

Ruth's rest ...

Ruth 2:13 *Then she said, Let me find favour in thy sight, my lord;* **for that thou hast comforted me,** *and for that thou hast spoken friendly unto thine handmaid, though I be not like unto one of thine handmaidens.*

Ruth stood at ease before Boaz, her benefactor and channel of God's blessing. Boaz had a way of speaking that seemed to usher away her fears. A deep, settled peace swept over her heart as she relished Boaz's words of kindness.

Initially, in this verse, she issued a request, "*let me find favor*"; this revealed her humility. She then offered a response, "*my lord,*" which reflected her heart's submission. Her words, "**for that thou hast comforted me,**" indicate a relaxation that had come to her soul.

The burden of the future had been lifted off Ruth's heart. She stood before Boaz as a woman at peace with her future confident that she was no longer left to fend for herself. She had found her benefactor. Ruth had discovered God's will for her life, and she was at peace in heart and mind.

The essence of Ruth's phrase would be similar to a person breathing a sigh of relief when discovering the relief of fears. Ruth truly could breathe a sigh of relief, as she had found both a benefactor and a place to belong.

Boaz comforted the heart of Ruth as she wondered about tomorrow. Boaz comforted the mind of Ruth as she concerned herself with provision. Ruth had no idea she would find such a level of protection in Boaz's presence and promises. Ruth's comfort came as she pondered the goodness of Boaz. His gestures of grace brought comfort to the heart of Ruth. Boaz offered comfort for Ruth that exceeded her expectations.

When she considered the goodness of his promises, protection, peace, and presence she could breathe a sigh of relief. That relief was expressed in the single phrase, *"for that thou hast comforted me."*

Are you the type of believer that frets over tomorrow? Do you spend your time holding your breath and never fully relaxing in the promises, protection, peace, and presence of God? Have you a sense of peace and comfort that controls your heart and mind? Do you know the perfect peace that comes to those who wait on our Eternal Boaz?

There are comforts abundant in the presence of the Lord. Relax. Breathe a sigh of relief today. Our Eternal Boaz has comforts for your soul.

Think about it...

Ruth's reassurance ...

Ruth 2:13 *Then she said, Let me find favour in thy sight, my lord; for that thou hast comforted me, and* **for that thou hast spoken friendly unto thine handmaid,** *though I be not like unto one of thine handmaidens.*

Ruth fondly reviewed the compassionate words of Boaz spoken on the terraced hillside of his harvest fields. His words became planted in her soul. His words were growing a harvest of peace for her formerly burdened heart.

Ruth needed to hear Boaz's message. She knew Boaz could have spoken the words to her through his servant, but Boaz spoke to HER. Ruth, aware that Boaz could have been glib welcomed his friendly tones.

Boaz was not too busy to speak to Ruth. Many things may have been on his mind and heart that day. However, none were as important as the friendly words he spoke to Ruth. Boaz's words comforted Ruth as she pondered his goodness and grace. Boaz's words assured her welcome in the field of his harvest and the field of his heart. Somehow, his words were not just the words of an employer. Boaz's words sounded as if he had become caretaker of her heart. Yes, Boaz had taken on a new responsibility with Ruth; he had become a friend of her heart.

Our attention is drawn to the phrase, *"thou hast spoken friendly unto thine handmaid."* Ruth discovered both friendship and fellowship as Boaz spoke. Boaz had spoken to her when he could have ignored her. His words embraced her heart and kindled her hope. Boaz could have given the facts to Ruth without any feeling, but he had spoken with friendship to Ruth.

Our Eternal Boaz does no less for us than what Boaz did for Ruth. Man's recorded history from the Garden of Eden onward reveals that God has spoken in a friendly way to His children. When the cool of the day arrived in Eden's garden, God's speech was friendly to Adam. When Enoch went on His daily walk with the Lord, certainly God spoke in friendly manner to him. When Abram searched for answers, God spoke as a friend to His friend. David found that God's words were friendly to him whether in green pastures, or in cold caves, or even in his palace. The friendliest words spoken by God to mankind were spoken in the events surrounding the cross of Calvary.

Friendliness ought to be our distinction as we walk this earthly course. When you speak to those lost in sin, is your speech friendly to them? Do you speak in a friendly way to your fellow servants of the Lord?

Clearly, we have both an earthly example in Boaz and an eternal example in our Eternal Boaz. Are you following the divine example of speaking in a friendly manner to sinners and saints?

Think about it...

Ruth's honest reply ...

Ruth 2:13 *Then she said, Let me find favour in thy sight, my lord; for that thou hast comforted me, and for that thou hast spoken friendly unto thine handmaid,* **though I be not like unto one of thine handmaidens.**

Ruth's reply reveals her inward struggle to grasp Boaz's offers of grace. She stated to Boaz, "*I am not like one of your maidens.*" The words were spoken from Ruth's heart as she considered herself in light of the others in the field who were working for Boaz. Her comments to Boaz were accented by her amazement at his desire to extend favor and exhibit friendliness.

The last phrase in the verse deals with Ruth's amazement with Boaz's offer of fellowship. Ruth's heart swelled with emotions that could hardly be conveyed with words Ruth knew her chief obstacle from fellowshipping with Boaz came because of her Moabite birth. When she looked at the others she saw herself as inferior because the others were Israelites by birth. Ruth could never change her birthplace. She could not change her background. Considering the natural obstacles to a relationship with Boaz, it was all the more amazing to receive Boaz's overture.

The story of Boaz and Ruth is a story that began in distant lands, but whose happy ending would be in the Promised Land. Their meeting was not by chance. They met because our

Eternal Boaz brought them together. Ruth was aware that she could not start her life over again to become more acceptable to Boaz. Boaz's offer of fellowship to Ruth gave her the opportunity, not to start her life over, but to make a new future.

Boaz, our principal character, desires to fellowship with a girl from Moab. He has many handmaidens from whom he could choose to bring into his fellowship. Why would one of the original inhabitants of Ephratah, now called Bethlehem, want to fellowship with Ruth? Boaz could choose anyone with whom to fellowship, yet, he still chose Ruth above all others. Boaz's choice left Ruth with a recognition of her own inadequacy and an appreciation of his fellowship.

Like Ruth's beginning, the believer's life began in a distant land. We were born far from Jesus Christ. Sin separated us from His righteousness. Our Eternal Boaz sought us out and brought us to Himself. There was nothing we could bring to the relationship; we were marred by sin. Yet, even with our marring and mistakes, He still offered us His favor, His friendship, and His fellowship.

Words fail in each believer's attempt to describe God's goodness. He saw us, He loved us, and He forgave us. The truth of God's offer of forgiveness and His desire to fellowship with us should make our hearts rejoice each day. Although our Eternal Boaz knows about our sin's marring, He still says, "You are forgiven, and it is forgotten - forever."

Our Eternal Boaz desired you. He moved Heaven and earth to fellowship with you. Draw near to Him this day in your prayers and in His Word.

Take time to recognize His covering of compassion in your life. Reflect on His goodness and the grace He has offered you. Although marred by many things, He will always love you!

Think about it...

A handmaiden to Boaz ...

Ruth 2:13 *Then she said, Let me find favour in thy sight, my lord; for that thou hast comforted me, and for that thou hast spoken friendly unto thine handmaid, though I be not like unto one of thine handmaidens.*

Ruth's choice of words indicated her heart's desire and devotion to Boaz and to his cause. Boaz had been SO gracious to her that she could hardly assimilate everything he offered and the manner in which he offered it. Boaz's goodness was not evident in just one statement. In a fountain of statements, Boaz showered her heart and soul with graciousness.

"Handmaid," was the one word that characterized Ruth's feelings. She willingly viewed herself as a handmaid to Boaz. The position of a handmaid in the culture of Israel is that of being a mere servant. Ruth did not seek to elevate herself to a position of grandeur, but rather to maintain a position of humility. She sought only to be counted as a servant/slave to Boaz.

Ruth saw herself only in the place of a handmaiden, and God elevated her to the role of a wife. She saw herself as a slave to Boaz's cause, and God placed her in the royal crown of His Son, Jesus Christ. Ruth had a simple plaque that hung over her heart's door. It read "Handmaiden to Boaz." She sought no other position for herself. She only wanted to be a slave to Boaz's harvest and his heart.

Believer, when last did you take a view at the plaque that hangs on the door into the chamber of your heart? What is the title you have given yourself on that plaque? Does it read that you are a servant to the Eternal Boaz? Does it read, "Slave to the heart and harvest of Eternal Boaz?"

I have seen believers hang a list of their credentials on their heart's door. They read: "Charter Member," "A Pillar of my Church," "I am a Sunday School Teacher," or "I am a Deacon." Many herald their level of giving on the plaque of their heart's door. Ruth's statement should serve as an "ego check" for every child of God. Far too often, we think of ourselves more highly than we ought to think.

The positions of servants and slaves in our churches are disappearing. Churches have traded servants and slaves for "hired help" and people who need their egos stroked weekly by the pastor. Are you a servant and slave for the harvest of Boaz? Are you a servant and slave for the heart of Boaz?

We need more servants and slaves then we do anything else in our churches. God does more with people who see themselves as lowly than He does with those who see themselves as great. Ruth started as a handmaiden, and God made her a homemaker in the line of the Messiah. Surrender your credentials today and get back to the splendor of servanthood.

Think about it...

Favored by Boaz ...

Ruth 2:14 **And Boaz said unto her, At mealtime come thou hither,** *and eat of the bread, and dip thy morsel in the vinegar. And she sat beside the reapers: and he reached her parched corn, and she did eat, and was sufficed, and left.*

Heaven's spectators, aware of God's Messianic plan, would have rejoiced to see Boaz interact with Ruth. It was God who sent every emotional sunrise and sunset into Ruth's life. God has a way of making the sun to rise over the horizon of a burdened soul and restore hope.

Ruth's story exemplifies one of those times when God displayed the rays of His in a person's heart. Though the Book of Ruth is thousands of years old, just reading how God touched Ruth in her darkest hour still thrills hearts today.

Our verse begins, *"And Boaz said unto her …."* Undoubtedly Ruth's heart began to beat faster as she saw Boaz was about to speak again. Each time he spoke to her she sensed an unquestionable passion in his voice. Oh, how he had stirred the embers of her bosom! She knew that he was a man sent from God to her. No longer would she have to fret over the necessities of life.

Previously, we have seen that Boaz had committed both his heart and his assets to Ruth. Boaz committed himself before God to meet the needs of her home and the needs of her heart. Boaz certainly sensed Ruth's tender heart as she poured out to him her gratitude and expressions of willingness. Boaz knew this special handmaid would be no ordinary servant. Boaz committed himself to look after supplying all she would desire.

Have you noticed that in all the recorded occasions where Boaz spoke to Ruth she never grew weary of listening to him? Boaz's words never became mundane to Ruth. She seemed to treasure every word he spoke. She found it pleasurable to hear from Boaz. Ruth discovered Boaz's words were meat for her hungry soul. Ruth learned that Boaz's words became strength for her journey.

Our Eternal Boaz graciously speaks today through His Word and His Spirit. Have you lost the preciousness of hearing from Boaz? Has your spiritual life become mundane? Have you no joy in Jesus? Determine today to return to the place where hearing from Boaz brings delight to your soul!

Think about it…

A relationship of grace ...

Ruth 2:14 *And Boaz said unto her, At mealtime come thou hither, and eat of the bread, and dip thy morsel in the vinegar. And she sat beside the reapers: and he reached her parched corn, and she did eat, and was sufficed, and left.*

The conversation between Boaz and Ruth continues and we discover more images to insert into the scrapbook of Ruth's heart. Things had not been the same for Ruth since Boaz brought her under the umbrella of his protection. One visit to the terraced hillside of Boaz's fields changed her life. Ruth's visit of faith to find a benefactor on the hillside outside of Bethlehem brought her into a relationship of grace with Boaz.

Boaz offered to Ruth a relationship of grace, and she accepted. From that moment forward, Boaz's grace evicted the loneliness, the hurt, and the fears from Ruth's heart. Meeting Boaz caused Ruth's fears to be replaced with a bright future. Ruth's relationship with Boaz replaced her hurts with comfort. Ruth's widowed heart had found a companion in the presence and promises of Boaz.

Because of the grace of Boaz, Ruth found that some things were missing in her life. Gone were Ruth's days of aching loneliness in Moab. Gone were Ruth's heart-wrenching visits to a graveside in Moab. Gone were Ruth's days of worrying and wondering about her tomorrows. She quickly discovered that the benefits of a relationship with Boaz were innumerable.

Ruth learned what believers discover when they come to God. Those that enter a relationship of grace with the Eternal Boaz find abundant benefits. God's grace removes their failures and replaces them with His forgiveness. His grace takes their fears and replaces them with faith. His grace provides a peace that passes all understanding. Truly, the benefits of a relationship with the Eternal Boaz are countless.

Friend, have you made a journey of faith like Ruth and found a relationship of grace with our Eternal Boaz? This journey is not to Bethlehem, but rather to Jerusalem's hillside. On a hill, outside of Jerusalem, called Calvary, many have entered a relationship of grace with the Eternal Boaz. Is there a place you can point to in your life where you made a journey of faith and like Ruth, found a relationship of grace?

If there is a point when you came to Him, rejoice! If there is not a place in your life where He saved you, turn to Him and find His saving and sufficient grace. The Eternal Boaz still takes Moabites marred by birth and blemished by sin and makes them His child in a relationship of grace.

I am related to the Eternal Boaz by His grace. Are you?

Think about it...

Mealtime with Boaz ...

Ruth 2:14 *And Boaz said unto her,* **At mealtime come thou hither,** *and eat of the bread, and dip thy morsel in the vinegar. And she sat beside the reapers: and he reached her parched corn, and she did eat, and was sufficed, and left.*

Ruth could hardly believe her ears; Boaz wanted her to eat with him at mealtime! Ruth's heart must have been uplifted as she considered the lord of this harvest wanted her to be near him when it was mealtime. Many workers were in his field working, but he chose for Ruth to come and be with him. Other widowed gleaners were in his field, but Boaz specifically chose her to come near and eat with him. This was not just for one meal; but from now on she was to gather at the appointed time and place for the purpose of fellowshipping with Boaz.

Mealtime in the harvest field was a time to gather and rehearse the morning's labors. Mealtime allowed workers to look toward what must be done before sunset. Mealtime was a time for gathering and resting for the workers It was a time of refreshment for both the heart and the spirit.

Ruth's mealtimes would not be spent in solitude as a stranger, because Boaz told Ruth, "*At mealtime come thou hither.*" In these five words, Boaz communicated his desire to fellowship with Ruth. In essence, Boaz told Ruth, "When your body is hungry, come to me for food. When your spirit is hungry, come to me for fellowship. When your heart is hungry, come to me for friendship."

Believers, we would do well to realize that our Eternal Boaz extends this same offer of fellowship to us. He longs to be with us at mealtimes. At His mealtimes, we can discuss the morning's labors and what needs to be done by the sunset of our lives. During His mealtimes, we can just enjoy His grace and goodness. How often do you permit yourself to miss mealtimes with our Eternal Boaz?

Every believer should anticipate mealtimes with The Eternal Boaz. We should not neglect one mealtime with Him. Your mealtime with Boaz should bring refreshment to your spirit and rest to your soul. The time you meet with God to begin and end your day is a mealtime to fellowship with Boaz. The time you gather at church should be a mealtime with Boaz.

Our Eternal Boaz has prepared something for you today! So, "*At mealtime come thou hither!*"

Think about it...

Come thou hither ...

Ruth 2:14 And *Boaz said unto her,* **At mealtime come thou hither,** *and eat of the bread, and dip thy morsel in the vinegar. And she sat beside the reapers: and he reached her parched corn, and she did eat, and was sufficed, and left.*

Truly, Boaz sought a unique level of fellowship with Ruth. Boaz recognized that Ruth's labors for him would make her weary in the work. He knew that she would encounter difficult moments where he would not be right beside her. He was aware that Ruth would need an encouraging word that would help her to go on as she labored for him. He could not always be right beside her. Boaz determined to place a word of encouragement in her heart. He told her, *"when your labors are ended meet me here for a meal."*

Boaz requested of Ruth *"At mealtime come thou hither."* He wanted Ruth to come to his side and to be near him. It was more than just, *"Would you get to this specific place?"* but rather, *"Ruth, I want you near my side and in touch with my heart. I want you to be right here with me when you finish the labors of the morning."* When the heat of the day was in full force, he wanted Ruth in his presence.

How precious it is to realize that Boaz wanted Ruth to be near him. Boaz had friends with whom he could eat. Boaz did not even need to come to the meal in the field. Boaz assured Ruth that when her labors were ended, he would be there waiting for her. Ruth could go back to the field and glean with a comforted, contented heart. She would go back to the field confident that in just a little while she would meet Boaz, and he bring comfort to her when her labors were ended.

Friend, if you are involved in your church's ministry, you know that at times your duty can become laborious. You are aware that working with people can breed frustration. You have come to learn that a misplaced expectation in people always brings disappointments. Circumstances have a way of diminishing our hope. The heat of the day will oftentimes sap our confidence in being able to finish with success.

We oftentimes forget that our Eternal Boaz is looking over the fields of our lives. We neglect the fact that He is watching with interest. We fail to remember that we have His invitation, after our labors, to meet Him for eternity. Our Eternal Boaz has prepared a place at His table, and in His home, for His laborers.

We have His word that a day is coming when our labors are ended where He will say, "*It's mealtime, come thou hither.*" Eternal fellowship will be had with the One from whose Word we have taken hope. We will experience Eternal fellowship with the One by whom we have been comforted. This is the promised rest to the worker of God.

What is weighing you down today? What has seized your attention away from His promises? What thing could possibly erode your confidence in the day that He will call us to His side forever? Take hope, weary worker; at mealtime, we will go home!

Think about it...

Bread from Bethlehem

Ruth 2:14 *And Boaz said unto her, At mealtime come thou hither, and **eat of the bread**, and dip thy morsel in the vinegar. And she sat beside the reapers: and he reached her parched corn, and she did eat, and was sufficed, and left.*

The name **Bethlehem-judah** means, *"house of bread in the land of praise."* This town, named for its production of bread, carries special significance in Bible history. Two kings would come from Bethlehem: one, an earthly king, and the other, the King of Kings. Rachel, the mother of Israel, would be buried there. Boaz, the benefactor in Ruth's life, would hail from there and be God's channel of blessing in Ruth's life.

It is this Boaz and his offer of bread that holds our focus for this day. Boaz cared for Ruth in every way possible. His words seemingly dissipated the lingering clouds of doubt and despair in Ruth's horizon. Boaz's words paint a portrait of his inclusion of Ruth into his favor. Boaz's words portray two hearts brought together by God's will. They were two hearts standing in a field, knowing that each of their tomorrows would never be the same.

These two certainly must have shared an unspoken hope as they examined their hearts in this moment. Ruth stood near Boaz's side as he presented his invitation to fellowship with him and as he explained his instructions for her to follow. Boaz's words pleased Ruth very much. She knew that this man sought to bless her heart and that he held no ulterior motives. Boaz was a man she could trust with her heart and her hopes.

Boaz directs Ruth's attention to the bread laid before his workers. It was bread from Bethlehem. This bread from Bethlehem would represent the call from God that brought Naomi and Ruth from Moab. The bread displayed God's goodness after a famine in the land.

The bread he offered replenished her energy and rewarded her efforts in the field. The bread from Bethlehem would have provided strength for her continued labors. This bread would also create anticipation for another meal tomorrow. Boaz encouraged her to eat because he knew he would have fresh bread for tomorrow. Ruth would learn that her labors in the field would require her to use the strength from the bread she had eaten at her mealtime with Boaz.

Similarly, our Eternal Boaz offers to us today the same invitation. God offers us, his adopted children, the bread of the Word of God. His Word replenishes the energy we expend laboring for Him in His harvest. The bread of God's Word rewards us for our efforts on His behalf.

When reading God's Word, we find that our strength is renewed and we are prepared to return to our labors for Him. When we eat of His bread, we are left with anticipation of another meal with Him soon. The Word we take in each day at our mealtime with our Eternal Boaz will benefit our labors. Once you have tasted His bread, you will want no other.

Think about it...

My position with Boaz ...

Ruth 2:14 *And Boaz said unto her, At mealtime come thou hither, and eat of the bread, and dip thy morsel in the vinegar. **And she sat beside the reapers:** and he reached her parched corn, and she did eat, and was sufficed, and left.*

Ruth gently took her place as Boaz had instructed her. Looking around her, she noticed the reapers with whom she had been gleaning that morning. Confidence marked each step as she made her way into the family of reapers. The reapers knew she had been taken from the ranks of the poor, foreign, and widowed. Furthermore, they saw she had been placed into the circle of fellowship with them.

The faces of the reapers changed as she crossed the unmarked boundary between poverty stricken and preferential status.. Ruth stepped into their circle of fellowship, found her place, and sat down by Boaz's reapers. The harvest family had a new member. They knew it was because of the work of Boaz.

Ruth's search for a benefactor came to an end in Boaz. Boaz abundantly exceeded any desire she had when she left Naomi that morning. Certainly, living *"under the wings in whom she had come to trust"* had blessings untold and joys unspeakable.

When Boaz took Ruth and invited her to be a part of his harvest her social standing among the field workers changed. She went from being poor to being preferred. She changed from one who was foreign to one who was family. She went from widowhood to being wanted by Boaz.

Ruth now had a sense of security that she had not known since Mahlon died. The day he died she lost more than her husband; she felt as though she had lost her heart. Her heart became disconnected after Mahlon's death. Yet, today, Boaz found the loose ends of her heartstrings and tied them to his own, and Ruth knew security again.

Oh, how it must have done Ruth's heart good! What a sense of belonging she must have felt as she looked around her and saw from where she had come to where she was now! Boaz had made a way for Ruth to have food for tomorrow, fellowship for today, and a family forever.

Believer, you must know that were it not for the work and will of our Eternal Boaz we would not be in the position we have today. The will of our Eternal Boaz is that all would come to Him. The work of our Eternal Boaz has made it possible for all to come to Him.

Never forget the day that you crossed the boundary from sinner to saint. Don't ever lose the value of just how precious it is to be in Boaz's family! As a believer, you have been given a position in Boaz's family that lasts forever. You are given provision from Boaz's field for your daily bread. You have a position in Boaz's fellowship with other workers.

What a privilege it is to be a part of His family, a partaker of His food, and a participant in His fellowship!

Think about it...

Morsels from Boaz ...

Ruth 2:14 *And Boaz said unto her, At mealtime come thou hither, and eat of the bread, **and dip thy morsel in the vinegar**. And she sat beside the reapers: and he reached her parched corn, and she did eat, and was sufficed, and left.*

Certainly, Ruth's heart swelled with delight as Boaz took careful detail to explain his desire for them to fellowship. She must have found great pleasure as he made it clear that she was to be in fellowship with him at her mealtime. Ruth would be able to be near Boaz and to receive nourishment from him at every mealtime.

Boaz's instructions about their fellowship time included a comment about taking morsels and dipping them in vinegar. This practice is used today by Arabs in the deserts of the east as a method of hydration. The people would dip their morsels of food and bread into a sauce. The sauce would provide them cool refreshment.

Boaz thought of everything and made it available to her. Ruth would not need to bring anything to this mealtime. All she would need would be given to her: bread, parched corn, morsels, and vinegar would be spread before her. Mealtimes with Boaz and his reapers would replenish her physical energy and refresh her emotional energy.

Fellowshipping with Boaz would bring her joys without measure. All she would need to do is arrive, get in her place, and feast on what was placed before her. Boaz made it easy for her and gave her his personal invitation. Ruth discovered that Boaz gave attention to even the morsels.

At mealtime, Ruth was to come from the field. She was to be seated by the reapers. Ruth was to take bread from what was prepared and not to worry about bringing any from home. The fellowship time promised to be refreshing for the body; however, there was an unspoken benefit for her heart, too. You see, the fellowship would bring a much-needed uplift to her heart. She would not be cast off to the side in Boaz's field; she was both welcome and wanted.

Our Eternal Boaz offers the same arrangement for His reapers today. God has given us the bread and morsels of His Word. He has given us fellowship with His Spirit in which to dip the morsels of the Word we find at mealtimes. This fellowships spurs us to seek even richer refreshing. It is our duty to arrive at the table during fellowship times and enjoy morsels from our Eternal Boaz.

Keep in mind the danger many believers face. In searching for morsels, they rush to His table of fellowship each day in the Word just to grab the morsels and never stay for the meal. Many have come to think the Word of God as a fast food chain where they can rush in, order a "Happy Meal" from God and drive off. Many expect that kind of relationship with the Word is exactly what God intended.

Friend, let your relationship with Him become a time of intimate contact, and not a "fast food" experience.

Think about it...

He reached out for me...

Ruth 2:14 *And Boaz said unto her, At mealtime come thou hither, and eat of the bread, and dip thy morsel in the vinegar. And she sat beside the reapers: and he reached her parched corn, and she did eat, and was sufficed, and left.*

This scene, to the casual observer, would seem unique. Here, gathered at the edge of the harvest, are what appears to be the lord of the harvest and his workers and a woman. They are in the midst of a mid-day meal.

Their fare seems to be not only adequate and but also abundant. Bread brought from Bethlehem has been broken. Vinegar from a dish is made available for the workers to dip bread in as they eat. Refreshing water is available to quench the worker's thirst. Young men stand nearby to draw more water if needed. Each worker was able to reach for the food he desired. The food had been placed there for the worker's benefit. The workers shared both in the food and in the fellowship.

Placed on the table before the workers is a dish containing corn. This corn has been roasted in the husk over a fire. Many preferred corn served this way. In order to eat it, they would remove the husks and either break off the kernels or eat it off the cob. Both the nutrients and the flavor were rewarding to the workers in the field.

Boaz was seated in the Middle Eastern fashion with his workers. At the table, all eyes would be toward Boaz; anything he did or said would be noticed. After all, this was his food, prepared for his people.

The reapers, and the new member of the group, all watched the lord of the harvest in wonder. Boaz purposefully reached across the spread of food laid out for his workers to get parched corn. His reach was not for himself. He took an ear of the parched corn and offered it to one person at this gathering. Boaz gave it to Ruth.

Boaz chose the ear he would give. Ruth, and the rest seated at the table, knew this gesture was special. No one else at this meal had been favored in this way. Boaz selected the husk, offered Ruth the corn, and she accepted it.

Boaz had honored Ruth in front of the reapers of the harvest. The honor was not for years of service. Nor was Ruth's honoring for the sake of productivity. Boaz honored Ruth because of his goodness.

Our Eternal Boaz is even more gracious to us than Boaz was to Ruth. God knows our every need and He supplies it; yet, more than just meeting daily needs, He selects and offers us parched corn in our daily lives. Look around your home and your heart. Have you no husks remaining from where our Eternal Boaz selected, roasted, and offered you gestures of His goodness? He did not have to offer you anything, but He did!

Friend, it is time we train our hearts and our heritage that follows us to look for the ears of parched corn He reaches for us. His reaching parched corn for us should make us as well as our children rejoice and find reassurance. Our Eternal Boaz loves us and is looking out for us. For every ear of parched corn He brings today, take a moment and reflect on His goodness.

Think about it...

Boaz satisfies my soul ...

Ruth 2:14 *And Boaz said unto her, At mealtime come thou hither, and eat of the bread, and dip thy morsel in the vinegar. And she sat beside the reapers: and he reached her parched corn,* **and she did eat, and was sufficed, and left.**

Boaz's invitation gave Ruth more than a place to eat; it gave her a place to connect with his heart and with his harvesters. It was more than just an invitation to a meal for Ruth. This was an invitation to a new way of life. It was here Ruth discovered that all she would ever need, Boaz could supply. That day, Boaz fed her food for her hunger and fellowship for her heart.

Ruth could look at the faces of those gathered around this humble fellowship of people and know that they all enjoyed Boaz's blessings and bounty. Ruth's position of being seated by the reapers, but within reach of Boaz, gave her no small comfort. Ruth found her hunger was satisfied with his provisions. She discovered her heart was satisfied with his presence, and her hope was satisfied with his promises.

A quick glance over her shoulder as she returned to her labors would have left Ruth with a sense of tranquility. The meal had restored her energy; she knew that the fellowship had renewed her mind.

Her departure from the fellowship and the food initiated a new thinking process. Inwardly, she must have contemplated the satisfaction that Boaz had brought to her life. She was satisfied with Boaz's blessings and bread. Ruth found satisfaction in his bounty. Boaz satisfied her heart and met all her needs.

Any who have ever worked on a project with a group of people and stopped for a meal can imagine their conversation that day in the field. There would have been a discussion of their labors that morning. They might have discussed what was happening in the community and what was transpiring among their friends and family. Surely, there would be laughter and lightheartedness during this meal; yet, all would be mindful of the unfinished task before them. They would enjoy the mealtime for the moment but would know they still had work to be completed. There was still a crop to harvest. There was still grain to thresh. There were fields to be gleaned.

For the believer today it would be wise to take a lesson from these nine words in our focus phrase, "*And she did eat, and was sufficed, and left.*" There are lessons of resting, replenishing, and returning for the labor of our Eternal Boaz. Ruth was called apart from her labors to rest. She enjoyed the way the food and the fellowship had replenished her emptiness. She enjoyed it all with an awareness of her unfinished responsibility. Ruth then returned to her labors mindful that only Boaz could satisfy her soul.

We too, have before us a harvest of souls that we must reap, glean, and gather. Let us feast and fellowship until we are satisfied. Then let us return and complete our labors, ever mindful of the day when our labors shall cease and we will have an eternity to rest and to rejoice. Laborer, never forget that only Boaz can bring satisfaction.

Think about it...

A heart for His harvest ...

Ruth 2:15 *And when she was risen up to glean, Boaz commanded his young men, saying, Let her glean even among the sheaves, and reproach her not:*

Ruth's first meal with Boaz was most memorable. Boaz selected Ruth to come to the meal. Boaz had served Ruth during the meal. Boaz had satisfied her with his bounty and blessings.

Ruth knew her responsibilities to fulfill the promise made to Naomi rested upon her own shoulders. Furthermore, Ruth knew she must get back to the fields to finish the day's gleaning. Though relishing in the favor of Boaz for the rest of the day would be fine with her, she realized that there were fields to glean. In an unrecorded silence, she removed herself from that special place of fellowship and food and returned to work.

The image of this gleaner rising to return to her responsibilities creates a vivid image in this author's mind. For the student of the Word, Ruth's behavior portrays for the student of the Word a clear view of her priorities, purpose, and plans. Ruth valued her lord's work above her own desire to rest. Ruth's purpose evidenced itself as she left the fellowship to labor in the fields. Ruth's plans become apparent when she departed for her duty. She knew that she had gleanings to gather in her lord's harvest so she could provide for Naomi and herself.

Boaz and the rest watched this special one under the wings of Jehovah's protection, graciously rise from the period of resting and return to her responsibility. Boaz knew she enjoyed his fellowship and favor. Boaz was impressed with her determination to do what was right. Boaz did not have to remind her of her duty. She just rose up and did it. Although they both would have loved to fellowship now, they knew that when the harvest ended there would time to do so.

For the believer, the beginning phrase from chapter two and verse fifteen reveals many lessons for living. Our own hearts find a wonderful example in Ruth's heart for the harvest. While many claim to enjoy the fellowship, favor and food of Boaz, they have no heart for His harvest. Some testify they cannot wait to spend forever in Heaven with Jesus, but they have no heart for His harvest.

Ruth's rising to her responsibility is our example that we should never allow our purposes, plans and priorities to become focused on ourselves. When we do allow "our will" to rise above "His will," we quickly lose our heart for His harvest. Do you have a heart for His harvest?

Think about it...

A place for Moabites ...

Ruth 2:15 *And when she was risen up to glean, Boaz commanded his young men, saying, Let her glean even among the sheaves, and reproach her not:*

The servants of Boaz listened with interest to the most unusual instructions from their master. Here the one who has a vested interest in the profitability of the harvest has told the servants, start to give away the profit. This gesture, to the calloused observer, would seem ridiculous. Yet, the servants, being obedient to Boaz, obeyed his command.

The servants were to allow Ruth full access to every part of the field. Normally, the corners would be the place a woman of Ruth's status would be lawfully permitted to glean. Yet, Boaz treated Ruth, not under the law, but under grace. Boaz's said, *"Let her glean even among the sheaves."*

Ruth, though a Moabite, had found a place in Boaz's heart, and now Boaz wanted a place in his harvest for this Moabitess. Boaz's grace permitted Ruth access to his harvest and his heart. It was his grace that provided Ruth favor and fellowship. Boaz's grace opened the way for Ruth's reward and redemption. Were it not for the grace of Boaz, Ruth's outlook and outcome would never have been the same.

The servants were commanded to yield to Boaz's desire to help this one who had come seeking a benefactor. Boaz desired for Ruth to have the freedom to roam in his fields. Boaz wanted Ruth to find fruit in his field. Boaz sought for nothing less than for Ruth to have found favor in his fields. Boaz recruited his servants and required them to help in this endeavor.

Ruth held a special place in Boaz's heart. She had come to Boaz's field seeking a benefactor. Instead, she found everything and more in Boaz. Boaz arranged everything around her to bless and to benefit her. Boaz did not exempt Ruth from work; he simply made the workload a little easier.

We too hold a special place in the heart of our Eternal Boaz. He has gone to great lengths to give us more than we ever thought possible to find in this life. Our Boaz has arranged every detail of our lives to bless and benefit us. He loves us with an everlasting love and made the way for us, as former Moabites once estranged from His fellowship, to live not under law, but under grace.

There is a place for redeemed Moabites in the heart of Boaz as well as in His harvest. Since He accepted and adopted you, have you been gleaning? Since His redemption, have you spent more time sitting or serving? Since coming under the shadow of His grace, have you labored for Him in His field, or have you just been looking around His field?

Servants of the Eternal Boaz, consider His commands to you today. Have you been obedient to His commands to tithe to your church? Have you been observant to his commands for the lost souls of man? Have you been occupied with his command to caring for His servants who go to fields abroad? Have you opened your heart to Him for daily fellowship in His Word? Let us occupy until He comes!

Think about it...

Serving without reproach...

Ruth 2:15 *And when she was risen up to glean, Boaz commanded his young men, saying, Let her glean even among the sheaves, and reproach her not:*

Boaz cared deeply for this recent convert to the God of Israel. He had been fully shown Ruth's importance to God's plan. God had enlisted the resources, respect and riches of Boaz to make a way for Ruth in Bethlehem.

Boaz's command to his men is punctuated by a unique phrase, " ... *and reproach her not.*" The young men may have found this request to have been unusual. The command could easily have been a threat to their wages if there payment were based on productivity. They also could have viewed Boaz's command as a threat to their role as harvesters.

Boaz's instructions were clear to his men. The workers of Boaz were to lift the restriction on Ruth's gleaning. Ruth, because of God's law of grace could come and glean in the corners of the field. Boaz's words granted her full access and gave her the needed authority to glean wherever there were grains that had fallen.

Boaz knew his men and he recognized their tendency to be hard on each other, not to speak of their treatment of the women. Previously, he had cautioned the men about their behavior. Boaz recognized Ruth's status. After all, she was a Moabite, and a recent convert to Jehovah. These things may have meant little to his men. Therefore, he sought to protect Ruth by his words. The words Boaz used to admonish his men indicated they were not to taunt, torment, insult, or wound Ruth.

The average church member could learn a valuable lesson from Boaz's command to his laborers. New laborers are not to be viewed as a threat to our own position on Boaz's team. Reproach should not come to the newest harvesters, but rather, upon their arrival, unanimous rejoicing should be offered.

Absorbed in their pride, many servants, think their own positions in church are threatened when new people come along. Usually the members will begin to identify themselves to the newcomers by their length of service in the church. Some church servants have been known to isolate newcomers with cynical statements, and critical comments.

Believer, you were once a newcomer in Boaz's field. You came and needed the fellowship and friendship of the other workers in the field. Have you forgotten from whence you have come? Has time erased your memory of the peace and protection you sought? Have you drifted from the manner in which The Eternal Boaz expects you to serve? If you are not careful, your pride can elevate you to a position higher than you really have in God's eyes. Take heed that pride does not replace humility in the service of our Eternal Boaz.

Believer, it is time we heed the earthly Boaz's command to Ruth. The fact remains that at one point in our existence, we too were brought to the Eternal Boaz's field by His grace. Too often, we who have been in the field for some time offer reproach to Boaz's workers, instead of rejoicing. May God forgive us for the reproach we have offered to the newcomers in God's field!

Let us return in obedience to the commands of Boaz and offer thanks and praise instead of taunting and tormenting. Let us encourage and welcome others rather than insulting or wounding the newest members in the field. Let us be what Boaz expects us to be!

Think about it...

Instructions for harvesters ...

Ruth 2:15 *And when she was risen up to glean, Boaz commanded his young men, saying, Let her glean even among the sheaves, and reproach her not:*

Ruth's departure back to the fields gave Boaz the opportunity to carry out further the plan God had fully shown him. When Ruth was out of hearing range, Boaz gathered his young men.

Because of the nature of Boaz's request, these probably were not the same young men that were instructed to draw water for Ruth if she became thirsty.

Boaz did not make a suggestion to these men on their responsibility to Ruth. Boaz gathered them on the terraced hillside of his harvest field and gave them a specific command. The command he gave them would instruct them concerning where they should go, what they should do, and what they should say.

Boaz's command to his workers would not be negotiable, for these were his harvest fields. He instructed these men to return to the fields in which they were familiar and look at them in a new way. They were to go back to the fields with the heart and eyes of Boaz and carry out his command.

Boaz's concern for Ruth became apparent as they listened to his words and assimilated their responsibility. Boaz specifically told them that Ruth was to be allowed unrestricted access within his fields. Normally the poor, the strangers in the land, and widows would be given permission to stay in the corners and glean. However, with Boaz's instructions, these men were to permit Ruth to glean among the sheaves in the field.

Boaz gave his men a specific command regarding what they were to say to Ruth if she came around the sheaves. This one command must have raised eyebrows for these men knew the profit from the field would be used up if they would allow her to come and go wherever she chose. They were told to not reproach Ruth for coming near the sheaves. They were, in fact, to encourage her to glean, as the next verse will indicate, by leading her close to the sheaves with the handfuls they would drop on purpose.

One day our Eternal Boaz, Jesus Christ, stood outside Jerusalem on a hillside and gave specific instructions to his disciples about His harvest. These men were to go to His fields, with His heart and His vision and accomplish His work. He told those disciples the same three things Boaz told his workers. He told these workers where they should go, what they should do and what they should say.

As a disciple of Christ, are you following His instructions for the harvest from Acts 1:8? Are you going to the places He told us to go? Are you working in the harvest like He told you to work? Are you carrying the message He said to bring?

The world is our harvest field. We have the message of hope and Heaven to deliver. We are to go to every nation and deliver the message of mankind's condemnation and His redemption. Our Eternal Boaz has a heart and vision for the whole world. Do you have His heart?

Think about it...

Reproach her not ...

And when she was risen up to glean, Boaz commanded his young men, saying, Let her glean even among the sheaves, and reproach her not: Ruth 2:15

Boaz spoke with authority to his men. Each man knew fully that Boaz's words were to be taken literally. Boaz commanded the young men to permit her to glean. The gleanings were not to have the ordinary restrictions that limited the stranger, the widowed, or the poor to the corners of the land and to what was lying in the way. Boaz's orders meant Ruth had been given unfettered access to his fields.

His words gave Ruth the clearance she needed to roam in the fields of Boaz and to pick up whatever fell from the grasp of the reapers. They were not to hinder her with their actions, attitudes, nor their words. Boaz specifically added, " ... and reproach her not." Typically the men would well be in their rights to defend the fields of their master against an intruder or a straying gleaner, however, the rules were different for Ruth. These men were not to utter a word of reproach to her.

The very phrase indicated to the young men Boaz's power, protection and passion for Ruth. Boaz's command to the young men displayed his power. He cautioned the men, which revealed his protection. His constraint of the men, revealed his passion for Ruth.

Apparently, according to Divine Law, the young men would be within their rights to make Ruth feel ashamed for taking more from the field than what was legally her right. Boaz's words made certain they were not to reproach her. That is to say, they could not scold, humiliate, nor insult Ruth for moving from the corners of the field to glean throughout the field.

Boaz's command gave Ruth the ability to roam throughout his fields without any fear of reprisal. Divine law gave Ruth access to the corners, but Boaz's command gave Ruth grace to go beyond the boundaries of the law to find his love. What the law permitted for Ruth, Boaz's grace extended to give her far more than what the law allowed.

Sadly, in the family of God, it seems reproaches come more easily from other believers than do rejoicings. Oftentimes, a new believer's zeal to rest and roam freely in the goodness of God's grace is met with scolding and sarcasm from long-time family members who have grown calloused. May the words of the earthly Boaz prompt us to consider the words of our Eternal Boaz, *"Let all bitterness, and wrath, and anger, and clamour, and evil speaking, be put away from you, with all malice: And be ye kind one to another, tenderhearted, forgiving one another, even as God for Christ's sake hath forgiven you."* (Ephesians 4:31-32)

Today, for each person you meet, live out these words from the New Testament in light of Boaz's command to his young men, "Reproach them not!"

Think about it...

Handfuls for her...

Ruth 2:16 And *let fall also some of the handfuls of purpose for her,
and leave them, that she may glean them, and rebuke her not.*

Boaz determined that things for Ruth were going to be easy.
He commanded his young men that the blessings of the
handfuls of purpose were to be for Ruth exclusively. The men
were not to extend this favor to any others in the field. They
may have known the other gleaners that had been in the field
for a longer time than they did Ruth. They have may have
even been related to some, but favoritism was not permitted
as they dropped these handfuls of purpose.

Boaz's command was not to be altered. He specified that Ruth
was to receive handfuls of purpose. His men would be in full
disobedience if they chose to take their master's bounty and
place it into the hands of someone they liked better. They
could not take it and give it to someone they felt had a greater
need. The men would be in error if they took the handfuls
and used it for themselves. The men who received these orders
knew full well that any other use of the bounty would leave
them in jeopardy with Boaz.

The men in the field were to take the bounty of Boaz and
place it before Ruth to comply with Boaz's commands and to
provide Ruth's needs. Boaz's men may have seen others with
needs similar to Ruth's; however, Boaz had specified who was
to receive the gift. Boaz declared the amount of the gift; Boaz
even determined the frequency of the gift. Nothing was left
for them to assume. Boaz had given his word.

You know, our Eternal Boaz has given a similar command for
believers today. We are to take the bounty He places in our
hands and give it away. We are not left without commands as
to where we are to give His bounty. Like the reapers of Boaz
were to give only to Ruth, so the believer is commanded to do
ALL his giving in one place, His local church.

The men in Boaz's field were to give to Ruth with regularity. The believer is under similar guidelines; we are to give as God has prospered us. We are not to choose when and where we will give. Nor are we to choose how much we will give. Boaz told his reapers to use a measure of a handful. Our Eternal Boaz has given us specific command in the same way; we use not the measure of a handful, but rather the measure of 10% of our increase.

How foolish we believers can become in matters of giving. God gives to us everything we have and yet, many times we think we can choose where we will give, how much we will give, and how often we will give. The amount, location, and frequency of our giving are given in Scripture. Your giving must be a priority not a preference.

Think about it...

Lessons in giving...

Ruth 2:16 And let fall also some of the handfuls of purpose for her, **and leave them, that she may glean them,** and rebuke her not.

Boaz's words to his men left them with little doubt. His men were to purposely drop handfuls in the path of Ruth. They were to be careful that Ruth would be the exclusive recipient. Each man would return to his row and return to his work. Each one knew the harvest belonged to Boaz. Boaz could choose to do with his harvest whatever he wanted. Each man knew Boaz would pay him a fair day's wage. He would see to it that none of his workers would lack because they obeyed his word.

The men were to walk down each row and purposefully drop bundles of blessing for Ruth to retrieve. Imagine the delight Boaz's workers would find as they not only chose the bundle of grain to drop, but also as they chose the precise location in which they would drop it. Traditionally, Ruth would be walking behind these men picking up here and there the occasional stalk and stem for future threshing.

Boaz's men were to leave the gift and continue with their work. They were not to linger with the gift and wait for Ruth's arrival to identify themselves as the giver, nor were they to give it and attach a little plaque to the bundle that would be in memory of their mother or father. The reapers were merely to leave them anonymously in a place and move on.

There is a valuable lesson for the believer determined to obey Boaz's commands. Clearly, we have been given commands to give to our church by our Eternal Boaz. We have been commanded to give a tithe from our increase and offerings from our heart.

As for Ruth, surely, delight would surge throughout her body as she would happen upon a bundle of barley. Delight would not only belong to Ruth, but also there would be a contentment that would belong to the men as they dropped handfuls of purpose for Ruth. I am quite confident it would become pleasurable to them, as they would see a look of contentment sweep across Ruth's face with each retrieved bundle. These men learned it IS more blessed to give than it is to receive.

When it came to giving, each man had within his heart the desire to follow the commands of Boaz. Do you? Have you learned the blessings that come only from obedient giving?

Think about it ...

Rebuking or rejoicing

Ruth 2:16 And let fall also some of the handfuls of purpose for her, and leave them, that she may glean them, **and rebuke her not.**

Boaz covered every detail with his men in relation to their special task of leaving sheaves of barley for Ruth. His men were to place the barley in her path. These emissaries of Boaz were not to hover over them but rather just to leave them for her to glean as she progressed though the field. Boaz's words gave both instructions to the men and a guaranteed insurance for Ruth that would prevent any rebuke as she gathered up provision for Naomi and herself.

Boaz's command left his workers with a clear indication of his intentions for Ruth and her future provision. He did not want the typically mean-spirited accusations and activities to bruise the newest rose in Boaz's garden of compassion. The temptation on the part of the workers of Boaz would be to scold her for being where she had not earned the right to be gleaning.

With ease, Boaz's workers could have used sarcasm as the newest member of the harvesting family had just been given full access to the fields and family of Boaz. The harvest-hardened workers of Boaz would not have struggled to offer sharp comments to the Ruth. They had to resist these feelings and serve as they had been instructed. The men in the service of Boaz knew clearly, Ruth's protection, provision and potential rested solely in Boaz.

In no small way is this same scenario played out in our churches today across this world. Many times, the harvest-hardened workers of the Eternal Boaz struggle with new people coming into the family. They feel endangered by the enthusiasm of the new believer. They sense an inadequacy with their own spiritual development and therefore, seek to make the new believer uneasy. They develop a territorial presence in their personal service for the Lord of the Harvest. The freshness of the new believer to Christian service threatens them.

My fellow harvester of many years, the command of Boaz easily serves as a caution and a calling. Let it caution us to rebuke not the newest Ruth that has been added to the harvest family. May it also call us to rejoicing and renewal in our own relationship with Boaz. Let us not grow used to the calloused personality that occasionally accompanies a long tenure in the field, but rather, let us fight back the carnal doldrums and experience anew and afresh the delight of being in the service of Boaz.

Have you recently erred by having offered rebuke to a Ruth instead of mutual rejoicing? Let the command of Boaz urge you to rectify this matter today.

Think about it...

Seeking His blessing over my bounty ...

Ruth 2:16 *And let fall also some of the handfuls of purpose for her, and leave them, that she may glean them, and rebuke her not.*

In the 24th chapter of Deuteronomy, God told the Israelites three things concerning their harvesting of grapes, olives, and grains. These instructions were to benefit those who were strangers, widows, and fatherless. God gave these instructions so there would be provision for these who could not provide for themselves.

If the farmer had vineyards, he was to gather grapes only once and not to glean them later. If a man had olive trees, when it came time to beat the tree's, trunks and branches to harvest the olives, they were not to return to beat the trees again. If a farmer had field crops to harvest and they had gathered sheaves in the field when they dropped a sheaf by accident, they were not to return after it.

God's provision in His agricultural laws for the strangers, fatherless, and widows came with a blessing. God specifically promised to bless anyone that blessed those that had been disadvantaged through death or by displacement. Boaz knew God's laws and desired to not only follow them but to also do more.

Boaz spoke that day with both local and divine authority to his workers when he told them to leave handfuls of purpose for Ruth in the fields. His workers were familiar with the rules about the accidental dropping of sheaves. They would never dream of returning to retrieve it, for every Israelite desired God's blessing on their life. Yet, on that day, they would be told to let some fall on purpose.

Today, Boaz is taking his men with him on the path of desiring even more of God's blessing in his life. He told his men. " When you go through the fields, I want you to drop some sheaves for Ruth." This instruction went beyond the boundaries of the law and entered the boundaries of love. The letter of the law said if a sheaf falls by accident, leave it. The letter of love said let some fall on purpose and watch it bless.

Boaz wanted Ruth to discover tokens of his love throughout her workday. Boaz's men were to drop them surreptitiously; Ruth was not to know or see them intentionally do so. What delight they must have found as they observed God's law, obeyed their master's word and enriched the heart of one who had only known disadvantages and displacement in her life.

Many Christians today neglect Boaz's example. Many times, believers seek to build their own nest egg and help few out along life's way. Boaz's thinking was simple, "Better I bless others from my bounty and let Him bless me with His bounty; than if I were to bless my myself with my own bounty and miss the blessings of His bounty.

What about you today? Are you hoarding the bounty He has given you? Are you one to follow the letter of the law when being observed? Are you of those who bless themselves and miss God's blessing? Let us return to the desire of Boaz and seek God's blessing over our own bounty.

Think about it...

Your will is my desire ...

Ruth 2:16 *And let fall also some of the handfuls of purpose for her, and leave them, that she may glean them, and rebuke her not.*

Ruth has returned to the work in the field and gleaned once again. Joy filled her mind as she reviewed words Boaz spoke during the meal they had shared. Oh, how his words still ministered to her heart and soul. It was easy to trust him; his words spoke peace to her heart. She found, as she drew near to him, hope's embers become re-kindled in the hearth of her heart.

With Ruth safe in the fields, Boaz instructed his men in a new method of harvesting. These men were well acquainted with the latest techniques and styles of harvesting. They were hired by Boaz because of their ability to harvest efficiently.

However, Boaz's instructions seemed counterproductive to anything they had heard or seen done in the harvest field. His first words were, *"let some fall."* There was no doubt; Boaz's words were clear. They were to let fall some of the handfuls of the harvest onto the ground on purpose.

Dropping the fruit of the harvest was not a natural act to them. Their skills were well learned. They knew how to swiftly strike the scythe to the stems and grab the falling crop in a seamless movement. Now, in their new instructions, Boaz is telling them, "After you have labored to retrieve some of my harvest, make sure you let some of it fall to the ground for Ruth."

Questions were sure to arise; but Boaz had spoken; his words and will must become their own. They were to let go of what they had worked hard to get, all for the sake of Boaz. The harvesters could not spend all their time cherishing every grain gathered as if it were their own crop. They must not fuss over what Boaz said to do. They were now to take some of their labors and let them fall for the benefit of another.

Many times, those who are working for the Eternal Boaz are hindered by pride. We look at our areas and admire our own accomplishments. This can be a real hindrance when God requires of us to take of what we have done for Him and give it to His work and to His workers. We love to delight in our abundance, as if it were our own.

This "pride-filled" mentality still affects our labors in the Eternal Boaz's field. Many times we see what we have done as our personal achievement, when in truth, the accomplishment is His. We are to be working in His harvest, with His tools, and His methods. We can claim no fruit as our own. When Boaz says, "Let some fall," we should reply with delight, "Your will is my desire!"

When Boaz asks for you to drop some handfuls of purpose for his workers, what is your reply and reaction?

Think about it...

Beating out – to share with others ...

Ruth 2:17 *So she gleaned in the field until even,* **and beat out that she had gleaned***: and it was about an ephah of barley.*

The goodness of Boaz was certainly brought to Ruth's mind as she took her rod to beat out the grains of barley from the stalks. Each strike to the bundles of barley yielded the precious grain that she desired from early in the morning at the beginning of her quest for a benevolent provider for her needs. Who would have thought in human terms that a Moabitish widow could enter a strange land, find favor with a landowner, and carry home much more than an ordinary person's gleanings for a day?

There is a thought worth considering from Ruth's efforts that day. Boaz had provided her the access, authority, and abundance to obtain the barley. All Ruth needed to do was get into the field and find what was available to her. Once she had procured the gleanings, she would then be able to beat out what she had gleaned. This process enabled her to bring the blessings home to share with Naomi.

Our Eternal Boaz has done the same thing for his adopted Moabite Children of Grace. He has given us the barley fields of His Word. His Word is a perfect crop, abundant with handfuls of purpose dropped on every page and on every line. The Holy Spirit is the servant set over the reapers and is available to us to show us the places from which to glean for the day. Once we have read in His Word and gotten a thought for the day, it is incumbent upon every believer to use the rod of meditation to beat out grains for our own sustenance and grains to share with others.

Have you ever been called upon to share a verse or a thought from the Word of God with a friend? Have you struggled because you skipped your reading that day? Have you ever read the words on the pages of the Bible, but did not sit down to beat out grains to gather for yourself and prepare some to give to others? By neglecting the time of meditating, (beating out) you are missing out of the best part of the barley fields of the Bible.

Many people fall into the trap of always relying upon others to beat out grains for you. They rely upon Pastors, teachers and books to beat things out for them and never attempt to make the effort to do so themselves. It is typical of our society to expect everything to be handed to us, and therefore, we are left with a spiritually shallow generation.

Believer, determine today to be one who not only receives beaten out grains, but also is able to do so on your own. Remember there are others in your life with whom you will be able to share grains from God's Word. Why not determine to always beat out with the rod of meditation a barley blessing for yourself and barley blessings to share with others?

Think about it...

In the field . . .

Ruth 2:17 So she gleaned **in the field** until even, and beat out that she had gleaned: and it was about an ephah of barley.

Ruth gleaned in the field. It would be rather easy to overlook the simplicity of such a statement. It would be even easier to avoid the obvious. No small attention should be made toward the middle words in this verse's first phrase.

Some might even wonder, "Where else, Sir, would one labor but the field?" It is clear if she were adopted into a relationship with the lord of the harvest's family and she had been inducted into the harvest worker role, what else would she do? One could ask, "She was laboring, is that not enough?" Friend, it seems that many have come to adopt the mentality that generates these questions. It is assumed that if you are laboring, it is enough. Candidly, it is not enough!

Careful readers should make a conscientious application to their own heart, as they ponder not solely upon whether they labor, but also upon where they are laboring. Christians today are often busy laboring in fields, but they are fields of their own making. They labor for their own causes and neglect the cause of Christ. Others today seem to labor in more than one field. Their labor in fields other than those of the Lord of the Harvest's, creates a weariness that hinders, or even halts, their labors for their Eternal Boaz.

Like Ruth, a believer has been adopted into a relationship with Jesus, The Eternal Boaz. They have also been inducted into His harvest field to labor. This should be enough to prompt the believer to stay in His fields, laboring for His cause.

Where are you laboring today, friend? Are you in a field of His making or your own? Have you spread yourself thinly, and His fields are suffering for it? Many would have scolded Ruth for getting into Boaz's family and then went about her own business as if nothing happened between herself and Boaz. Why then would you hold a standard for Ruth and another for yourself?

Determine today to labor in the field He placed you and not in a field of your own making.

Think about it . . .

Seven and a half gallons of grace

Ruth 2:17 *So she gleaned in the field until even, and beat out that she had gleaned: and it was about an ephah of barley.*

The fruits of Boaz's grace lay before her and the next phase of her work began. Though the day had slipped to the evening hours, she began to beat out what she had gleaned. Ruth's gleanings could not be left unattended that evening. She spent her day not having to work as hard as she thought she would.

It seemed that ever since the midday meal that her work became very easy. Could it have been the more time she spent with Boaz the easier her labors became? Could it have been the meal Boaz shared with her sustained her so much that she had strength beyond her own measure to accomplish the task? No matter the answer to the aforementioned questions, the truth remained she had an abundance of wheat for a normal gleaner.

The Old Testament laws pertaining to these matters only permitted gleaning after the wheat had been gathered and bundled; however, Ruth was permitted to glean among the reapers. Her gleanings yielded seven and a half gallons of wheat. This would have been an extraordinary amount. It was the grace of Boaz that brought this amount. And in that amount, she discovered her satisfaction in the provision of the Eternal Boaz.

The focal point in today's verse should not spotlight Ruth's efforts, but rather, should highlight the grace of Boaz to one he has made his own. Ruth's testimony before the servant set over the reapers was one of a diligent, dedicated, and determined worker. Today's gleanings represent the interest of the God of Israel under whose wings she had come to trust. Her gleanings symbolized Boaz's intention to provide care and comfort to her.

Ruth's gleaning would not be complete until she had beaten out the grains of barley. This beating would yield the nourishment and supplies she and her mother-in-law required. Each grain of barley indicated an answered prayer, an attentive provider, and an active promise. Ruth had sought God for supply and He had answered. She pursued God and He gave her a provider. Ruth knew that since she was under His wings, His promises were sure. This beating time was certainly a blessing time for Ruth.

As you go about this day, working with His blessings of barley in your life, consider each grain a representative of an answered prayer, an attentive Provider, and an active promise. He loves us with an everlasting love. Ruth carried home seven and a half gallons of barley that day. How much are you carrying home today?

Think about it . . .

Gleaned until even . . .

Ruth 2:17 *So she gleaned in the field until even, and beat out that she had gleaned: and it was about an ephah of barley.*

Boaz made it clear his intention to this soon to be gem in the crown of the Messiah. It was Boaz's intention to protect, provide, and perceive her every need. Just this morning Ruth,, a recent widow and displaced Moabite, set out to find a place to glean for today and found much more than a field. She discovered Boaz's fields, his friendliness, his food, and a future.

Ruth quickly settled into her former position before sharing the noon meal with Boaz. The meal was certainly refreshing. It was not her meal that she reflected upon, it was the provider of her meal. His words of comfort and charm became her meditation as she returned to the field.

Ruth hardly noticed how quickly the minutes became hours. When the joy of Boaz is your strength, time is immeasurable. The Word of God indicates that she stayed in the field working until it was even. Gleaning until evening sounds melodic in its expression. However, this work was not easy, nor was it effortless work; this was earnest work. Yet, with her meditations upon Boaz's grace, her desire to give her all could be understood.

The efforts of the morning and the events of the noonday meal led to earnest working until the last ray of sunlight crossed the barrier between daylight and twilight. The night would be here soon when none could work. She knew what was going to be done could not wait.

Ruth's zeal for Boaz's harvest and his heart set a real standard for harvest workers. It is clear if the workers of the Eternal Boaz would make His grace their meditation, their zeal for His work would increase exponentially. The Lord of the harvest said Himself, "I must work the works of him that sent me, while it is day: the night cometh, when no man can work." Ruth's example and the Savior's edict must be our main concern.

Harvest worker, have you become weakened and laid aside yourself? Has the tint of the evening's sunset on the horizon made your labors decrease? Do you work with the same inner zeal as you did the first day upon entering the family of the Eternal Boaz? Let the phrase from today's verse spur you on to a newfound zeal.

Think about it . . .

A blessing reserved . . .

Ruth 2:18 *And she took it up, and went into the city: and her mother in law saw what she had gleaned: and she brought forth, and gave to her that she had reserved after she was sufficed.*

With her labors ended, Ruth begins to gather her beaten barley grain to begin the journey home. No mention is made here that she had to acquire from Boaz a means of getting the barley home. It seems that Ruth's confidence in the LORD God of Israel caused her to bring a vessel or the means to carry home the grains of God's goodness. The volume of seven and a half gallons of grain would be a great amount to convey back to Bethlehem, yet, she was prepared to receive God's provision.

Ruth's faith in God to provide both a field and food is an encouragement to observe. She left home that morning expecting God to provide ALL her needs. Ruth needed a field in which she could glean, though the barley harvest was just beginning. Many people would have already secured their places with the landowners. Yet, she knew the God of Abraham, Isaac, and Jacob could sustain her every need. Ruth needed a fellow to view her through eyes of grace instead of eyes of race. Ruth needed food for today and God made a way.

Ruth's commitment to the God of Israel and Naomi was not a light-hearted arrangement. Upon her exodus from Moab, she did not merely get caught up in the emotions of the moment and frivolously state that she would follow the Lord God of Israel. Ruth's commitment was not forgotten when the good times came in fields and fellowship with Boaz.

During the meal, Boaz gave Ruth corn that had been parched for her to enjoy. Ruth took this extra blessing for herself and also for Naomi. Ruth's love for Naomi prompted this selfless, generous act. She wanted every good thing that came to her to come to Naomi. When Ruth returned back to the field she had to keep the parched corn safe. When she made her journey home she had to secure its safety.

Ruth saw her blessings as blessings to be shared with the others in her life. Upon her return to the city, Ruth's reserved portion for Naomi was pulled from its secured location and presented to her. Naomi knew that Ruth did not have to do this; she certainly was touched by her kindness. Boaz had blessed Ruth with handfuls of purpose of barley and kernels of parched corn. Ruth chose to share this goodness with Naomi. Ruth's simple deed of reserving a "parched corn blessing" for Naomi must not be overlooked in our daily lives.

Today, we receive many blessings from our Eternal Boaz that we should keep a portion back for the Naomi's in our lives. Certainly, God has placed a Naomi in your life. Your Naomi might be a family member, a friend, someone in your church, or at a nursing home. Why not take the parched corn of God's blessings and share it with a Naomi today?

Think about it . . .

Bringing barley to others . . .

Ruth 2:18 **And she took it up, and went into the city**: *and her mother in law saw what she had gleaned: and she brought forth, and gave to her that she had reserved after she was sufficed.*

Ruth's journey from home that morning was one filled with hope, faith, and trust. Ruth's prayer when she left home that morning indicated her hope and trust. Hearing Boaz's testimony in the middle of the day encouraged her faith. Now this journey home is one filled with satisfaction in the one true God of Israel.

She left home seeking to find grace in human eyes. That day she found grace both in human eyes and Heaven's eye. Ruth left seeking ears of corn and came home with gallons of barley. She went out looking for daily provision and found divine provision. Ruth's heart was full as her hope was fulfilled. Ruth's faith was made sight by the barley in her hand. Ruth's trust was confirmed as she strode home, certain that the wings of the Lord God of Israel had once again guided her to a place of provision.

When Naomi returned to Bethlehem, she declared she went out full and had returned home empty. Straying out of God's will drained her. Straying from God's Word depleted her. Straying from God's ways exhausted her.

Now we see Ruth left home empty, and returned filled with bounty from Boaz. She came back with more than enough barley for today's provision and tomorrow's provision. She had slipped into her pouch the parched corn she had received from Boaz during the noon meal.

It would have been easy for her to consider that Naomi would never have known about the parched corn, but this was not Ruth's way. We see Ruth's human commitment to Naomi in chapter one verse sixteen. Ruth made a heavenly commitment to God in chapter one verse seventeen. These commitments precluded her from withholding the parched corn from Naomi now.

Ruth knew that beyond her local barley field was a hungry person who needed to have bread. She gathered the precious seed and walked to her home place. Upon her arrival, she offered it to her mother-in-law who gladly received it and glorified God for its arrival.

You know, we who have received the goodness of God's Word are obligated to rise out of our barley fields and go where there are people who are hungry and bring the seed to them.

Our churches today are full of "barley-gatherers," however, we lack many "barley-givers and barley-goers."

When last did you take the barley of the Word of God and head into a city, village, or home and present to them barley and parched corn? Since you have the Seed of the Word of God, and you know where there are hungry people, why not head there today and take them the Word of God?

Think about it . . .

Grace AFTER knowledge . . .

Ruth 2:19 *And her mother in law said unto her, Where hast thou gleaned to day? and where wroughtest thou? blessed be he that did take knowledge of thee. And she showed her mother in law with whom she had wrought, and said, The man's name with whom I wrought to day is Boaz.*

It would have been easy for Naomi to reflect upon the disasters that entered through the door of her home since her departure from God's will more than a decade ago. Naomi knew God's hand of discipline could not only touch her husband and children, but she knew it could affect others too.

Naomi was not ignorant of Ruth's desire to search for a place of provision. Naomi knew when Ruth left that same morning that "the odds" would be against her. Throughout the day Naomi could have wondered of Ruth's welfare. "Would she find a field where she could glean? Would she be accepted in that field? How much grain would she be able to bring home for their sustenance? Where would the God of Israel lead her daughter-in-law? How would she be accepted? Who would she meet? What would happen?"

They were living in troublesome times. Many in their region lived according to the laws of their own creation and not their Creator's laws. *"In those days there was no king in Israel: every man did that which was right in his own eyes."* Judges 21:25

Naomi's response may reflect her day of pondering and praying for her precious daughter-in-law. Ruth's arrival with such an abundant bounty of grain prompted Naomi's reaction of two questions and one blessing for their newfound benefactor. Such responses define our thought today, "Grace AFTER knowledge."

Ruth's benefactor took knowledge of her. After he learned of her family, her fate, her frustrations, her flaws and even her faith, he showed her grace. Knowing Ruth's inadequacies, he STILL showed her his grace. He could have ignored her, but he invited her into his field and family. He could have rejected her, but he opened his heart and harvest field. He could have despised her, but he offered her provision and protection. He offered grace after he took knowledge of her. Boaz showed grace AFTER he took knowledge of Ruth's cause, condition and country.

This very thought should thrill the heart of every convert from the land of Moab. You were once flawed, far from God and a failure. Our Eternal Boaz took knowledge of you and even AFTER that, He showed His grace. He knew whom we were, what we were, and where we were, and He loved us anyway. He knew me. Yet, He loved me. What generosity! What goodness! What grace!

Let your meditation this day be like Naomi's, *"Blessed is He that did take knowledge of me!"*

Think about it . . .

168

*Hope*Hope breaks across Naomi's horizon . . .*

Ruth 2:18 *And she took it up, and went into the city:* **and her mother in law saw what she had gleaned:** *and she brought forth, and gave to her that she had reserved after she was sufficed.*

Naomi's life, since she left Bethlehem the first time, had been dramatically altered. The days of raising children in the Promised Land were exchanged for burying two sons in the deserts of Moab. The anticipation of growing old with her husband, Elimelech, and watching their grandchildren play and grow up in the faith was crushed when Elimelech was interred in Moab's plains.

Now she had returned to the God of her childhood and the land of His promise with a daughter-in-law remaining in Moab. No, her life was not the same. Her plaintive mourning over joys buried in Moab was echoed upon her return to Bethlehem. She announced to all who were stirred upon her arrival after more than a decade, *"Call me not Naomi, call me Mara: for the Almighty hath dealt very bitterly with me. [21]I went out full, and the LORD hath brought me home again empty: why then call ye me Naomi, seeing the LORD hath testified against me, and the Almighty hath afflicted me?"*

She desired her name be changed from delightsome one to disappointed one. Her very name stood as a monument to her husband's decision to leave Bethlehem and her decision to remain in Moab after her husband's death. Though her decision to remain in Moab had drained her of her delights, Moab could not detain her in its shackles of death, disappointment, and discouragement.

Naomi's departure from Moab to come to Bethlehem revealed her awareness of God's dealing in her life. God had worked in her life and she saw the emptiness of her home, heart and hope. She declared to them God's working in her life and how His working testified against her. (Ruth 1:21) She knew that He dealt very bitterly with her. The darkness in Naomi's soul from chapter one of Ruth's book is now chased away as the sunlight of God's provision breaks across the horizon of her tomorrows with Ruth's return from the fields.

Naomi saw what Ruth had gleaned and deep within her bosom she knew this visit from the Almighty was a visit of bread and blessing, not bitterness. She received the barley and the parched corn from Ruth. It had been a decade or longer since she had known this kind of blessing. The Almighty's grace is beginning to replace the emptiness and disappointment with bread, barley, and blessings.

Ruth's return with God's provisions was more than just a trip home. Naomi saw it as the beginning of God's replacement warranty taking affect in her life. Naomi returned to Bethlehem heartbroken. Now, with Ruth's return, God honored His Word and began to replace the missing elements in her life.

Have you a blessing to share today? Has God touched your life? Someone needs to hear of His visit in your life. Proclaim today His goodness; it may mark the beginning of a turnaround in someone's life.

Think about it . . .

Recognizing blessings . . .

Ruth 2:19 *And her mother in law said unto her, Where hast thou gleaned to day? and where wroughtest thou? blessed be he that did take knowledge of thee. And she showed her mother in law with whom she had wrought, and said, The man's name with whom I wrought to day is Boaz.*

Naomi could keep silent no longer! Certainly something must have happened with Ruth today – she just had to know. Where did you glean today? Where did you beat out your gleanings? Before Ruth could utter a response, Naomi declared her gratefulness and said, "*Blessed be he that did take knowledge of thee.*" Ruth seized her opportunity to explain it all. Seven and half gallons of barley lay spread before Naomi. Parched corn is placed in Naomi's hand as she declares the events of the day in her own way. Listen as she could have declared it:

Mom, I left home today and sensed in my heart the guiding hand of Jehovah. Just like you have been teaching me about the way He guided our people to the Promised Land, so too I sensed His hand guiding me to glean in a certain field. I prayed that God would let me find grace in someone's eyes and let me glean. I arrived at God's field for me and met the servant set over the reapers. I asked him if I could glean today in his field. I declared to him my status, relationship, and testimony. I made it clear I was Moabite by birth and Israelite by faith. I related to him my financial position and marital status. I thank God for his provision in the law for me because the servant gave me access to his master's field.

About noontime the owner of the field came. He spoke with such tenderness. What spoke to my heart was that he called me daughter. The owner told me to plan on going nowhere else for the rest of the harvest. He knew all about my conversion, my commitment to Jehovah and to you. He said that he had been shown fully all about me. I was so humbled by his compassion and kindness; I thanked him and wondered why he would favor me so. He made it clear to me I could leave the corners of the field and work right around the reapers. He then invited me to share the midday meal with him. (That is when he gave me this parched corn to eat. I saved some of it for you!)

It seemed from that moment, my day got easier and the work went faster. Everywhere I could look it seemed I found grain to pick up. The next time the master and I speak I must tell him about the carelessness of his workers. After lunch it seemed they became careless with the grain, even wasteful. When the afternoon passed, I found myself with all this grain. So I began to beat the grains. I tried to be careful and not waste a grain. My excitement to come home and share these blessing with you spurred me on to finish. When I finished beating out the grain, I had this much to carry home.

Mother, I know you wanted to know the name of the man who is this Master. Certainly you are correct; he did take knowledge of me. His name is most unusual in sound; I understand it means, "quickness." Certainly he was quick to respond to my needs. I am so grateful to Jehovah for leading me to this man. Mother, his name is Boaz.

God had arranged their meeting and gave them each a heart for the other. All of it was done in His time to bring together these two hearts. He brought Boaz and Ruth to the intersection of loneliness and hope, and they found each other. Their meeting was not by chance: no, this was a meeting that secured the line of the Messiah and thwarted Satan's attempt to extinguish the salvation of mankind.

How well do you recognize God's blessings in your life? Can you see how He has woven the threads of your life to make a beautiful fabric for His honor and glory? Pause today to recognize and testify of His blessings.

Think about it . . .

Show and tell . . .

Ruth 2:19 *And her mother in law said unto her, Where hast thou gleaned to day? and where wroughtest thou? blessed be he that did take knowledge of thee. And she shewed her mother in law with whom she had wrought, and said, The man's name with whom I wrought to day is Boaz.*

The childhood game of show and tell comes to mind as the last sentence of this verse is read. The verse indicates that Ruth answered Naomi's questions with a visual and verbal response. The visual response is not recorded for us save that she directed her attention toward something. Then she offered Naomi a verbal response and identified Boaz.

Ruth stood before her mother-in-law and showed her a clear identifier. This would distinguish with whom she had been working. Students of the Bible would love to extrapolate what she possibly could have shown Naomi.

In the cultural setting, relying upon those who are authorities for this time period, she could have been given a garment that identified her as one of Boaz's gleaners. She could have also had some that identified Boaz vessel with her to convey the barley grains home. It is possible, that some other indicator had been displayed before Naomi, but it would leave any onlooker without question, Ruth had been with Boaz.

Ruth would long remember the experiences of this day.. Her heart was filled since Boaz had taken up residence there. This served as a comfort to her. It would be hard to guess which thrilled Ruth more the visual presentation or the verbal one of having been with Boaz. Either way, both would have been thrilling to witness.

Ruth's voice proclaimed the thrilling phrase, "*The man's name with whom I wrought to day is Boaz.*" The words penetrated the silence in Naomi's home. A home that knew well of God's discipline, now has encountered God's delight. A home that once declared barrenness and bitterness, now must see that bounty and blessings have come since their choice to return to God.

This show and tell was not just a normal display of an item and a short story to accompany it. No, this show and tell represented the sovereign and providential will of God. Ruth's verbal and visual display revealed that Boaz had been identified as her benefactor. His gracious response to her needs reveal her adoption and acceptance. Boaz chose to associate himself with Ruth, a Moabitish homemaker in the line of Christ.

Converts to the Eternal Boaz know well that they too have visual and verbal identifiers to distinguish their Benefactor. They have God's Word that declares they are His. They have The Holy Spirit to comfort, guide, and teach them. They have His 'ephahs' of barley (2:17) that confirm His adoption, acceptance, and association with them.

Do you have something for show and tell today in the classroom of your life? Perhaps you need to show someone today the visual blessing of a recent 'ephah' with which He has blessed you.

Meditate upon His Word and commune with His Holy Spirit and ask God to give you something today to show and tell.

Think about it . . .

Where? Oh, where? . . .

Ruth 2:19 *And her mother in law said unto her, Where hast thou gleaned to day? and where wroughtest thou? blessed be he that did take knowledge of thee. And she showed her mother in law with whom she had wrought, and said, The man's name with whom I wrought to day is Boaz.*

The events of Naomi's day are not recorded for us in the text. It would be safe to conclude that Ruth crossed her heart and mind more than once throughout the day. "How much would she bring back?" "Would she bring any grains back?" "How far would she have to go before someone would permit her access to their fields?" Naomi certainly must have looked forward to hearing from Ruth upon her return from her first day of gleaning.

Ruth, too, must have been preparing in her heart and mind as each step drew her closer to home. God had been so kind to her today. She wanted to tell everything and not miss a detail. Ruth came through the threshold of the door and began to display the bounty from Boaz. Naomi found herself overwhelmed by the rewards received from the hand of God.

Naomi knew the amount Ruth returned with exceeded Ruth's own ability and achievements. These gifts exhibited someone's charity, and she recognized it immediately. Someone out there in her homeland had taken the time to learn about her daughter-in-law and responded with grace.

Naomi's questions for Ruth reveal a truth we must not overlook. Ruth could have attempted to glean in any field she chose. Had Ruth gone to another field, she would have been frustrated beyond measure and found herself fruitless in her labors. Had she chosen her own field, she would have not met Boaz.

God had saved and delivered Ruth from Moab not for her to find her own provision, but to learn to trust Him for His provision.

Naomi's questions should make the growing believer consider his own gleaning and gathering. Where are you gleaning? Are you in a field of your own choosing, or His choosing? How bountiful are the fruits of your labors? Are you experiencing all the blessings of God's goodness?

If you are making your own way and seeing your own meager fruits for your labors, let Naomi's questions provoke some thoughts in you. Am I in God's field or my own field? Am I gleaning my own fruits or His fruits?

Where, oh where, are you gleaning and gathering?

Think about it . . .

A kinsman inspected. . .

Ruth 2:20 *And Naomi said unto her daughter in law, Blessed be he of the Lord, who hath not left off his kindness to the living and to the dead. And Naomi said unto her, The man is near of kin unto us, one of our next kinsmen.*

Naomi's words reflect how quickly she was mentally working her way through the family tree. Boaz was a kinsman, but just how close was he? She began to consider, "*The man is near of kin unto us.*" Certainly it was the thought of the Levirate laws (laws of the kinsman-redeemer or Goel) and Boaz's placement in their family brought about the next phrase, "*one of our next kinsmen.*"

Cautious hope sprang within their hearts. Would they be sentenced to live with their property within reach of their arms, yet, still beyond their grasp? Would there be no Goel willing to stand for them?

These two phrases of "near of kin" and "one of our next of kin" help us to see the turmoil in Naomi's heart. Naomi saw the provision of God's grace and His preparation of in the heart of Boaz. Yet, with this development of the closest kinsman must have put her in a quandary. Ever the matchmaker, Naomi is forced to declare upon careful inspection, Boaz is close to us, but to fulfill the requirements of the Levirate laws there is one closer.

Boaz's placement in Elimelech's family tree is not clear from this text, but without question, he was family. Some Old Testament Rabbi's teach by conjecture that Elimelech and Salmon, Boaz's father, were brothers, which made Naomi a niece of Boaz. No matter the manner of the relationship, Naomi, the city elders, and the nearer kinsman, all recognized Boaz was a rightful kinsman.

Before salvation, the believer stood before God separated and in need of redemption. The law, our means to follow God's ways, was a next kinsman to us. Yet, the law could in no way serve as our Goel. However, Jesus Christ, as a declaration of His grace stepped in and announced He would be Goel for mankind. He paid the price of our redemption with His own blood.

What a delight for the children of God to look back upon what Jesus has done as our Goel! Today, we must share with someone that one's own righteous attempts to purchase their redemption will never work. Each "someone" must be told of our Goel. Whom will you tell today?

Think about it . . .

A kinsman introduced . . .

Ruth 2:20 *And Naomi said unto her daughter in law, Blessed be he of the Lord, who hath not left off his kindness to the living and to the dead. And Naomi said unto her, The man is near of kin unto us, one of our next kinsmen.*

Naomi's worshipful recognition of God's kindness led to her recollection of the kinship of Boaz. Her worshipful inspiration led to wonderful instruction for her disciple in the faith. Naomi now must step into her role as instructor of this Moabite in the Divine provisions for the widowed and orphaned in this world. Let us listen as she could have taught her spiritual charge.

"Mother, what exactly do you mean when you say Boaz is a near kinsman (Goel) to us?"

"You see dear, God gave us His laws to govern us in times of peace and persecution. God wanted us to know what we should do at all times. His law is perfect.

In His law, He has established a principle that protects people in our situation. God instituted the rule of a kinsmen redeemer to assist those who have been in dire straits. A Goel, a kinsman, is the nearest living blood relative. It is the Goel's responsibility to restore the rights of another and to avenge any wrongdoing. God designed his law for a Goel to assist his next of kin when they encounter difficulties in matters of finance, murder, and slavery."

"As God's people, if we cannot redeem our own inheritance, it becomes the duty of the Goel to redeem it for us. If we had sold ourselves into slavery, a Goel could redeem us, his relatives, from slavery. If an Israelite, is murdered, a Goel would avenge his relative's death."

"Mother! Jehovah is so good! I left the house today looking for the wings of Him I had come to trust and of all fields for Him to have directed me, to, I was led to the field of Boaz, our near kinsman. Oh, I wish I could say the words that could properly express my joy!"

"Truly dear, God is good to His people!"

Because of the laws of the kinsman-redeemer, Elimelech's name and lands would not be left in desolation. The women in his family would not be left without claim to their lands they had left more than a decade ago. God had visited His people in Bethlehem in giving them both bread and a redeemer.

In the Garden of Eden, six millennia ago, mankind sold himself into slavery of sin. This slavery held man in captivity. That same day, Adam became aware that he could not redeem himself. God, in his kindness, looked at our hopelessness and offered man a Goel to redeem us. Four thousand years later Jesus Christ took on human form to become our Goel to God. Calvary's cross became the place where He declared His position as our Goel to redeem us from the slavery to which we had sold ourselves.

We easily could just read over this and say, "Oh, isn't that nice," and move on to the next thing. Yet, we must not ignore that we were sold into slavery and stood without a Kinsman Redeemer. Our Eternal Boaz became our Goel and provided redemption because He loved us.

His declaration to redeem the world unto Himself must be our motivation to share with mankind. There is a clear message of hope in His declaration to redeem. What else could be more important this day than to find someone still sold into slavery and tell them of their Goel.

Think about it . . .

Call me Mara???

Ruth 2:20 *And Naomi said unto her daughter in law, Blessed be he of the Lord, who hath not left off his kindness to the living and to the dead. And Naomi said unto her, The man is near of kin unto us, one of our next kinsmen.*

Could this be the same woman who concluded chapter one with the words, *"Call me not Naomi, call me Mara: for the Almighty hath dealt very bitterly with me. I went out full and the Lord hath brought me home again empty: why then call ye me Naomi, seeing the Lord hath testified against me, and the Almighty hath afflicted me?"*

Had Ruth's demonstration reversed Naomi's desire to change her name? Did Ruth's declaration prompt Naomi to check the gauge of blessings in her life to see that she had gone from empty to full? When Ruth testified of Boaz, was it enough to make Naomi change the testimony of her heart about the Almighty being against her? Was Ruth's hope enough to make Naomi see that the afflictions of this life are to make us better, not bitter?

Naomi had genuine concerns for her family's name. Elimelech's children had died. No one remained to carry on her husband's name. (Deuteronomy 25:5-9) Naomi had entertained thoughts of her daughter-in-law finding happiness again in marriage. (Ruth 1:11)

Naomi had seen other women in the community who had celebrated life with their grandchildren. She would not be able to do this. Daily, she was condemned in the courtroom of her own conscience for stepping out of God's will. Now with the entrance of Ruth carrying into her house reminders of God's kindness, she finds forgiveness and freedom from the Almighty. Naomi's outlook now is transformed; her dismay (*Mara*) becomes delight (*Naomi*).

Are you a Naomi that lives in Chapter One – living in the shadows of bitterness, barrenness and brokenness? God's kindness, extended to His obedient children, will change dispositions and determinations. Naomi, why not move to Chapter Two and let Him convey His kindness to you?

Think about it . . .

His mercy endureth forever . . .

Ruth 2:20 *And Naomi said unto her daughter in law, Blessed be he of the Lord, who hath not left off his kindness to the living and to the dead. And Naomi said unto her, The man is near of kin unto us, one of our next kinsmen.*

"Blessed be he of the Lord, who hath not left off his kindness to the living and to the dead." Naomi's words in this sentence indicate the liberation of her spirit and the declaration of a certainty of hope for tomorrow. She, for the second time in as many verses, recognizes the return of God's goodness and she offers praise to God for not leaving off His kindness.

She remarked that God's kindness had been extended to both the living and the dead. God's love, when it takes action, is seen in His deeds of kindness. If love had feet and hands, they would be named kindness. God's kindness changed Naomi's perception.

Naomi learned that His kindness turns bitterness into blessing; exchanges barrenness for bounty; replaces affliction with affection; drains hopelessness from the heart and refills it with hope.

Naomi's worship in this moment of blessing teaches us that God's kindness is not limited solely to those who walk this sod. His kindness can be extended to those who have passed from the earthly life too! *"His mercy endureth for ever."*

Naomi recognized that God's kindness had remembered her husband who had erred in leaving Bethlehem. She appreciated how God's kindness remembered Mahlon who had made a mistake with his stay in Moab. She discovered God's kindness had touched Ruth in the redemption of a Moabite. The family name of Elimelech would be carried to future generations. She now recognized that God's kindness had touched her life both in Moab and in Bethlehem.

This lesson would be enough to help a believer to recognize the merciful kindness of God if considered on its own merit. Yet, when you consider Naomi's worship it touched more than those who were in the room and those who read its account. Ruth's great grandson, David, will spend many a day recognizing the mercies and kindnesses of God throughout the book of Psalms. Always remember, just like Naomi set a pattern for David, your worship is setting the pattern for those who follow in days to come.

Why not take a moment today, and in personal worship to our God, try to identify His kindnesses to you? Look in your heart, and then check your home for portraits of His kindness. God's kindness must be reviewed often, otherwise we will become accustomed to it and undervalue its worth. Then, when you have taken inventory of His kindness, show the list to those who make up your family and establish a pattern of worship for them.

Think about it . . .

A Protector and Provider . . .

Ruth 2:21 *And Ruth the Moabitess said, He said unto me also, Thou shalt keep fast by my young men, until they have ended all my harvest.*

Boaz's message to Ruth had not fallen on deaf ears. It did her heart good to rehearse his message of hope and help to Naomi. All that Boaz said to her gave her the security she needed and desired. Her confidence in leaving home that morning to find grace in the eyes of a benefactor had been buoyed by Boaz's charity.

Boaz had in his employ, young men who were vital to his harvest. These men would gather the crops from the fields for Boaz. Boaz's command to the young men gives indication of the vulnerability of Ruth and the values of their society. The book of Judges indicates that in their society, every man did that which was right his own eyes. This lawless behavior created a society with no values. Therefore, Boaz had cause to give five clear commands to his employees.

The young men were told not to touch Ruth, but rather to serve Ruth water when she thirsted. Boaz commanded them to let Ruth glean more than just the corners; she was permitted full access in his fields. The young men were cautioned not to reproach her; they were not to charge her with a fault by using severe or harsh language. Boaz's workers were instructed to purposefully drop handfuls and leave them for Ruth to retrieve. Boaz spoke a second time to the young men and told them they were to offer no rebuke to Ruth for her gleaning and gathering beyond the normal boundaries assigned to the woman of her status.

Although their society's values were at their lowest, Ruth's vulnerability was at its highest. Ruth's arrival in Bethlehem as a widow, and impoverished stranger increased her defenselessness. Under Heaven's rules women were to receive care, comfort, and honor. Yet, under the heathen's rules women were scorned, chastised and owned. The key to understanding it all is the shielding umbrella God placed in each woman's life to uphold His rules. Until marriage, a woman was under her father's provision and protection. After a woman married, she came under her husband's umbrella of protection and provision.

Clearly, God prepared Boaz to become Ruth's protector and provider from lawless men with selfish goals. Boaz took his charge seriously. His instructions and preparations made it plain to all around him that he was here for Ruth's protection and provision.

Similarly, when our Eternal Boaz returned to Heaven, He left His Holy Spirit with us. The Holy Spirit, Heaven's representative in Christ's absence, protects and provides for His children. The lawless deeds and desires of men will not penetrate the Holy Spirit's umbrella of protection.

When the values of this world seem to threaten, and you, like Ruth, seem most vulnerable, remember you are not without a Goel. Jesus Christ our Provider, Helper, Healer, and Friend is with you THIS day. The words, deeds, or accusations of lawless men cannot change this special privilege.

Think about it . . .

My men . . .my harvest

Ruth 2:21 *And Ruth the Moabitess said, He said unto me also, Thou shalt keep fast by my young men, until they have ended all my harvest.*

Ruth continued to relate to Naomi the message of Boaz. Calm authority characterized his words. Ruth came needing safety, security, and supply. Boaz made it clear that Ruth would have all she would need.

Ruth certainly found comfort in Boaz's use of the word "my." Four times in this chapter the word "my" is used. Boaz's first words to Ruth were "my Daughter." Then he told Ruth "Follow my maidens."

The focus verse today reveal Boaz's use of the word "my" twice. First, he said to Ruth, "Stay fast by **MY** young men." Boaz saw the workers in the field, not just as hirelings; they were **his.** The men in the fields were not free agents that would come and go; they were **his.** The men in the field were identified as young, they were not scorned because of their age or achievements; they were **his.**

Boaz was not ashamed to be identified as the lord of their harvest. He was not embarrassed to include his workers as ones who would be close to his heart. He called them, "my young men." His investment in the harvest did not distance him from the workers, but rather drew them to him. His communication to Ruth made it clear the young men belong "to me."

The second use of the word, "my" in this verse is connected to his harvest. He told Ruth, "*Keep fast by my young men, until they have ended all my harvest.*" Boaz had a vested interest in the harvest. This was not just another harvest field, it was "my" harvest field. Boaz did not ignore the harvest field as just another one in his possession, but he took ownership of harvest. Boaz's investment in the harvest led to his interest in the harvest and his affection for the harvesters.

Children of the Eternal Boaz would do well to heed this simple thought. You are part of His harvest. You are his laborer, his harvester. He has an interest in both your person and productivity. He invested much in his harvest and in you. He spoke to disciples and mentioned to them this same thought in Matthew 9. He referred to "His laborers" and "His harvest." Our Eternal Boaz loves us dearly and longs for us to complete His harvest.

Boaz had invested much in his maidens, his harvest, and his men. With all of his investment he had much interest. Jesus said it this way. *"For where your treasure is, there will your heart be also."* His treasure is in His children and in those who could be His children. Take comfort this day in the truth that, *"My beloved is mine, and I am his."* (Song 2:16)

Think about it . . .

Ruth the Moabitess . . .

Ruth 2:21 *And Ruth the Moabitess said, He said unto me also, Thou shalt keep fast by my young men, until they have ended all my harvest.*

"Ruth the Moabitess." It has been 19 verses since we last read that line. It certainly should not be ignored; its placement in Scripture is important. The Holy Spirit, in the midst of Naomi's and Ruth's worship and wondering made sure we would remember the grace of Boaz. It was the grace of Boaz that brought her to this place, It will be his grace that will bring her from Moab to Motherhood.

Ruth never assumed herself to be worthy of Boaz's kindness. Ruth knew she was unworthy of Boaz's goodness and grace, yet, she never was presumptuous or proud. When she first came to Boaz's fields, she began with a prayerful request for permission to glean from the servant set over the reapers. When Boaz spoke to her, she fell on the ground and spoke to him from a heart of submission. When she returned to the fields to serve in her new found relationship, dedication and devotion marked her movements. Ruth's decision to stay and separate the grain from the stalks indicate her faithful stewardship.

Although her name, "Ruth the Moabitess," would always linger, her newfound position in the faith of the Eternal Boaz and in the fields of the earthly Boaz would shine brighter. Ruth, one who once belonged to a country afar off, has now been brought near. The lifestyle, language, and loves of Moab have all been buried in the past. Yes, the Moabitess moniker would remain because of birth; her faith in the one true God of Israel would make her "Ruth, the homemaker in the line of Christ."

Friend, Ruth's story is the story of every sinner who comes in repentance and faith to Christ. The titles of "Ruth the Moabitess" and "Sinner Saved by Grace" are synonymous. It was in leaving Moab and cleaving to the One True God her life was transformed and she was taken from foreigner to family.

What has happened in your life? Can you point to a moment in time where you came to him as a sinner and He saved you by His grace? Sin has abandoned, orphaned, widowed, and bankrupted many a person. However, any that ever come to Him in faith have never been refused nor rejected. Redeemed, forgiven, and saved are wonderfully descriptive titles that belong to every sinner saved by grace.

Does the title, "Sinner Saved by Grace" belong to you? If it does not, turn to Him in faith today and accept him as your Redeemer. If the aforementioned title does belong to you, when last did you worshipfully praise Him for the transformation He brought to your life?

Think about it . . .

A kinsman inspires . . .

Ruth 2:21 *And Ruth the Moabitess said, He said unto me also, Thou shalt keep fast by my young men, until they have ended all my harvest.*

The childhood home of her deceased husband, Mahlon is the setting for Ruth to tell her Mother-in-law of her first day with Boaz. What a unique moment for both women! Many moments of celebration and joy had been celebrated within this home. Naomi had experienced many joys in this home. Naomi could look around this very room and see the bygone days of little boys toddling around the room echoing with bursts of laughter.

Now in this home, her deceased son's wife relates the events of the day where she met a near kinsman who opened both his harvest and his heart to this Moabitess. Ruth bubbled over with joy as she related to Naomi of the goodness, grace, and gifts of Boaz showered upon her. Naomi knew Boaz had kindled the embers of love within the heart of this young woman.

Ruth's jubilation is detected in this phrase. One can almost hear a daughter sharing with her mother how her heart had been stirred in that moment. Phrases, sentences and words could not flow fast enough. Ruth did not want to forget to tell Naomi anything. Ruth's phrase, *"He said unto me also"* is worthy of spiritual consideration.

In Chapter Two, Boaz, as it is recorded in English, spoke one hundred sixty three words to Ruth. Though we were not there, we can be sure that Ruth told Naomi every one of those words and more. Boaz's words brought comfort, consolation, and celebration from the first as he called Ruth, "my daughter." He offered Ruth access, adoption, and acceptance. Boaz counseled Ruth as he spoke of his harvest that she would be secure and supplied with all she would need. He gave Ruth the warmth and welcome she desperately needed when he spoke of her faith in God.

The sinner saved by grace will find similar excitement as they reminisce in the goodness of the Eternal Boaz. The children of the Eternal Boaz are blessed indeed. They rejoice in their adoption, acceptance, and association in Boaz's family. The children of God, like Ruth, have many "He said also(s)" to share. It is MORE than grace just to be in the family. Yet, each child of God gets all this and Heaven too!

Consider all the "also" things He has said to us in His Word. We receive also forgiveness, fellowship, friendship, and forever. Pause this day to reflect and rejoice in His goodness!

Think about it . . .

Keep fast . . .

Ruth 2:21 *And Ruth the Moabitess said, He said unto me also, Thou shalt keep fast by my young men, until they have ended all my harvest.*

Ruth sought to convey to her mother-in-law every event of that day. So much had happened to her heart since she met Boaz. The emptiness since the death of Mahlon left an ache that could not be assuaged. Now, she was sure the bloom of love began to open once again. Its familiar fragrance permeated the recesses of her mind and heart and she began to bloom. The words flowed with devoted pride as she delivered Boaz's message to Naomi. "*Thou shalt keep fast by my young men.*"

Boaz's words revealed his affection for Ruth. This precious gem, soon to be inlaid in the Messiah's crown, has been treated with dignity and honor by the region's most honorable citizen. His words were simple. She was not to leave the side of the young men whom he had disarmed from any vile intention. Ruth could stand in any field belonging to Boaz and not fear rebuke nor reproach from anyone.

The workers in the field knew full well that Ruth had taken residence in the heart of Boaz. They could not explain it; they just knew it. The workers in the field had a direct charge from Boaz. "Work and finish my harvest."

Ruth's charge to keep fast is not solely for her benefit. Consider the benefit it was for the workers. Boaz's workers needed Ruth's presence; it served as encouragement to them. The Lord of the harvest did not leave them alone in the field. He remembered them and sent them the token of His affection. Ruth's presence among the workers provided edification for them.

The workers of Boaz would enjoy hearing how Boaz was caring for Ruth. They could relate to her their experiences of his goodness to them. Her presence met their need, built them up, and kept them going.

Boaz's words, "Keep fast by my workers" still deliver a clear message today to God's children. Consider your church home as a type of Ruth for just a moment. Your church has been given a command to keep fast by His workers – the missionaries serving on the mission field. Ruth was to keep fast by them. She needed them and they needed her. She was not to be distracted by other offers. Other things could not delay her. She was to keep fast to his people for her benefit, for their benefit, and his benefit.

Keep fast by His workers, dear Ruth. It is there you will find friendship, fellowship, and fulfillment. Keep fast by His workers, dear Ruth. All you need is found in His fields with His workers caring for His business.

Think about it . . .

The end of the harvest . . .

Ruth 2:21 *And Ruth the Moabitess said, He said unto me also, Thou shalt keep fast by my young men, until they have ended all my harvest.*

As lord of the harvest, Boaz could see the entire harvest. He was there when it was just grain to be scattered. He was there the day the first worker arrived. He would be there to take care of winnowing out the grain at harvest's end. Though he left the harvesting under the care of his servant set over the reapers, he did come to inspect their presence and performance. He visited them to encourage and edify them in their labors for him.

Boaz's words spoke to Ruth and revealed his ability to view not just the present condition of the harvest but the day when it all would be gathered. Boaz was waiting on his men to end all his harvest. Boaz had more than one field. The laborers could look around and say we are almost done here, but then they would recall, Boaz has other laborers in other fields harvesting. The harvest would not end until it had ended in all fields.

Boaz could easily have ended the harvest at anytime. Yet, ending the harvest early would have abandoned crops that could have been harvested. Boaz heart was on the harvest and his eyes were on the day when it would be completed. He told Ruth she could stay until it was ALL over.

Our Eternal Boaz also sees the end of the harvest. He was here before there was even a field. He knows every laborer by name. He has placed each one in the field and cares for them. When the harvest ends He will be there to winnow out the grains from the chaff. He will know what is really barley and what is not.

The Eternal Boaz has left His Holy Spirit here as the servant set over the reapers. Yet, he is not without making his presence known in the harvest field. Many times the workers of the Eternal Boaz could testify how He has made His presence known in their area of the field. He cares about our outcome and all opportunities in the harvest.

There is coming a day when ALL the harvesting will be ended. Those in every part of His harvest field will end His harvest. The day for gathering will come.

When all the harvest is gathered there can be no more gathering; let us then gather while we can. Our Eternal Boaz can see the end of the harvest, keep your eyes on Him and keep harvesting.

Think about it . . .

Affliction or affection . . .

Ruth 2:22 *And Naomi said unto Ruth her daughter in law, It is good, my daughter, that thou go out with his maidens, that they meet thee not in any other field.*

Naomi watched and listened in amazement at the provision of Jehovah displayed through the kindness of Boaz. Seven and a half gallons of barley lay before her perhaps on the table or on the floor. Her daughter-in-law stood before her bubbling over with exuberance, as she detailed each moment of her interaction with Boaz.

Naomi could no longer keep silence. Commentary and counsel must be given. What would she say? How should she say it? She began, "It is good."

The words of a few days before must have echoed in her heart. *"The Almighty has dealt very bitterly with me."* I went out blessed, and now I have returned bankrupt. I went out with a good testimony in Bethlehem, and now I have returned with Heaven's testimony against me. I left home delighted, and have returned disappointed. Since my arrival in Moab, I have been in His classroom of affliction; but now, upon graduation, I find this to have been His classroom of affection.

Dear friend, the goodness of the Lord will always manifest itself. When Naomi came home from Moab, she could not see one good thing around her. Her disappointments abounded; her heart was heavy. Little did she know, that her return to God's will led to the restoration of the Messianic line. Certainly, all things **do** work together for good to those who love God and are called by Him.

When Naomi recognized this moment was really God's classroom of affection she graduated from the classroom of affliction. Are you struggling today with a heavy burden?

Remember this, God always will chastise his children, not because He desires to afflict, but because He cares for us. Your affliction is to draw you back to Him. You are not apart from His affection.

Think about it . . .

Now I'm standing on the mountain. Looking back, I can se when I was in that lowest valley His strong hand was leading me.

Oh, it's good to see the sunshine and to taste sweet victory; God has made this trial a blessing–oh, the grace He gives to me.

Terry Tidwell

Found in other fields . . .

Ruth 2:22 *And Naomi said unto Ruth her daughter in law, It is good, my daughter, that thou go out with his maidens, that they meet thee not in any other field.*

Truer words could not have been spoken. Naomi told Ruth, "*It is good, my daughter, that thou go out with his maidens, that they meet thee not in any other field.*" Naomi knew personally the shame, reproach, and regret that comes to those who leave the place of God's provision for places of their own provision.

Images of her own flight to Moab could have splashed on the screen of her mind as she and the love of her life left more than a decade ago during a famine. Naomi knew enough from her own experience; never let yourself think that it will be better in any other place than God's will. The famine that touched Bethlehem spoiled more than the crops that year. The famine also spoiled their confidence in God's ability to provide. Elimelech led his family to another field for provision, the fields of Moab.

Naomi knew the reproach she bore because of it. She did not want Ruth to endure the same. Since coming to the place of God's blessing, Naomi sought to guide Ruth from potential mistakes she could make. Naomi knew Ruth had found the best of God's provision. God had provided Ruth a harvest, a home, and a heart to love again.

Many had passed Elimelech's fields since his departure to Moab. Any who passed and saw his absence from the field God had given him, knew that he could be found in a field in Moab, a field of his own making. His decision to go to his chosen field ended up killing him.

Yes, Naomi knew enough to tell Ruth, "Don't seek your own provision. If the crops fail, God won't fail! If famines come, so will His faithfulness. If disaster looms across the horizon, so will His daybreak. Just be faithful to His field!" Everyone in Bethlehem, except Naomi, had a story to tell of God's provision in a famine. She missed His faithfulness in a famine once, and she did not want Ruth to make the same mistake.

Today, it would be good to apply this lesson to your own heart. Have you noticed how you tend to look around at other fields when your own looks bleak, or when God is blessing someone else more? Take heed, this behavior has led many to the burial grounds of Moab.

Let Naomi's memories of Moab be the catalyst to make the determination to avoid the shame of desertion in the midst of a famine!

Think about it . . .

My daughter . . .

Ruth 2:22 And Naomi said unto Ruth her daughter in law, It is good, my daughter, that thou go out with his maidens, that they meet thee not in any other field.

The delight that pulsed through Ruth's being, would be hard to measure, as she heard for the second time in one day the phrase, "My Daughter." Yet clearly, she must have been at an all time high. Three times this day she had heard the phrase, "My daughter." She heard it two times from Naomi in verses two and twenty-two, and once from Boaz in verse eight.

Ruth's journey from the land of her birth to the land of her belief is well documented in this book. Her decision to come to Bethlehem meant she arrived beset by social stigmas. She was Moabite in her heritage; this troubled most Israelites. Ruth's arrival as a widow left her without a covering of a man and susceptible to dangers from many sides. Ruth's Father and Mother remained in Moab; she was by herself.

On the 67-mile journey to Bethlehem she made her profession of faith and confession to cling to Naomi for the rest of her days. Yet, these decisions were initiated from her toward others. The law would force field owners to let her glean the corners; however, none would be forced to take her as a daughter.

The beginning of Ruth's day was marked with Naomi's commission to her, "Go, my daughter." Ruth set out to follow the Lord's leading and to honor her commitment to Naomi's commission. In the midst of her workday, Ruth heard again the phrase, "my daughter," from Boaz. This phrase came when Boaz first met her in his fields. He could have said, "Widow Woman," or "Moabite"; however, he chose to reveal his compassion and said to her, "my daughter"

Now at the close of the day, Ruth heard Naomi say again, "my daughter." This time the phrase sent a message of comfort to Ruth. She could be comforted by the fact that nothing had changed since they had been apart from each other for the day. With her labors ended, Ruth heard Naomi confirm, "you are my daughter."

The sinner who has come to God in faith, believing, knows the same adoption and acceptance Ruth knew. What comfort it is in our commission to know He calls us His own. In our labors for Him, He calls us His own. Even when the day is done and our labors for Him are over, He call us His own. Child of God, you are not alone, He loves you and calls you His own.

Let not one of life's struggles discourage you, disappoint you, or even bring dismay. The Lord of the Harvest calls you His own. The Holy Spirit, our Comforter, calls you His own. There is a day coming for all of His laborers when He will call His own to be with Him. Friend, live in this comfort today!

Think about it . . .

His daughter . . .his maidens . . .his fields . . .

Ruth 2:22 And Naomi said unto Ruth her daughter in law, It is good, my daughter, that thou go out with his maidens, that they meet thee not in any other field.

Naomi and Ruth found the priceless contentment that comes from being in God's will. It was the hand of God that had seen them both through the days of departures and difficulties, diseases and death, as well as discouragement and depletion. Those days have been exchanged for a new day of return and rest, recovery and rejuvenation, and rejoicing and re-supply.

Like most women's hearts, Naomi found great delight in seeing two people find the path that leads to lifelong happiness with each other. Naomi was not the matchmaker for Boaz and Ruth; she was merely an encourager to the participants. The matchmaker for the Messiah's line was God himself. He arranged the events that brought the couple's hearts together. They found each other in the same field of service. No one brings people together like God.

Naomi's endearment and excitement became a time of education for Ruth. Carefully, she sought to instruct Ruth about serving with a kinsman, staying with his workers, and keeping separate from the distractions of other fields. Naomi knew what was happening was far broader and went much deeper than two people whose hearts had been drawn to each other. This was the hand of God working all things together for the good.

Naomi knew Boaz's acceptance and affection toward Ruth merited faithfulness in return. Ruth's instruction from Naomi is worthy of consideration. "Stick with his maidens and stay in his fields," paraphrases Naomi's instruction to Ruth. The implication from her instruction indicates that a level of shame would mar her from seeking satisfaction in any other field with anyone else's fellowship.

What a simple life lesson for the believer today! Those who are adopted by our Eternal Boaz should follow the same instructions. Stay in the fellowship of those who are his workers and serve only in the fields of the Eternal Boaz. Many "Ruths" today seem to be glad to be in the family, but find it an imposition to be in the fellowship of Eternal Boaz's workers and in the field of service He assigns.

If you are His child and struggle with faithfulness in your attendance to His house and with the acceptance of responsibility for His house, then you must heed Naomi's instruction to Ruth. *"It is good, my daughter, that thou go out with his maidens, that they meet thee not in any other field."*

Are you in fellowship with people who are not in association with the Eternal Boaz? Are you in a field of your own making and not of His assignment? When you are His child, you should be with His people, in His field.

Think about it . . .

Committed to the harvest . . .

Ruth 2:23 *So she kept fast by the maidens of Boaz to glean* **unto the end of barley harvest and of wheat harvest***, and dwelt with her mother in law.*

Ruth's daily trips to Boaz's fields began in the months of early spring and ended in the heat of summer. In those fields she met and made friends with Boaz's maidens. She found her place of employment not a burden, but rather, a blessing. It was there she found friendship, fellowship and financial provision.

Ruth exhibited a testimony of faithfulness before Naomi and Bethlehem's other residents. Ruth came to town a stranger, and became familiar through the grace of Boaz. She came to Bethlehem with nothing, and now she was given a position in his field, a purpose to fulfill, and provision for her family. Ruth knew her arrival at the beginning of the barley harvest was God's provision. Ruth knew that this place and its people were God's will for her life. It was His wings that brought her there. His wings brought her here and provided to her safety, security, and supply.

Ruth's testimony in Scripture states that she stayed for both the barley harvest and the wheat harvest. When the one harvest ended, and the next harvest began, she still kept fast to his maidens and gleaned until all the crops were harvested. Every former citizen of a spiritual Moab should be captured by this thought: Ruth's position and provision in the fields of Boaz was all a work of grace. Ruth did not allow the good times to take her from her responsibility. She remained committed to his maidens until the work was done.

Ruth's commitment to the harvest is needed still today. Every forgiven sinner must realize the need for further harvesting. We cannot quit until the Lord of the Harvest calls us in and declares the harvest to be over. Sadly, dear friend, you may have begun in one harvest and deserted. Perhaps you finished in the first field never came to the next harvest field. May Ruth's commitment be our commitment.

Is your testimony equal to Ruth's? Are you committed to Him to stay until He calls us home? Why would you be content to work only in one harvest? Is He content with your level of activity in His harvest? Have you backed away from a previous level of commitment? If so, a renewed commitment to Him will ensure completion of His harvestings.

Think about it . . .

A promise kept...

Ruth 2:23 *So she kept fast by the maidens of Boaz to glean unto the end of barley harvest and of wheat harvest; and dwelt with her mother in law.*

There is something special about a promise made between two people. It is more than the words of commitment; it is the bond that comes between the one to whom it was promised and the one who made the promise. Ruth had made a distinct promise to Naomi her mother-in-law. Many things had changed in Ruth's life since she had made the promise to Naomi; yet, none of these changes dissuaded her promise.

In the previous chapter, Ruth made six promises to Naomi. " . . .*for whither thou goest, I will go; and where thou lodgest, I will lodge: thy people shall be my people, and thy God my God: Where thou diest, will I die, and there will I be buried: the LORD do so to me, and more also, if ought but death part thee and me.*"

Ruth made Naomi promises from the heart on that fateful day. A day filled with both hope and heartbreak. Ruth promised wherever Naomi would go, she would be with her. Ruth gave a promise of fellowship; anywhere Naomi would live, she would live with her. Ruth made a promise of family; Ruth was replacing her people with Naomi's people. Ruth determined that God's people would be her people. Ruth made a promise of faith; Naomi's God would now be her God. Ruth gave a promise of finishing; Ruth would stay until death and would later follow Naomi in death. Lastly, Ruth made a promise of a funeral. She would not be seeking to be buried by her husband or people of her birth in Moab; she committed to a funeral that would bury her in Israel.

Many believers today err in their commitments to the Lord. Many have never offered the Lord the promises Ruth offered Naomi. Have you promised to follow Him, fellowship with Him, and replace your family with His family? Have you promised to live by faith? Have you promised to finish the row in His harvest He has assigned to you? Have you promised faithfulness until death?

Reader, have you noticed the tendency to only make promises that are comfortable, convenient and cost nothing? May God help you to be keep ALL the promises you have made to Him.

Think about it . . .

A promise remembered...

Ruth 3:1 *Then Naomi her mother in law said unto her, My daughter...*

Naomi had not forgotten the words of Ruth spoken to her on the border between hope and hopelessness. Ruth's commitment to the heart of Naomi brought an unmistakable bond between them. This bond went beyond family; it was a joining together of faith.

Naomi would not soon forget that this Moabitish girl promised, against hope, to stay with her until death separated them. Ruth's promise had come when there was no barley harvest, no Boaz, and no promise of a better day. Now, with the barley harvest past, and Boaz on the horizon, Naomi found that The Almighty had begun to fill the cup of joy in her heart again. Naomi's bitter words from days gone by melted in light of the Boaz's compassion and Ruth's commitment to his harvest and his heart.

As the mutual interest and affection between Boaz and Ruth kindled, Naomi found hope breaking across the horizon of her heart when she pondered the goodness of Jehovah. Later, her own great-great grandson would write many times in the book of Psalms, "The Lord is good." Truly, the goodness of God stirred her heart. Naomi began to see and to know that The Almighty had sought to bring her back to himself. What she had formerly defined as The Almighty's bitter treatment now was becoming clear: it was not bitter treatment at all.

The consolation in the opening statement of this chapter should make you contemplate your own situation. God sought Naomi's best by bringing her home to redeem their family's name and restore the line of Christ. He had remembered His promise to Abraham, and Isaac, and Jacob; His promise to them extended to her and, now, to Ruth. Ruth's promise to Naomi reminded her that God had been so very good to them.

Now as the goodness of God began to shadow yesterday's bitterness, Naomi sought to become Ruth's mother, matchmaker, and mentor of the faith.

With greater ease than a few months before, Naomi was able to remember Ruth's promise. The Lord does arrange the course of our lives to bring about many events; these events are meant to bring Him into better focus.

What do you do when faced with circumstances far greater than yourself? Do you focus more quickly on the problems of the day, or on the promises of the Divine? Oh that we were quick to remember His promises!

Think about it . . .

Everything beautiful in His time . . .

Ruth 3:1 *Then Naomi her mother in law said unto her, My daughter, shall I not seek rest for thee, that it may be well with thee?*

With Naomi's arrival home, it was easy for her to remember the joys she and her dearly departed Elimelech knew in this the land of their birth and the home of their youth. Days of happiness in courtship, and as a couple, were all about her. She could walk through the town and see places where she and her husband had spent walking together and wondering what all of their tomorrows held. Dreams of growing old in the land of their fathers certainly had to be their destiny. Their faith in the Almighty had always been enough to sustain them until the famine came. Elimelech's decision to go away from all they had ever known had come to bear a bitter fruit.

Now she had eaten the fruit of that detour of her life and knew its bitterness. With that fruit gone, and the bitterness slowly ebbing, a new fruit sprang up on the tree of her life. This fruit would be a way for her to enjoy the blessings of love once again in her home. The joy of love once known in this home and heart must now be re-awakened in her adoptive daughter. Naomi knew the joys of love must be rekindled in Ruth's heart.

Ruth's devotion to Boaz's harvest and heart started the matchmaking wheels turning in Naomi's mind. That Naomi wanted to help Ruth discover the hope for their tomorrows is revealed in her first words to Ruth. She began, "My daughter." Her use of the words "my daughter" revealed that Naomi saw hope breaking across the horizon of a new day as her husband's name might be redeemed and restored in Boaz.

Naomi has called her "my daughter," for the third time. She called her "my daughter," when Ruth took a journey of hope to seek grace in the eyes of an unknown benefactor (2:2). The second time Naomi called Ruth "my daughter," took place when she counseled Ruth about her faithfulness to Boaz's harvest. This occasion of calling Ruth "my daughter," reveals Naomi's desire to bring the heart of Ruth and Boaz together.

What a thought! Only in the economy of God could delight replace disappointment and death. It is with God alone that one could find serenity after sorrow. The plan of God can one day write a chapter of marriage plans that would make the pain of a Mara experience be forgotten. Solomon, the great-great-great grandson of Naomi, would hold God's pen and summarize a moment like this as he wrote, "*He hath made every thing beautiful in his time.*"

Today's misery can be tomorrow's merriment with surrender to God's Word and will. He does make all things beautiful in His time. Surrender today to His will, and enjoy the fruits of obedience in the days ahead.

Think about it . . .

Seeking rest for a friend . . .

Ruth 3:1 *Then Naomi her mother in law said unto her, My daughter, shall I not seek rest for thee, that it may be well with thee?*

A deposit of hope is made in the heart of the hopeless when you consider Naomi's words. Naomi has assumed spiritual, financial, and familial responsibility for Ruth. It would have been very easy for Naomi to ignore the needs of Ruth's heart. Naomi could have spent her days nursing the painful past of yesterday. Naomi's arrival home encompassed tales of departures, death, and disappointments. These events and memories would have kept her confined to the prison of her sorrows. Yet, it was the goodness of God that carried her from the prison of sorrows to the place of supply.

Naomi learned a lesson after more than ten years in Moab, that one must not spend one's days wishing one could make a new start. Instead, Naomi sought to make a brand new end. Instead of seeking her own pampering in pouting, she turned her heart toward God and He changed her misery into a ministry. Naomi's words lend us insight to her forgiven and healed heart. With conviction, she confesses that she desires rest and reward for Ruth.

What if you learned to do the same thing? Align yourself once again with God's will and Word. Let the keys of His grace and goodness and release you from your prison of sorrows and unlock your shackles of misery and mistakes. Once freed, set your heart on Him. Find someone within your spiritual charge. Determine now to bring them out of their prisons of sorrows into a place of rest and reward.

Far too often a disobedient believer ends up serving himself as he wallows in self-pity and sorrow. It is the obedient believer that desires to serve others. Naomi found comfort in serving Ruth by seeking a reward and rest for her daughter-in-law.

When will you begin to do the same? How long will you remain serving self?

Think about it . . .

Of our kindred . . .

Ruth 3:2 *And now is not Boaz of our kindred, with whose maidens thou wast? Behold, he winnoweth barley to night in the threshingfloor.*

The very phrase, "of our kindred," evokes a myriad of images each portraying the sovereign hand of God. The significance of its placement in Scripture must not be overlooked. From the first day when Ruth came to the fields to seek an earthly benefactor, her Eternal Benefactor had already worked in earlier generations to provide her benefactor.

The first glimpse of God working to provide Ruth a benefactor is first seen in the Garden of Eden. Here, in a scene where sin entered into the world, accompanied by his fateful companion of death, God begins to provide to Ruth a benefactor. Man's sin brought both a penalty and a promise from God. The penalty was separation from God, yet, the promise was salvation. The penalty brought death, yet, the promise was of a Deliverer. The penalty affected Satan, yet, the promise brought God's Son. The penalty left mankind in a mess, yet, the promise brought the Messiah. This one scene established that the Messiah would come from God into the family of man.

Another scene on which one should reflect to see how God's provision of Ruth's benefactor is at Mt. Sinai when God gave the law to Moses. His law established that a widow from a marriage without fruit would have a way to keep her husband's name alive. God made it clear not to let a family's name be extinguished in Israel.

The effect of this law would allow a widow without an heir to marry her husband's brother in order to keep his family name alive. In God's law this is called the Levirate marriage. (Deut 25:5-6) When God established this law, it made it possible for Ruth's kindred to redeem her husband's and father-in-law's name. This restoration provided Ruth an earthly benefactor in Boaz, and the family of man an eternal benefactor in Jesus Christ. The Levirate marriage of Ruth and Boaz restored the line of the Messiah, broken by Elimelech's disobedience.

A third scene in your consideration of God's provision of a benefactor for Ruth should focus on the days of Moses and Joshua. God allowed Moses to send two faithful spies into the Promised Land. These spies met a woman named Rahab. She received the spies with gladness and became a recipient of God's grace in His judgment on Jericho. She would later marry a man named Salmon and give birth to Ruth's benefactor. (*Matthew 1:5*)

God's hand in providing a benefactor for Ruth and Naomi is seen clearly in Naomi's words to Ruth. "***Is not Boaz of our kindred?***" Ruth and Naomi had hope because of God's promise in the garden, His provision in the law and His protection in the Promised Land. Each of these shielded the family line for a Kinsman Redeemer to provide redemption to the family of Elimelech and the families of earth.

Friend, the hand of God, which has worked from eternity past, is working today in your life. Should thing look bleak and beyond hope, take into account His commitment to you and His Word. As you walk through the seemingly isolated events of a day, take time to gratefully consider His promises, provisions, and protection of you. God used yesterday to prepare today's blessing for you.

Think about it . . .

A maiden's fellowship

Ruth 3:2 *And now is not Boaz of our kindred, with whose maidens thou wast? Behold, he winnoweth barley to night in the threshingfloor.*

Naomi's words kindled heartfelt emotions as Ruth listened. Certainly the words could have found a lodging place in her heart for a moment. Yet, words like these are words best stored in the heart to treasure in days to come. Naomi's words struck the chords of friendship and fellowship in Ruth's heart.

It was not that long ago, now measured in months, that Ruth arrived from Moab. Providentially, she arrived in the harvest season. She was accepted in the field and assigned to a group of Boaz's servants to work for him. His acceptance and assignment gave her the secured status of a maiden of Boaz.

When she met the other maidens in the harvest field, she discovered the blessing of harvest fellowship. Ruth enjoyed being accepted as his maiden in spite of her marred heritage, missing husband, and monetary holdings. She came to the fellowship of maidens with nothing but a grateful heart and willing hands. They accepted her and, of, course she accepted them.

Ruth's assignment was to abide fast by Boaz's maidens. (2:8) Naomi encouraged her to be faithful to his harvest. She did not want Ruth to experience the shame of being found in the fellowship of other maidens doing other things in another harvest. (2:22) Ruth's commitment to Boaz's heart and harvest made her faithful to both the barley and the wheat harvest. (2:23)

An interesting parallel is seen between the days of Ruth and our day. We who have been saved from sin are accepted in the family of God and assigned to a group of believers in a specific location, a church. Your church is where the servants and handmaidens of Boaz conduct His harvest business. Some believers think that church membership and faithfulness to the house of God does not apply to them. Some enjoy the acceptance in the family of Boaz, but think that the assignment to a group of believers is superfluous.

There are even others who will join a church and never lift a finger to work in the harvest. They believe that attending the worship services, tithing, and coming to prayer meeting is doing their part in the harvest. Doing these things are the matter of character and commitment in the heart of any forgiven servant or handmaiden. Involvement in the harvest business is no problem for those who are appreciative of His acceptance and adoption in His family; however, it is a problem for those who have lost their appreciation for the Eternal Boaz!

Where are you in this parallel? Are you among those who are spiritual spectators? Are you among those who are spiritual participants? How faithful have you been to the Eternal Boaz?

Think about it . . .

Knowledge of Boaz. . .

Ruth 3:1 *And now is not Boaz of our kindred, with whose maidens thou wast? Behold, he winnoweth barley to night in the threshingfloor.*

Chapter three of this Inspired Journal of God's preservation of the Messianic line of Christ, details for us Naomi's pursuit of rest for Ruth. Naomi saw Ruth, as the wife of her deceased son, her traveling companion, and the sole convert from her sojourn in Moab. Ruth had unknowingly endeared herself to Naomi. Even the women of the community even recognized Ruth's worth as they reminded Naomi that Ruth's value was more to her than that of seven sons (4:15).

Ruth's commitment to fulfill a promise made in the desert reaped far more than she could ever have dreamed. She committed that day to be true to the heart of her in-law, as well to the home of Israel, the Hope of Israel. God honored and rewarded Ruth's commitment; He gave Naomi a dispensation to look beyond her grief and to become an instrument of His grace to bless Ruth's life. Naomi's mission was clear; she was to seek rest for Ruth.

She set out to fulfill this divine mission by taking knowledge of the activities of Boaz. Since the harvest was nearing completion each neighbor would be taking their turn at the community threshingfloor. The community threshingfloor was the location where harvesters brought the fruits of their labor. Here they would winnow their harvest. Winnowing was the process of taking out the chaff, the unwanted elements, from the grain. In the evening the west winds would carry a steady gentle sea breeze suitable for this task.

Naomi, aware of the winnowing schedule, Boaz's activities, and the provision in the law of God for marital arrangement, began to fulfill her mission. Her mission would not be difficult since Ruth had already found Boaz's heart to be a comfortable place.

Ruth listened as Naomi spoke, *"Behold, he winnoweth barley to night in the threshingfloor."* Naomi knew the heart of Boaz was the harvest. He would winnow tonight. It would be the opportune time to arrange the meeting of kinsman-redeemer with the one who needed redemption. There was nothing illicit in this meeting; it would simply be a meeting to present herself for redemption. Her arrival, no matter the hour, would be welcomed.

What about you today? Have you presented yourself to our Eternal Boaz for redemption? He desires all men to come to Him for redemption. He will accept all who come to Him.

Perhaps you know personally of the redemption of Boaz; yet, would He say you share His heart for the Harvest?

Think about it . . .

No chaff in His harvest . . .

Ruth 3:1 *And now is not Boaz of our kindred, with whose maidens thou wast? Behold, he winnoweth barley to night in the threshingfloor.*

Boaz was known for many things in his community. He was a businessman, an employer, a man of prestige, and a man of the harvest. His investment in the harvest was great. He may have hired others to take part in the harvest, but, when it came to winnowing, he would do that himself.

You may recall winnowing was the process of taking out the chaff, the unwanted elements, from the grain. His investment in the grain was clear. He knew what chaff was and what grain was. He knew how he wanted it handled. He trusted none other than himself with this task of separating out the good from the bad.

West winds would carry a steady gentle sea breeze suitable for this task. If he waited for east winds, they would come in gusts. The north wind would be too strong. He waited for the night hours to do his work of winnowing. The chaff would not survive the process of heaving the grain in the air. The steady east wind would gently blow away that which looked like the harvest but was not really the harvest. When Boaz's crops went to the marketplace, people knew they could expect a pure grain. Boaz was in charge of the quality control; no grain would be lost, and no chaff would make its way to market.

Our Eternal Boaz does the same in His work with us. He knows who is part of the harvest and who is chaff. He sees chaff in our lives and brings us to the threshingfloor. In the night hours of our lives He allows a steady breeze to winnow out of us what He does not desire. We are His harvest, and He is in control of our outcome. It is amazing how much chaff clings to us, and how much He desires to have a pure harvest.

You will not successfully resist His winnowing process; He will be successful in winnowing you. Perhaps today you are struggling with His winnowing. Trust Him He knows you, the breeze you need, and the best hour of the day for your winnowing. When the chaff is gone, you are most valuable to Him for His work.

Think about it . . .

Her cleansing. . .

Ruth 3:3 Wash thyself therefore, and anoint thee, and put thy raiment upon thee, and get thee down to the floor: but make not thyself known unto the man, until he shall have done eating and drinking.

Five instructions were given to Ruth by Naomi that would enhance her fellowship with Boaz. Naomi knew what was both culturally and physically appropriate for Ruth to do. Naomi recognized that Boaz's work would be completed at night. She knew he would remain at the threshingfloor to protect his harvest. She knew how to touch the heart of a man and gave instruction to Ruth accordingly.

She said to Ruth, "*Wash thyself therefore, and anoint thee, and put thy raiment upon thee, and get thee down to the floor: but make not thyself known unto the man, until he shall have done eating and drinking.*" No longer did the dust of Moab cling to the feet of this widowed girl. Rather, it was the dust of daily living that clung to her.

She had been in the presence of Boaz many times as a worker. They had shared conversation and meals in the heat of the day, however, this proposed meeting was not to discuss the matters of the harvest, but rather the matters of the heart. The washing in this verse is not ceremonial, but rather the normal daily kind, however, the motive behind the cleansing is worthy of our attention. She was not cleansing herself for the work of the harvest, but rather for the lord of the harvest. Her motives were, "I want nothing clinging on me but my desire to please him." She was not attempting to please him with her productivity in the harvest, but rather to please him with her purity of heart.

The purpose of her cleansing was to be pleasing to his heart. The process of her cleansing was to remove that which would distract him from her heart. She had no need to cleanse away Moab, since Jehovah had seen to that upon her profession of faith. This cleansing was to take away the dirt from daily living so her communication with Boaz would not be hindered by the soil of the day.

Friend, the connection between cleansing and communication in our relationship with the Lord is glaringly apparent. Remember, there is the soul cleansing by faith in the finished work of Christ; that is a unique cleansing of the life. However, there is a need for the daily cleansing of the heart. That is a daily cleansing needed for daily living. Cleansing is needed for clear communication between one and the Lord of both the Harvest and one's heart. When the heart is cleansed, the fellowship is enjoyed the most. How sweet is your fellowship with Him? Is it time for some heart cleansing?

Think about it . . .

Therefore . . .

Ruth 3:3 *Wash thyself therefore, and anoint thee, and put thy raiment upon thee, and get thee down to the floor: but make not thyself known unto the man, until he shall have done eating and drinking.*

Naomi, who wore the crown of wisdom that comes to some from length of days, shared with Ruth the summary of God's goodness in one word – "therefore." This is the first time in the book of Ruth that the word "therefore." is used. Accordingly it is worthy of mention concerning its placement and as well as its purpose. This word generally points to a rehearsal of the facts, emotions, and ideas just presented and leads its listener to a decision.

Naomi's message was intended to lead Ruth to a place of decision. She wanted Ruth to see it was the right time to take the next step on God's path of provision. It was God's hand that made this plain path for Ruth to follow. The path that left from Moab led straight to the heart of Boaz. Neither woman knew it at the time, but Naomi, one who knew what it was to have God's fullest blessing, now spoke words to help Ruth make a decision.

Naomi's *"therefore"* in the midst of her instructions to Ruth showed her that since these facts existed, and God's hand had led her thus far, that it was time to take the next step. Ruth had stepped out of Moab and into the status of a maiden. Now, it was time for Ruth to step from being a maiden into being a mother in the line of the Messiah.

Naomi's *"therefore"* in verse three rehearses Ruth's promise. (3:1) Naomi's question, *"Shall I not seek rest for thee . . .,"* was to remind Ruth of the reward of her promise. Ruth's promise made to Naomi on Naomi's pilgrimage of hope, now had found its reward.

Naomi's *"therefore"* in verse three reviews Ruth's position. (3:2) Boaz was a kinsman to Naomi. This familial relationship provided to Ruth an occupation and an opportunity to restore her husband's name. Ruth had worked in Boaz's field; this familiarity gave them an awareness of the sovereign hand of God in their lives.

Naomi's *"therefore"* in verse three reminds Ruth of Boaz's proximity. (3:2) Boaz was working that night in the threshingfloor. He was working with the very grains of the harvest with which Ruth had worked. His heart was focused on the winnowing and Ruth's heart was to become focused on the winnower.

Naomi knew the time had come for this determined younger heart to find delight once again. Because God had led Ruth to this place, *"therefore"* it was time for her to prepare to present herself to Boaz. My reading friend, we too should take Naomi's *"therefore"* and rehearse the goodness of our Eternal Boaz and prepare to meet Him.

Think about it . . .

Her anointing . . .

Ruth 3:3 *Wash thyself therefore, and anoint thee, and put thy raiment upon thee, and get thee down to the floor: but make not thyself known unto the man, until he shall have done eating and drinking.*

Naomi's five-part explanation to Ruth on the preparation to fellowship with Boaz resumes with this next phrase, " . . .*and anoint thee* . . ." With Ruth's body cleansed from the dust of her environment, Naomi's instructs her to anoint herself. It would have been useless for Ruth to attempt to go straight to the anointing without washing. The washing was needed to make the second step for fellowship with Boaz truly worth the effort.

The anointing Naomi mentions is the application of oil to the skin. The oil, oftentimes scented, would serve as a lotion and a protector to the skin. The fragrance would be added for the pleasure of the one in the presence of the anointed. The anointing, coupled with the cleansing, would set that person apart from those who had not done the same. In Ruth's day this anointing was used to prepare for worship, (2 Samuel 12:20); as well as preparation to meet a king (2 Samuel 2:14). However, Ruth's purpose was to meet the one who would become her kinsman-redeemer.

The instructions for Ruth were clear. Naomi could not do this for Ruth. The responsibility of preparation belonged to Ruth. Ruth received the instructions for fellowship, but unless she followed them personally, the best fellowship would not occur. It was Ruth who would need to wash off the dirt. It would be Ruth who would need to wipe on the fragrant oil to delight Boaz. There were no shortcuts for fellowshipping with Boaz.

Anointing was critical for Ruth's preparation. It set her apart from others in the field of his harvest. It also set her apart to the field of his heart. Yes, there would be others that night who may have anointed themselves that evening for other purposes, but Ruth's anointing was for one purpose. She wanted Boaz to find her acceptable in their fellowship.

Ruth's desire to prepare to meet Boaz is worthy of consideration for those who are in the family of God. It should be the chief delight of each child of God to make similar preparations for his own fellowship with The Eternal Boaz. Once the washing of confession is done, let us seek to anoint ourselves with the fragrances most pleasing to our Eternal Boaz. The things that make us fragrant to our Eternal Boaz are our praises (Hebrews 13:15), our giving (Hebrews 13:16), our prayers (2 Thessalonians 1:11) and our faith in Him. (Hebrews 11:6)

How is your fellowship with the Eternal Boaz? Are the fragrances most appealing to Him adorning your life?

Think about it . . .

Her raiment . . .

Ruth 3:3 *Wash thyself therefore, and anoint thee, and put thy raiment upon thee, and get thee down to the floor: but make not thyself known unto the man, until he shall have done eating and drinking.*

Ruth's heart felt reassured as Naomi continued her instruction. Each step of the instructions were to prepare Ruth for fellowship with Boaz. First, Naomi spoke of a cleansing, then a of consecration, and finally she spoke of a covering for the body. Each step held its own significance as she readied herself for Boaz.

Ruth's raiment before moving to Bethlehem was that of a Moabite. Her birthplace influenced her dress. When Elimelech and his family moved to Moab, Ruth had the raiment of her father's house. She dressed in traditional Middle Eastern garments with the look of a Moabite. Her status as a widow would have influenced her choice in raiment. Dwelling in the land of Jehovah as an Israelite widow would have brought a change in the look of her clothing.

Ruth now was being instructed to put on her raiment to fellowship with Boaz. Not the raiment of a Moabite, nor the garments of a mourning widow, but rather the attire of a woman presenting herself for redemption by a kinsman. She carefully chose the garment. She would want the article of clothing to attract him to nothing else but "*the hidden man of the heart*" (1 Peter 3:3-4). Her cleansed, anointed body was to be draped in raiment which would be pleasing to both the lord of the harvest and the Lord of her heart.

The instructions Ruth received from Naomi indicated the raiment was in her possession. She did not have to go buy it or borrow it; she had it. Furthermore, the instructions reveal it was her personal responsibility to get dressed to go fellowship with Boaz. Ruth wanted to do what was right and do it in the right way. What good would it do to bathe, and to anoint, but to dress in a manner displeasing to the lord of the harvest?

Reader, there is a resemblance in Naomi's instructions to Ruth and James' instructions to believers. Consider James 4:8: James gives direct commands about fellowshipping with our Eternal Boaz. He declares cleansing and purifying to be vital parts of drawing near to God. As it was Ruth's choice to choose to put on the garment of presentation of her heart, we too must choose which garments will be worn in our fellowship with Him.

With the cleansing and consecration done, let us cover ourselves with the garment of praise (Isaiah 61:3) to enjoy sweet fellowship with our Eternal Boaz. As a believer, you would already have the garment of righteousness; let us retrieve the garment of rejoicing which follows cleansing and consecration, and adorn and present ourselves to Him today for fellowship.

Think about it . . .

Her destination . . .

Ruth 3:3 *Wash thyself therefore, and anoint thee, and put thy raiment upon thee, and get thee down to the floor: but make not thyself known unto the man, until he shall have done eating and drinking.*

This evening would be one like no other experienced in their lives. Boaz and Ruth had been in daily contact with each other throughout the harvest. She had eaten meals with Boaz; she had sipped refreshments from his vessels. She had eaten morsels prepared in his kitchen. Their casual, daily contact was always in the context of the harvesting. Yet, this contact would not be like any of their previous encounters. This evening's contact was a planned meeting to bring Ruth's tender and innocent heart to the righteous lord of the harvest for his consideration for kinsman redemption.

Naomi's instructions gave Ruth the precise directions to prepare herself to approach Boaz and to enter his fellowship. The next steps involved directions on how to arrive and present herself to Boaz, a treasure of God's grace. Her words are unmistakably clear; *"get thee down to the floor."* Two ideas present themselves in this phrase of instruction to Ruth. The first idea is the reference of going down to the floor. They were in the city of Bethlehem, on the hills summit, which created the need to go "down" to Boaz. The other indication in Naomi's instructions was to go to the floor. Generally, one community would have a floor where its residents could bring their harvest and winnow out the chaff.

Ruth had worked in the harvest long enough to know the location and purpose of the threshingfloor. She could have passed it each day on the way to the fields. She could have seen it in the process of gathering the handfuls of purpose left for her. No harvest would be complete without a visit to the threshingfloor. Boaz would be there as this was the evening he would be finishing his inspection and protection of his harvest.

Ruth's arrival at the threshingfloor would come after she finished some winnowing of her own. You see, Ruth's preparation to fellowship with Boaz involved a winnowing process. Her cleansing, anointing, and dressing were the removing of the chaff of hopelessness to reveal grains of hope. She winnowed from her heart the hopelessness of widowhood, loneliness, and disappointment. The grain left on the threshingfloor of her heart was the hope of redemption and companionship.

There could be no presentation of Ruth for kinsman redemption unless she would leave home and get to him. There could be no appreciation of Ruth's effort to present herself to Boaz unless she got to the floor. There would be no birth of the Messiah without this presentation of a winnowed heart.

Reader, this exciting portion of Scripture brings many thoughts to mind. In your heart today, does God need to winnow your heart? Has the chaff of daily living clouded the grains of promise and hope? Why not today, through prayer of confession and praise to our Eternal Boaz, allow Him to winnow from your heart the chaff?

Furthermore, there is coming a day at the threshingfloor of our Eternal Boaz. It is the Bema Seat judgment where He will separate from us the chaff of wood, hay, and stubble to reveal gold silver and precious stones. Let us commit to being prepared for this threshingfloor.

Think about it . . .

Preparation, then presentation . . .

Ruth 3:3 *Wash thyself therefore, and anoint thee, and put thy raiment upon thee, and get thee down to the floor: but make not thyself known unto the man, until he shall have done eating and drinking.*

Ruth listened as the instructions came forth. She knew there were three things to be done to prepare for herself for fellowship with Boaz. Her cleansing, consecration, and covering were to prepare herself for close fellowship with Boaz in accordance with Naomi's instructions for preparation. There were two other things she had to do to fellowship with Boaz. These were part of Naomi's instructions for presentation.

Ruth understood clearly; she was to make her way down to the threshingfloor and wait. Her entrance into the threshingfloor would not be some theatrical moment where the lovely young lady dramatically enters the room for all to see. This would not be an inappropriate display of pride or arrogant ploy to draw attention. She was to hasten to the floor of threshing and wait for the right moment.

Were some today to have been in Ruth's place they would rush into the threshingfloor and show themselves off to the servants, Boaz, and anyone else. This was not a moment to display the beauty of her presence, but rather the beauty of her heart. Ruth was to get to the threshingfloor and to secret herself away until the right moment. Her presentation was not for the helpers of the harvest, but rather for the lord of the harvest.

The winnowing process was surely being completed upon her arrival. Boaz would have his meal prepared so he could eat it after the winnowing process. Ruth could watch as he went through the stages to stop the work for the night. He ate his meal, surveying the work done for the evening, and certainly was satisfied. Rest would come with ease, as those who labor with their hands know well. The gentle breezes from the east which helped him winnow would also caress him as he slept.

Certainly, Ruth would watch with anticipation and wait for things to unfold as Naomi said. Perhaps, she would rehearse the words from our focus verse in her mind. She was to wait until he had finished eating and drinking to present herself to him for acceptance into his fellowship. She was not to rush, nor linger. She was to present herself when the time was right.

The best fellowship known between harvest workers and the Lord of the harvest occurs when there has been heart preparation by the worker before the heart presentation. Reader, with our Eternal Boaz, He is always ready for us to present ourselves to Him for fellowship in prayer.

When was the last time you took such care to present yourself to Him? When was the last time you anxiously awaited getting to fellowship with Him? Our Eternal Boaz is always available to us through prayer.

Think about it . . .

Seeing in the dark . . .

Ruth 3:4 *And it shall be, when he lieth down, that thou shalt mark the place where he shall lie, and thou shalt go in, and uncover his feet, and lay thee down; and he will tell thee what thou shalt do.*

Arranging a meeting between two hearts that had met at the divine intersection of God's will and human attraction brought Naomi the filling of joy that Moab had drained from her life. Certainly Naomi's age had not removed her from the delights of seeking the happiness between two hearts that pined for each other. Each instruction of Naomi led Ruth closer to the moment where she would present herself to Boaz for fellowship and kinsman redemption.

Nothing else would exceed Ruth's desire to come to Boaz and seek redemption of her family's name. The names of Elimelech and Mahlon, Ruth's deceased husband would find redemption if Boaz would accept Ruth. Before any of this could happen, Ruth had to prepare to meet him. She then had to pause to present herself to him.

Ruth could not do this all at once; she needed to wait until he had nourished himself and had laid down for the night. Boaz would be tired from his labors and would enjoy his rest. With the meal being completed, he would seek a comfortable spot on the threshingfloor to rest for the next day's activities. Scripture indicates for us Boaz had no idea of Naomi's planning and Ruth's presentation. Ruth was there waiting to ask the biggest request of her life. This night would long be remembered by both of them.

Naomi told her to wait, watch, and remember the spot in her mind so she could present herself. This watching him from her concealed position taught her about his mannerisms and movements. She had seen him in the environment of the harvest where she learned his movements and saw his activities. Now, in this different setting, she watches him satisfy his hunger and wonders if he will be satisfied with her heart. When he settled down for the night, she was to mark the place so when the lights were gone out she could get to that place and present herself to him.

This simple thought of marking the place for when it got dark ought to stir the heart of every harvest worker. Occasionally, the light surrounding a situation in which we work may become dimmed or obscured. We may even reach a place of darkness in the work we conduct for our Eternal Boaz. We would do well to spend time with Him while it is light so that when it gets dark we can find Him and fellowship with Him. Mark His place today. You may need to find Him when this day gets dark.

Think about it . . .

Purity and humility . . .

Ruth 3:4 *And it shall be, when he lieth down, that thou shalt mark the place where he shall lie, and thou shalt go in, and uncover his feet, and lay thee down; and he will tell thee what thou shalt do.*

Naomi finally reached the part that Ruth longed to hear. Naomi knew that Ruth's eagerness cultivated by waiting, must be tempered by her instruction. Finally, after all the preparation at home, and the patience to find the right moment, she now heard the instruction that was sure to settle deep in her heart. "Thou shalt go in." These four words gave her the license, at the right timing, to enter into the presence of Boaz.

She would enter surreptitiously while Boaz slept. His work ethic gave him the right to a good night's rest. Likely, sleep would come without effort. Should he have known the events that would unfold, sleep may have remained out of reach. For, waiting in the shadows this evening was a young maiden from his field who desired to be redeemed by this gentle man with a heart of gold.

She would enter without pageantry and without seduction. She would enter with purity in her mind and humility in her heart. She could not have fellowship with Boaz if she physically remained outside the threshingfloor or if she had remained within Naomi's house. She had to enter into his presence to place her petition into his hearing.

The child of the Lord of the Harvest would do well to remember that entrance into His presence should be marked with the same characteristics as Ruth's entrance. She came with purity in her mind and humility in her heart. Yes, the New Testament writer of Hebrews instructed believers to come boldly to his throne; this is the matter of access, not necessarily of asking.

We should never feel entering His presence should be skipped because He might be too busy. Rather, we should, with boldness, come to the place of asking. Yet, as Ruth, we should be clothed with the garments of purity and humility in our requests. Ruth teaches believers the right way to approach Boaz. She came with a boldness in her steps to the threshingfloor and entered his presence with humility and purity.

How do you come to our Eternal Boaz? Has timidity or boldness marked your access to Him? When you arrive, does purity and humility drape your heart?

Think about it . . .

Uncovering his feet . . .

Ruth 3:4 *And it shall be, when he lieth down, that thou shalt mark the place where he shall lie, and thou shalt go in, and uncover his feet, and lay thee down; and he will tell thee what thou shalt do.*

The instructions from Naomi to Ruth in the minds of 21st century readers may seem a bit unusual. She was told to continue to wait until Boaz had finished eating, drinking, and lying down. At that time, she would go into that area and *"uncover his feet."* This simple action would be significant in that setting. Keep in mind this action was completely pure, and nothing about it was illicit.

Secular historians indicated that such action was taken by a wife to her lawful husband. Such action would display her subjection and modesty. The position she would take was rather a unique one as she was uncovering the place she would lay down. She would lay at Boaz's feet perpendicular to him. Ruth's heart, decorated with purity and humility, now takes overt action in her desire to be redeemed by this kinsman. Her directive from Naomi was simple; she would make a place to lie down at his feet. The covering over Boaz as he slept offered a bit of warmth from the gentle breezes. When she removed this covering, it would be a method to wake him and offer an opportunity for him to make a decision concerning redeeming Ruth as a kinsman.

Her action of uncovering the feet of Boaz indicated that she had a need only Boaz could fill, and she desired that he would fill it. Her uncovering of his feet is easily likened to a child of

God going to Him in prayer, with a heart decorated with humility and purity. It is a joy to the believer who uncovers the feet of our Eternal Boaz. At His uncovered feet, the believer presents to Him their petitions, discovers God's power, and learns the surety of His promises.

Reader, when last have you sought out our Eternal Boaz in prayer and uncovered His feet? How long ago was it when you last placed yourself before Him in subjection to His Lordship over your life? When last have you come to Him and placed yourself at His feet to accept His will for you? Today, determine to take a moment and uncover the feet of our Eternal Boaz and present yourself to Him. Many have come to the Eternal Boaz and sought his redemption as their kinsman, have you? None have ever been refused.

Think about it . . .

Portraits at the cross . . .

Ruth 3:4 *And it shall be, when he lieth down, that thou shalt mark the place where he shall lie, and thou shalt go in, and uncover his feet, and lay thee down; and he will tell thee what thou shalt do.*

Ruth listened to Naomi's precise instructions.. Naomi's directives to Ruth detailed to the need for cleansing, consecrating, and concealing herself as well as the importance of coming to his presence to present her petition.

In this verse we have meditated on three areas. First, we considered her entrance to the threshingfloor. Then, we thought about her drawing near to him. Most recently, we pondered the uncovering of his feet. Now, the last item of her instruction is very simple; she is to lie down at his feet.

Her lying down was not at his side, but rather, at his feet. You may recall we considered earlier when she uncovered his feet, it was to prepare a place for her to lie down. A careful look would let you see a cross by the placement of her body to his body. Although Boaz sought rest that night from his labors, Ruth sought redemption for her life.

What better place than a cross to find rest and redemption? Ruth had been drawn by the grace of Boaz and driven to him by her love for him. Placing herself at his feet to reveals her implicit trust in him and her submission to his heart.

The completion of this deed reveals a beautiful portrait with many images to consider. The first image portrays her submission to the lordship of Boaz; whatever he chose, she could accept. We would do well if we considered how well we are in submission to our Eternal Boaz's lordship.

Another image in this portrait displays Ruth's surrender to the love of Boaz. She trusted Boaz. She knew in his presence no harm nor ill could come to her from him or from any outside force. His love for her and her love for him created a wonderful shelter from any adversity.

A third image in this portrait of the cross is Ruth's satisfaction with the liberty she received from Boaz. She came for rest and redemption and in Boaz, she found liberty. Today, people would scoff that Ruth had liberty in this relationship. Ruth found liberty in her subjection to Boaz. This subjection led to his promise of provision. Her subjection did not enslave her to Boaz, but rather, gave her liberty she had never known.

Similarly, our Eternal Boaz, on the cross outside of Jerusalem, provided lordship love, and liberty for those who come to Him in faith. The images of the portrait of His cross should never be far from our daily thinking and living. When last did you pause in the art gallery of His divine goodness and meditate on the portrait of the cross and the images it displays?

"But drops of grief can ne'er repay The debt of love I owe;
Here, Lord, I give myself away–'Tis all that I can do!

At the cross, at the cross where I first saw the light,
And the burden of my heart rolled away,
It was there by faith I received my sight,
And now I am happy all the day!"

Isaac Watts – Ralph E. Hudson

Think about it . . .

Naomi's promise . . .

Ruth 3:4 *And it shall be, when he lieth down, that thou shalt mark the place where he shall lie, and thou shalt go in, and uncover his feet, and lay thee down; and he will tell thee what thou shalt do.*

God's sovereign hand orchestrated this moment. Naomi's declaration of despair upon her return home (1:20) was reversed as now she revealed her renewed devotion to Jehovah's will. (3:4) She clearly stated that upon Ruth's fulfillment of these matters, *"He **will** tell thee what thou shalt do."* Upon Naomi's teaching, Ruth in faith, prepared her body, spirit, and soul to meet with Boaz. She came without reservation to him.

How was Naomi able to know these things? While she was in Moab God ensured Naomi's knowledge of The Eternal Baker's bread in Bethlehem. He would enable Ruth to be persuaded of Boaz's knowledge of the next step. Boaz, if you recall, had been fully shown of Ruth's situation. (2:11). Now we see Naomi was fully persuaded that Boaz would have a response for Ruth. (3:4)

Boaz held the answer to the largest question in Ruth's heart; *"Will you redeem me and the name of my husband, Mahlon, and his father Elimelech?"* Naomi's training had given Ruth the guidelines for her preparation. She also had given Ruth the guarantee that Boaz would answer the question of her heart.

Naomi's promise of a guaranteed answer is also a wonderful comfort to every child of God. Every believer can come to our Eternal Boaz and mark the space where He lies and by asking in prayer we can uncover His feet and we will find He will tell us what to do.

Through the New Testament writer, James, displays the image of her promise in his writing with different words. *"If any of you lack wisdom, let him ask of God, that giveth to all men liberally, and upbraideth not; and it shall be given him."* James 1:5

Reader, do you struggle with what to do about a situation in your life? Ask our Eternal Boaz and He will tell you what you should do!

Think about it . . .

Peaceful obedience . . .

Ruth 3:5 *And she said unto her, All that thou sayest unto me I will do.*

When reading our focus verse for this day, one can become struck by the fact of the rarity of Ruth's speech. This book that bears Ruth's name is full of dialogue, yet, in the whole book, there are only eleven recorded conversations where she speaks. In fact, less than ten percent of the words recorded in the whole book are spoken by Ruth.

Ruth's confession of faith on the desert road from Moab revealed her confidence in the power of the God of Israel. Her statement on the doorstep of Naomi's house in Bethlehem revealed her confidence in the provision of Israel's

God. Her conversation with Boaz in the field revealed her confidence in the protection of the God of Israel. On the evening ending her first day's harvesting, she spoke with Naomi and revealed her confidence in the promises of God. Her words in this discussion with Naomi reveal her peaceful confidence found in Israel's God. *"All that thou sayest unto me I will do."* The deep settled peace in Ruth's heart is unmistakably seen as she receives the instructions from her mother-in-law and without negotiation, hesitation or question. She had no need to doubt God, Naomi, or Boaz; she would do what she was asked.

Naomi taught Ruth how to prepare and present herself to fellowship with Boaz. The moment of response rests in Ruth's hands and heart. She chose nine words that illustrate her peaceful confidence which had been shaped by her past experiences with the God of Abraham. All she was taught she would do.

Certainly, these nine words come with a lesson to the children of the Eternal Boaz. No matter the length of your Christian sojourn, you have seen enough of God's omnipotence to see you through difficult days and discouraging nights. Your trust in Him for salvation is enough foundation for you to place your life's course in His hands and say, *"All that thou sayest unto me I will do."*

When you trust Him for your provision, protection, promises, and power; why distrust His peace? You **can** say with Ruth, *"All that thou sayest unto me I will do."* When His peace governs your heart, you will have the calm assurance needed for full submission to His work. Does His peace manage your life? Do you find you trust Him with eternity but doubt His ability in the present? Will you say to Him today, *"All that thou sayest unto me I will do?"*

Think about it . . .

Answers at midnight . . .

Ruth 3:6-8 *And she went down unto the floor, and did according to all that her mother in law bade her. And when Boaz had eaten and drunk, and his heart was merry, he went to lie down at the end of the heap of corn: and she came softly, and uncovered his feet, and laid her down. And it came to pass at midnight, that the man was afraid, and turned himself: and, behold, a woman lay at his feet.*

Ruth had listened carefully to all that she was told to do. Naomi knew that if Boaz was to be presented with Ruth's petition, nothing should be a distraction to him. Ruth devoted the time needed to present herself to Boaz. No one could ever know all Ruth's thoughts, but one wonders if it might have been like this:

"Yes, Mother! I will do it. I will gladly accept this responsibility. Oh, how wonderful Jehovah is to have made this provision in His law for a soul like me."

With delight she headed to bathe; the time spent cleansing her body would give her the time to prepare her heart for the moment of meeting Boaz as lord of the harvest and lord of her heart.

"I hope he is pleased with me. I did try to work earnestly in his employ. I know he has shown his care for me in the matters of the harvest, but now this is all about matters of the heart."

With care she cleansed away the dust of the harvest and the despair from her heart. Her time of washing helped wash and pack away all of the memories of Mahlon, Moab, and the misery of widowhood.

"This is a new day! God has given me a way to honor my husband's name while giving me hope for my heart! What fragrance will I choose? I hope it is not too strong nor to subtle. I hope he will find it pleasing."

Her skin glistened as she carefully applied the perfumed oil. The fragrance of oil from the apothecary seemed just right. Its soothing quality was experienced both on the skin and in the room as the subtle fragrance from the perfume permeated the room.

"You know, it seems the time of washing and anointing had a way of calming the heart as much as it did cleansing the skin."

Now the challenge of the ages for all women came; *"What will I wear? Certainly, he would appreciate this selection!"*

The raiment of a godly woman was meant to draw him to her heart. She did not need to display her flesh to appeal to his flesh. She would simply dress to attract Boaz's heart to her own.

"What a beautiful evening!"

The harvest evening, lit with moonlight, brightened her pathway down to the threshingfloor. Each step toward the threshingfloor brought her further from Moab and closer to God's man for her life. She could see him now in the distance; the lamps would light the threshingfloor and reveal the object of her affection.

"Boaz," she might have thought within, *"Oh Boaz . . . My Boaz! I must wait until he has finished with his work. I wish I could bring him his meal, but perhaps that day will come soon. I must find a corner in the darkness and wait until he is sleeping as the reward for a hard day and after he has enjoyed a good meal."*

The soft breezes could have easily carried her perfume to Boaz; so she positioned herself accordingly and watched as this man worked, ate, and prepared for bed.

"Look at that heap of corn. How is it that such a heap of corn could be there? He has made sure I have had plenty yet God has blessed him so. He has worked so hard today! He seems quite content with the day's work and the harvest's ending. Oh, look at him now! His eyes have gotten heavy. He is making a spot for himself now. When those lamps go out, it seems I will have five steps or so to get to his feet. I will mark this spot in my mind and walk softly to the place. I wonder how long it will be until he awakes and discovers me there."

"Naomi, made it clear; this is a proper way to present myself to him. I will uncover his feet and lie down. By lying at his feet I will show him that I am not an improper in my motives; I just want to know if he will redeem our family's name."

With tender care she softly walked from her place of concealment to his feet.

"Oh, here is the spot. I will lift the covering ever so gently. I want him to awake but not quite yet." I want to treasure this moment to its fullest. Lord, I thank you for saving me from Moab. Thank you for your goodness in letting me meet Boaz. Lord, whenever you choose to wake him, may I be pleasing to him. Please allow him to accept me and fulfill my need of a kinsman-redeemer. May your will be done in my life.

She was not sure if the chill she felt was from the breezes or the excitement that raced through her. His feet were just below her bosom, never had she been so close to him. Being there with him was enough to warm her heart.

"Oh, when he awakes; what will be his first words? Will he be angry? Will he accept me?

It seems in such moments time would stand still. Minutes seem as hours; hours seem as days. Midnight approached as thoughts of tomorrow filled Ruth's mind.

"No matter the hour, his answer is worth the wait. I will wait and be ready for his answer."

The midnight hour would not prevent a response from Boaz; nor does the midnight hour hinder an answer from our Eternal Boaz. Oh, child of God with your heart cleansed from the dirt of this world, you can find him in the darkness and in the hopelessness of any hour, midnight included. You can retrieve the answer for your heart's question.

Think about it . . .

My Goel . . .

Ruth 3:6-8 And she went down unto the floor, and did according to all that her mother in law bade her. And when Boaz had eaten and drunk, and his heart was merry, he went to lie down at the end of the heap of corn: and she came softly, and uncovered his feet, and laid her down. And it came to pass at midnight, that the man was afraid, and turned himself: and, behold, a woman lay at his feet.

"Oh, he is stirring now. He is turning over. I wonder if this is the moment for which I have waited. Yes, it is. Oh no! I have startled him. Boaz stirred as he felt there was someone in the threshingfloor with him. Not knowing in the darkness if some marauder has come upon him. Momentary fear seizes him, he calls out, *"Who art thou?"*

Ruth couldn't help but smile. Inwardly she thought, *"I have lain there this whole time and he just recognized a presence in the threshingfloor."*

Ruth was there that night to ask Boaz to be her kinsman-redeemer. Her heart was joined to his heart months ago during the barley harvest. She remained through the corn harvest and was delighted to serve with him. Nothing more would please her more than to have him accept her.

Boaz wondered as a pleasant perfume reached his awakened senses. *"Is it a woman? Why would a woman be in the threshingfloor? Who is she?"* A myriad of concerns came to mind.

Quickly, she responds to properly identify herself and to calm his fear. Naomi's recorded instructions to Ruth did not include these words; however, what she said was perfect. In eighteen words she presented herself, her heart, and her heart's desire. *"I am Ruth thine handmaid: spread therefore thy skirt over thine handmaid; for thou art a near kinsman."* She introduced herself as Ruth, his handmaid. She said, *"I am Ruth thine handmaid,"* not Ruth the widower; not the Ruth the Moabitess, nor as Ruth a promiscuous woman. By identifying herself as handmaid to Boaz it revealed the passion of her heart – she loved him.

"From the first day in the harvest field when God's wings led me to your harvest field, I have cared for you. Your kindness and words embraced me from the first day. I have felt close to your heart ever since that moment. I remember thinking that when Mahlon died, my heart died with him. However, being with you these last few months has kindled a flame inside. The words flowed easily, *"I am thine handmaid."* Boaz, I belong to your harvest. I would love to belong to your heart.*

My heart is pounding out of my chest. I must tell him in this moment: I can wait no longer. I must let him know I am here for pure reasons and to present my petition. *"Spread therefore thy skirt over thine handmaid; for thou art a near kinsman."*

To the average Western reader, this phrase hardly sounds romantic, nor does it sound like a request that indicates her willingness for his marriage proposal. Yet, in truth, that is what Ruth's words meant. Ruth sought his skirt to cover her, not because of the breezes of the evening, but because she desired his covering as the head of her life. This idea comes from a little chick seeking shelter under the wing of its mother as it senses impending danger. Her words indicated she came to Boaz seeking for his protection as a husband and for the promise of his heart.

Ruth knew the word to use, "*Thou art a near kinsman,*" to the Hebrews one word would cover it all, Goel. "*Boaz, I want you to be my Goel.*" *My heart has been toward you as lord of the harvest, but now, you must know that my heart is toward you as a kinsman-redeemer husband. I wish you to be my Goel.*"

Boaz knew she was asking him to fulfill a provision in the law of God** as a kinsman-redeemer. The Goel, was established by God as one who would step in for a family member, however distant, to assist them in time of need. A kinsman-redeemer could redeem a slave from his enslavement. He could serve as the avenger for a murdered family member and bring that perpetrator to face the penalty for his crime. A kinsman-redeemer would be sought to purchase back family land due to be forfeited. As provided by God's law the Goel would also marry a childless widow so the family name would not be extinguished. **(*Leviticus 25:25,48; Deuteronomy 25:5-10 Numbers 35:19*)

Ruth chose Boaz to be her Goel. She sought the one to whom her heart had been drawn. Ruth told Boaz, "You are my Goel." She met the qualifications of the law. Ruth was a childless widow. She had land in her husband's name through inheritance which was for sale, ostensibly to meet financial needs (4:3-5). In matters of the heart, grief had held her as slave since Mahlon's death, so she needed a Goel. Ruth sought him because of his kindness first extended to her. She needed a Goel, and she desired her Goel to be Boaz.

Reader, your heart must be thrilled this day as you have read this account and recalled your own need for a Goel. Our Eternal Boaz loved us when we could not even love ourselves. He loved us first before we even knew how to love Him. He offered himself on Calvary's cross to pay the law's requirement for sin.

This selfless, loving deed was his offer to be our Goel. We were enslaved to sin. We had no means to redeem ourselves. Our Eternal Boaz became our Goel so we could be his bride. He came to this earth as a man with like passions, yet he did not sin. He is my Kinsman-Redeemer; is He yours?

Think about it . . .

Rewards, reassurances, and reflections. . .

Ruth 3:10 *And he said, Blessed be thou of the LORD, my daughter: for thou hast showed more kindness in the latter end than at the beginning, inasmuch as thou followedst not young men, whether poor or rich.*

With emotions collected and fears abated, Boaz's reply indicated he fully understood Ruth's petition, even though he had been awakened from sleep at midnight. His words must have sent a calming peace to Ruth's waiting soul. Boaz's response to the precious handmaiden lying at his feet came with a three part message. His message spoke of divine reward, daughterly reassurance, and deep reflection. Imagine Ruth's delight in knowing Naomi was right; he **did** know what to say.

Boaz began, "*Blessed be thou of the LORD.*" Her arrival heralded the Lord's blessing to Boaz; he desired God's blessing for her. You may recall when Boaz first came to the harvest field, the reaper's reply to Boaz's salutation was, *"The Lord bless thee."* Now with her arrival, the lord of the harvest is offering her the same greeting. This greeting signaled to her that she was in a spiritual company and should feel protected. The human mind would love to take the scene as what is before us and read into it far more than what occurred. The opening reply is hardly the way an illicit and immoral meeting would begin.

Without stopping for a breath, Boaz declares a message of daughterly reassurance. Ruth was coming to him for the protection of a husband and to hear the words, *"My daughter,"* brought reassurance to her heart she was accepted by Boaz. Ruth's position at his feet indicated her submission to his will. Boaz's words disclosed his acceptance of her. Never before had Ruth been so vulnerable in one moment and so secure in the next moment. Boaz had called her, *"My daughter"* upon her arrival to his harvest field. Now, with her arrival to the threshingfloor of his heart he give the identical answer to her request for a kinsman-redeemer. His words gave her the reassurance that she was accepted and appreciated.

Boaz's words also reveal that he had given deep reflection on this moment prior to her arrival. His words were not an instant assessment at midnight. Rather, they were the summary of moments of deep reflection. The previous chapter makes clear God had shown Boaz fully the matters relating to Ruth. Perhaps Boaz had thought about being able to be a kinsman-redeemer to Ruth. Yet, perhaps he wondered why she would choose him, seeing there were younger men in whom she might have an interest.

Boaz knew the right things to say. How this must have elevated Ruth's emotions. His rewards, reassurances, and reflections were all deposited in the bank of Ruth's heart for safekeeping and appraisal.

He cherished Ruth's preparation of the heart and position at his feet. He stated that she had shown him more kindness than even at the beginning of their relationship by choosing him over any available younger or richer man. The focus of this book has been on Boaz's kindness to Ruth, yet, the focal point of Boaz has been on her kindness to him.

Undoubtedly, Ruth's heart embraced Boaz's words She had not realized how her actions had been received as kindness to him. He was kind to her first. It was fitting for her to be kind to him. Ruth's initial kindness toward Boaz possibly occurred when she chose to stay in his fields. Ruth also had stayed through the barley harvest to the reaping of the corn. Yet, her arrival now was perceived as a greater kindness than the aforementioned deeds.

Boaz saw what Ruth did for him as kindness, an act of mercy. It would be easy to overlook how Boaz received Ruth's heartfelt actions toward him. She merely sensed his kindness and gratefully responded. Even at this midnight hour, he with clarity remembered her kindness to him and declared the opportunity to be a kinsman-redeemer exceeded all other deeds. Boaz's mercy overshadows anything Ruth possibly could have done for him, yet did not overlook her heart's devotion to him from the beginning.

The child of God would do well to consider 1 John 4:19, "*We love him, because he first loved us.*" Our Eternal Boaz extended grace and mercy to us, yet have we ever considered how he interprets our responses as acts of kindness to Him? Yes, He loved us first, but the reciprocity of our love to Him does not go unnoticed, rather it is appreciated.

How are you loving him? When last did you place yourself at the feet of The Eternal Boaz and bask in His love for you? What was the last loving thing you did for Him?

Think about it . . .

Kindness to Boaz . . .

Ruth 3:10 *And he said, Blessed be thou of the LORD, my daughter: for thou hast showed more kindness in the latter end than at the beginning, inasmuch as thou followedst not young men, whether poor or rich.*

Boaz's words of rewards, reassurance and reflections had no sooner entered Ruth's hearing than he elaborated on his purpose. Boaz said, " . . .*for thou hast showed more kindness in the latter end than at the beginning, inasmuch as thou followedst not young men, whether poor or rich.*" Ruth must have smiled with humble delight. Yet, could she have ever thought that she could exhibit kindness to Boaz? How could this be?

Boaz's words, as always, were precise and self-explanatory. Boaz noted an earlier kindness and a latter kindness. He determined that the latter kindness, her presentation to him at the threshingfloor, superseded her earlier kindness. The origin of her earlier kindness is left for speculation by the reader; however, the focus is on her kindness this evening at the threshingfloor.

Boaz considered himself too much older than Ruth to be appealing to this widow. After all, there were younger men who may have caught her eye. However, Boaz had not only caught her eye, he had also caught her heart. A younger man would not be her choice. This was not a choice of age, of ability, nor of appearance. Rather, it was a choice of acceptance. Ruth knew he loved her when she was at her lowest and in her greatest hour of need.

Genuine affection is not the glamorized image portrayed in films or television. Genuine affection is often realized when a kind look combines with unconditional acceptance. This realization for Boaz occurred first in the harvest field and now, at the threshingfloor. Boaz saw this as nothing less than her kindness to him. This was Ruth's genuine expression of affection for him. Though he knew his heart for her, her arrival and announcement sent a clear message of kindness to his own heart.

This is a rather stirring thought to ponder. As Boaz revealed Ruth's kindness to him, we should also let our thoughts dwell a moment on our Eternal Boaz. What kindnesses are we rendering to our Eternal Boaz? Ruth rendered kindness to Boaz when she followed him. Does our Eternal Boaz see kindness from your walk with Him? When you follow your heart, your kindness is directed toward another. However, when you follow His heart, this sends a message of kindness straight to the heart of our Eternal Boaz!

Did our Eternal Boaz hear a message of kindness from you yesterday? Will He hear one today?

Think about it . . .

Six words before 'I do' . . .

Ruth 3:11 *And now, my daughter, fear not; I will do to thee all that thou requirest: for all the city of my people doth know that thou art a virtuous woman.*

"*And now, my daughter, fear not . . .*" with these six words Boaz prepares Ruth's heart to receive his declaration of love. He wanted her to know how important she was to him. He wanted her as he explained the initial difficulty in his full commitment to be her Goel. He needed her to know when he would act.

Boaz's words are more than just an announcement of their new beginning, it is a message to calm her fears. They are the six words her heart needed to hear. Perhaps Ruth held her breath as he spoke.

For the third, and last, recorded time in this book that bears her name, Boaz says, "my daughter." This term, when spoken by Boaz, displayed the contents of his heart. It delivered to her a message of affection, acceptance and assurance. It was appropriate for him to address her in this fashion, for it was an indicator that his intentions were pure and his motives were right. Hearing the phrase, served as a comfort to this widowed stranger in Israel.

"*Fear not. . .*" How appropriate for Boaz to say! Today Ruth graduates from daughter in the harvest to darling of his heart. Ruth's fears of being a widow for life and struggling to survive in a harsh political and economical environment will now be whisked into the wind. Her loneliness and mere survival day to day will be evicted with his six words.

For the child of God, we too had a moment when our Eternal Boaz looked at us and spoke similar words. Throughout Scripture His "*fear not*" has cancelled fear, brought courage, and renewed hope. The darkest clouds escape when hope breaks across the horizon to shed light on the promises of God.

Does your future seem uncertain? Consider Edmund S. Lorenz, the hymn writer's words; *Are you anxious what shall be tomorrow? Tell it to Jesus alone.* Our Eternal Boaz cares deeply about what is on our hearts. His reply is still the same; "*and now, my child, fear not.*"

Think about it . . .

When his word is enough. . .

Ruth 3:11 *And now, my daughter, fear not; I will do to thee all that thou requirest: for all the city of my people doth know that thou art a virtuous woman.*

Remember, thus far during the evening Ruth's only words are, "*I am Ruth thine handmaid: spread therefore thy skirt over thine handmaid; for thou art a near kinsman.*" Her announcement revealed her humility. Her request showed her need for covering, both socially and physically. Her statement about Boaz near kinsman status displayed her knowledge of God's provision in the law for a Goel.

Boaz's response to her words indicated he understood her vulnerability and, subsequently, his responsibility. As a handmaid, she needed his acceptance. As someone over whom he would spread his garment, she needed his adoption. As a near kin to him, she needed his assurance.

God's law established a principle that protected Ruth in her childless and widowed situation. God instituted the rule of a kinsmen redeemer to assist those in dire straits. The Hebrew word for kinsman-redeemer is Goel.

A Goel, a kinsman, is the nearest living blood relative. It is the Goel's responsibility to restore the rights of another and to avenge any wrongdoing. God designed the law for the Goel to assist his next of kin when they encounter difficulties in matters of finance, murder, and slavery.

Boaz's words must have immersed Ruth in a soothing calm as she heard Boaz say, "*I will.*" Boaz's words said, I will accept and adopt you. I give you the assurance that I will make all things work together for your good. Boaz's agreement to come to her aid as a Goel protected Ruth, and, although he did not know it he was protecting the Messianic line.

Boaz's promise to Ruth is reminiscent of God's promise to believers in Romans 8:28, *"And we know that all things work together for good to them that love God, to them who are the called according to his purpose."* God is able to work all things together for good. Whether barren, penniless, widowed, or empty, God is not hindered by our circumstances when it comes to the good He wants to bring.

Reader, you have the word of our Eternal Boaz who can make all of life's negatives bearable and a blessing. The sole requirement of The Eternal Boaz is to love Him and live His way. Ruth did not have to fear when Boaz stepped in and committed to help, nor do we!

Think about it . . .

A testimony of virtue . . .

Ruth 3:11 *And now, my daughter, fear not; I will do to thee all that thou requirest: for all the city of my people doth know that thou art a virtuous woman.*

Ruth could not have imagined a more comforting response than what she received. Had Boaz stopped with just his commitment to be all that she needed, it would have been more than enough. Yet, Boaz's commitment came with a compliment that certainly warmed Ruth's heart in a way she may not have known or dreamt. Boaz said, *"for all the city of my people doth know that thou art a virtuous woman."* Boaz's words from the threshingfloor could not have honored Ruth's heart anymore.

Virtuous, the very word he chose, indicated he saw beyond the threshingfloor and all the way back to the dusty border between Moab and Israel. That day, when she made her choice to fulfill her deceased husband's role of caring for his mother, she also determined to follow the God of Israel. Her words to Naomi would not remain on the desert sand, but would make a journey to both the heart of God and of Boaz.

Boaz's words make it clear. Her virtue was apparent to the people of Bethlehem. They watched as Ruth cared for Naomi. Her concern for Naomi went on display at the moment of her arrival, and the people in town saw the virtue in this girl from Moab. The country of her birth would have normally made the townspeople discount instantly any visible virtue. Moabites were one of the incestuous sons of Lot, and enemies to the people of God. Yet, Ruth's virtuous manners overcame the social boundaries. Her confession of faith on Moab's border enabled the people to see a Moabite woman by birth, had become Israelite by faith.

Boaz's sense of Ruth's virtues came from her conduct in his harvest fields. Ruth's steadfastness to work in Boaz's fields revealed her worth to him. She did not try to go to other fields, nor did she just try to get by for herself. She sought provision for her Naomi. She did not stay for one harvesting she stayed for the harvest of barley and wheat.

Ruth's journey of hope to the threshingfloor that night armed with her request and plea for a Goel allowed Boaz to sense the virtues of her compassion and character. Only one word could describe the life of Ruth - virtuous.

Reader, you have before you today a very simple illustration of the value of virtue. Virtue is that special quality of doing what is right and avoiding the wrong. Do the all the people of your community know you are a virtuous person? When our Eternal Boaz makes the assessment of your life will you be valued as virtuous? Peter's epistle instructs the believer to add to his faith, virtue. Like Ruth after her profession of faith, have you made the addition of virtue to your faith?

Think about it . . .

"A kinsman nearer than I. . ."

Ruth 3:12 And *now it is true that I am thy near kinsman: howbeit there is a kinsman nearer than I.*

"I am thy near kinsman" What comfort Ruth must have sensed. This Gentile gem, mined from the desert sands of Moab to be a jewel in the crown of the Messiah, the Saviour of the world, found hope in the words of Boaz. However, Boaz's words came with a sharp point that certainly deflated Ruth's hopes and heart.

Ruth's heart must have felt the blow. Everything she felt and thought in this moment of security seemed in jeopardy. Didn't he say he would be her Goel? Hadn't Boaz said that he would take care of it all? What happened to the promise of the fulfillment of each need?

This man of honor, spoke with certainty. He said, *"I am thy near kinsman."* God's law was clear. Boaz knew that she chose him, not this other relative. She requested of him the liberation of her deceased husband's honor, but that was not the sole request. She also sought the deliverance of her own heart. Ruth's heart was toward Boaz, not a different relative. Would her dreams of a lifetime with Boaz be dashed now by a technicality?

The law made clear that the legal right belonged to the closest relative. Boaz knew another relative legally stood in the way of the deliverance of her heart. He offered himself as Ruth's Goel. Though he had the ability, the law still had to be fulfilled. He would seek the nearer kinsman and give him the opportunity to do his part. Boaz promised her, "If he will not, I will."

Mankind faces a problem similar to Ruth's. The relative that had the right to be Ruth's Goel had the first claim on Ruth.

The law has first claim on every person born into the world. Yet none could ever fulfil every point of the law. This desperation is similar to what Ruth felt. The other relative that Boaz had to seek could not do the part of a Goel. Like Ruth had a Boaz who would be her Goel, mankind has a Boaz who is our Goel.

Jesus Christ, our Goel offered and gave His righteous life on the cross to fulfil every point of the law. Every attempt of man to redeem his own lost state is met with frustration and failure. Mankind's desperation is exchanged for hope when they trust Jesus as their Eternal Goel. It is in Christ alone that man finds the redemption of his heart.

Your sin nature stands between you and God. Like the relative of Boaz which declined the offer to provide deliverance, the law must decline to provide deliverance, as it cannot save anyone. Any confidence that good deeds alone will bring forgiveness will meet with disappointment and death. The only hope mankind has for salvation is in the redemption of Jesus Christ, our Eternal Boaz!

Think about it . . .

A promise to sleep on. . .

Ruth 3:13 *Tarry this night, and it shall be in the morning, that if he will perform unto thee the part of a kinsman, well; let him do the kinsman's part: but if he will not do the part of a kinsman to thee, then will I do the part of a kinsman to thee, as the LORD liveth: lie down until the morning.*

The cover of darkness hovered over Boaz and Ruth. The midnight hour was upon them as decisions affecting the rest of their lives were contemplated. Ruth listened as Boaz's words comforted, confused, and calmed her simultaneously.

Boaz proclaimed he wanted to be her Goel. Then he spoke of the technicality of the law that would eliminate him from fulfilling that role. The law indicated the proximity in age or blood to the deceased relative would give the closest one the opportunity to be a kinsman-redeemer.

In the stillness of the night, with Ruth's heart surely beating fast, Boaz instructs her to stay the night and lie down, remaining at his feet until the morning. When the sun rose that morning they would see what would happen in the matter of the kinsman who was nearer. Ruth could have thought, "He may be nearer, but he could not be dearer than my Boaz. I will pray that the God who brought our lives together will allow our hearts to be together."

Boaz's concluding words on the matter spoke volumes to her heart. "*As the LORD liveth: lie down until the morning.*" His words brought the reminder to her that God, the Great I AM, the Source of Everything, the self-existing God of Israel, controlled this moment at the threshingfloor and would take care of it. Boaz's counsel to Ruth would have an immediate effect as well as a delayed affect on their family. Solomon, their son four generations later, would write in the Inspired Text "*He giveth his beloved sleep.*" (Psalms 127:2) God would see to it that this difficulty would be overcome while they slept.

The threshingfloor of Bethlehem held two searching hearts that honorably desired to be together. Those hearts found delightful rest that night. They drifted off to sleep knowing that God was working things for their good and they could rest in His ability.

Are you able to rest in the promises of God? Do the worries of tomorrow prevent your sleep from arriving each night? Allow Boaz's words to Ruth help your own heart: "*As the LORD liveth: lie down until the morning.*"

The next night that brings woes and worries of what might be at dawn, remember this: the only thing that is sure to be tomorrow is not a what, but Who.

Think about it . . .

Whispers at dawn. . .

Ruth 3:14 *And she lay at his feet until the morning: and she rose up before one could know another. And he said, Let it not be known that a woman came into the floor.*

The hours from midnight until the darkest hour before dawn passed without recorded conversation. Certainly, they could have spoken, but we do not know if they did so. We do know that she remained at his feet through the night. Nothing illicit would occur as Boaz, honorable in deed, and Ruth, honorable in her devotion to him, would follow what was right, instead of what might have felt right in the moment.

It would be very easy to imagine that sleep may not have come for either of them that night. They could have easily shared their hearts and plans for the future through the hours between midnight and dawn's arrival. However, the moment came where it was the best thing for Ruth to go back home and wait for a word from Boaz.

While the residents of Bethlehem slept, they were unaware of Ruth's presence at the threshingfloor. Yet, Boaz and Ruth knew the reproach that could be brought by the townspeople if they saw her returning home after being out all night and coming from area of the threshingfloor. They decided she rise early and go home. This decision protected their honor and kept the matter above reproach.

Ruth began to rise and leave. Boaz spoke to her in what is perceived as a whisper. Boaz thought it best for Ruth to do as she was intending. Prudent discretion guided them in this moment where she would part from him and await his response at Naomi's house.

He said, *"Let it not be known that a woman came into the floor."* He was not casting her out in rejection for that would have been done at midnight. Boaz was concerned for Ruth. He wanted her to avoid the questions and discussion by the residents of Bethlehem.

Ruth needed to know that what she was going to do was the will of Boaz. She did not want to act on her own desires. Boaz knew that and whispered to her at dawn the words she needed to hear to face a day of uncertainty. Her husband's inheritance and family name would be placed on the auction block for someone else to lay claim to her heart. She needed to know that going home was his will.

Boaz's whisper at dawn may not sound like a comfort at first reading. However, consider it closely. She needed to know she was doing the right thing, and Boaz gave her clear indication that it was and also gave her his guideline.

Have you ever spent the night wondering what might be the next day? Have you ever pondered whether or not your decisions were in God's will? Our Eternal Boaz still whispers at dawn for those who listen. The Bible will whisper to the listening heart the confirmation of His will when our nights are at the darkest.

Think about it . . .

Pausing to be filled. . .

Ruth 3:15 *Also he said, Bring the veil that thou hast upon thee, and hold it. And when she held it, he measured six measures of barley, and laid it on her: and she went into the city.*

Ruth stood to leave. Her heart was reassured of his midnight commitment to her for the morning. With morning fast approaching she prepares herself to vacate the threshingfloor to return to Naomi. Boaz delayed her departure and requested she take her veil and hold it out. This veil by all indications is the hyke still worn in the Middle East. Then it was worn by ladies and persons of distinction. It is said to measure five feet by eighteen feet and could easily be used as a pallet for sleeping.

Boaz, in the preceding verse revealed his concerned for the protection of her honor. Now he exhibits his concern for her provision. In Chapter Two Boaz gave her parched corn at the mid-day meal for her satisfaction in the field. Now we see him give her threshed barley for her sustenance in the future. This blessing was from his heart to hers. She sought nothing from him; it was enough to be protected by Boaz. Yet, she now finds the blessing of his concern as he gives a token of his concern for her well being.

Boaz asked her to open her veil so he could fill it with barley. When he measured it out, it came to six measures. This would be approximately 15 gallons of barley. This was twice the amount she came home with from her day of gleaning in the field with Boaz.

You can imagine Ruth with arms extended and Boaz filling her veil with barley. The bounty was all she could receive; the verse states that he laid it on her. It is certain she walked with great care back to Bethlehem.

Ruth's hands were full with blessings from Boaz. How comforting to know that David, her great-grandson, would write in a psalm that our Eternal Boaz daily loads us with benefits. (Psalms 68:19) Ruth opened her heart and God gave her a kinsman-redeemer. She opened her veil and God gave her blessings she could barely contain.

In your haste to 'get going' as the day breaks, do you pause in the presence of the Eternal Boaz for Him to fill you with His provisions? The believer should pause each day and seek the filling of His Holy Spirit for daily living. The veil of our lives empties quickly as we carry out our responsibilities. Why not pause daily in the presence of the Eternal Boaz and seek His filling so we can make it through every day?

Think about it . . .

Heavy burden – light load. . .

Ruth 3:15 *Also he said, Bring the veil that thou hast upon thee, and hold it. And when she held it, he measured six measures of barley, and laid it on her: and she went into the city.*

Ruth left the threshingfloor and headed toward the city. Just a few hours ago she made her way, her carrying her heart of hope. She came to the threshingfloor to present herself to the one whom her heart was toward. She came seeking a kinsman-redeemer and now leaves with his promise of arranging things today.

It is amazing how promising a sunrise looks when hope fills your heart. Boaz, the kinsman of her hope and the keeper of her heart, made a commitment that on this day he would meet her need. Ruth's first steps as she bid goodbye to Boaz must have been hard as her heart was tethered to Boaz; yet, she had to go to wait for him at home. Boaz saw to it that she had a visible symbol of his promise with her. He traveled with her in two ways. Ruth carried his presence in her heart and she carried his provision in her veil.

Boaz instructed her to go home to Naomi and he would come again to get her. Ruth left with the promise of his return and provision until the final redemption, and that was enough for her to wait. Boaz measured six measures of barley, approximately 88 pounds of barley for her to carry to Naomi. The barley was not the price for a bride, nor was it a payment to curry favor. The gift was given simply because he cared for her and desired to share his best.

The weight was heavy, but the load was light. She could carry it. Boaz laid it on her and she was able to take it home in its entirety. It seems some loads are not that heavy when your heart is in it. She journeyed home into the city carrying what some would say was heavy, but if you asked her, Ruth may have said, "How could what Boaz gives be too heavy for me? I am going to wait for his arrival at Naomi's and make myself ready for him."

Similarly, the believer has been told to occupy and prepare for His coming here in Naomi's house, on earth. He has supplied us with provision and a promise of His redemption. Like Ruth we are to go to our assigned place and fulfill his assignment until He arrives. Our Eternal Boaz is coming again. He has given us provision to sustain us until He comes. We must occupy until He arrives.

Furthermore, Ruth's journey home with the barley finds its New Testament equivalency in Jesus' statement to the disciples in Matthew 11:30. Christ's invitation to those who labored and were heavy laden was to come and discover the joy of rest. He promised that whatever the responsibility, His burden would be light. Ruth had a heavy burden to the carnal mind, but the load was light when you consider the source of strength and supply.

Fellow traveler on this spiritual journey, is your load heavy? When the load is heavy you may be carrying your own burden; His burdens are always light. Have you grown weary waiting for our Eternal Boaz to arrive? *"And when these things begin to come to pass, then look up, and lift up your heads; for your redemption draweth nigh."* Luke 21:28

Think about it . . .

The earnest until his return. . .

Ruth 3:15 *Also he said, Bring the veil that thou hast upon thee, and hold it. And when she held it, he measured six measures of barley, and laid it on her: and she went into the city.*

Ruth's heart was certainly lighter on this trip into Bethlehem than it was on her first trip to Bethlehem with Naomi. Grief and heartache marked each footprint in the sand as they journey back to the land where God gave bread to his people once again. However, the footprints on the path this day are marked with hope and expectation.

Gone are the days of wondering how they would survive. You may remember Ruth met Boaz by divine appointment as she sought a poor person's opportunity to glean in the fields to find daily sustenance. Boaz offered her a place to glean in his harvest, and she stayed through both wheat and barley harvest. She gleaned more than his harvest for here she gleaned his heart.

Now standing in the threshingfloor at the dawn of a new day, Boaz sends Ruth home to Naomi with a token of his promise to seek her redemption. The gift was more than just provision for mealtime. The gift revealed the very devotion in his heart for Ruth. Though they would have to be apart for some time, he felt a gift to her would be a comfort and a reminder of his promise to her.

In the identical way Jesus left the gift of His Holy Spirit for those who are His children. Jesus told His disciples that the Holy Spirit would abide with us until He returned for us. Like the grain from Boaz to Ruth served as an earnest payment until his return with news of their wedding celebration, so the Holy Spirit is to believers.

Paul wrote to the Ephesians in chapter one, verse fourteen, *"Which is the earnest of our inheritance until the redemption of the purchased possession. . ."* We are Christ's purchased possession. We have our redemption in our Eternal Boaz. The Holy Spirit is with us until the return of our Boaz. When He returns, it is for our wedding, the union of the church and her Goel, Jesus Christ.

If Ruth doubted for one moment anything Boaz had said, all she would do was remember his words and look at the 88 lbs of barley he sent as an earnest gift. When believers today struggle with doubts and dismay about His return, all they must do is to review His Word and look at the earnest they have been given until their final redemption.

Have you fears that overwhelm? Consider the earnest of our redemption, He is our Comforter and will remain with us until our redemption.

Think about it . . .

My daughter – his darling. . .

Ruth 3:16 *And when she came to her mother in law, she said, Who art thou, my daughter? And she told her all that the man had done to her.*

No matter how you might visualize it, Ruth's arrival must have been quite a sight. Considering she left adorned from within and without for Boaz, she arrived back with her veil laden with barley threshed by him. This young lady, carrying a load of grain, wearing with her finest clothing, arrives at Naomi's door.

As dawn broke across the horizon on what was to be an exciting day Ruth would have had some difficulty making a quiet entrance into Naomi's house. She had so much to tell Naomi. Scripture is silent on the manner of Ruth's greeting. Nonetheless, her presence is detected in the house.

Naomi calls out to her, "*Who art thou, my daughter?*" Naomi's question was not to discern Ruth's identity, but rather to whom she belonged. She wanted to determine whether or not Ruth was betrothed to Boaz.

Had Boaz agreed to be the Goel for the family of Elimelech? Would the stain of past failures be erased by the provision of Jehovah's laws? Would there be a wedding that would ease the memory of the three funerals they faced in recent? Naomi's question sought to learn Ruth's status, "You were the darling in his harvest, but dear Ruth, are you the darling of his heart?"

Ruth's words are kept from us in this verse. We are told, "*she told her all that the man had done to her.*" Certainly she related every important detail about the evening and the commitment of his heart to her. Her words must have sent to Naomi's heart the message that God was delivering bread again in Bethlehem. As Ruth revealed every detail, Naomi knew it was the hand of God that had done this work. Nothing was too hard for Naomi's God! He, the Forgiver of all mistakes, the Healer of all hurts, and the Lord of all harvests had stepped into her life and would restore her husband's name in a kinsman-redemption.

Ruth knew the joy of Boaz's acceptance and revealed the details to Naomi. For the believer, there was a day in his life where the Lord of Glory interrupted the daily routine and He made His love known and established him as the darling of His heart. Paul wrote it this way, *"But God commendeth his love toward us, in that, while we were yet sinners, Christ died for us."* Romans 5:8

Do you have a testimony that declares that you are the darling of His heart?

Think about it . . .

Not empty in heart or hands . . .

Ruth 3:17 *And she said, These six measures of barley gave he me; for he said to me, Go not empty unto thy mother in law.*

With great detail, Ruth's words gushed forth as she shared with Naomi the goodness of Boaz to her. The only detail we are given in the accounting of the past few hours is that Boaz instructed her not to go back empty to Naomi's house. The Holy Spirit gave us just what we needed to know in the text.

The absence of every other detail makes this, her one statement, significant. *"These six measures of barley gave he me; for he said to me, Go not empty unto thy mother in law."* Boaz wanted Naomi and Ruth to have everything they needed during the waiting period. Though he was only going to be gone just throughout the day, he did not want to leave them without his provision.

Boaz's concern for their sustenance makes it easy to see the honor he held for Ruth and Naomi. Naomi was the only real guardian Ruth had in Bethlehem. Boaz wanted Naomi to know his intentions were pure, and that he remembered Elimelech. His words make us realize that traveling back with just the testimony of the day was not enough. Ruth must not go empty handed. Boaz gave her exactly what he felt expressed to Naomi the message that redemption was on the way.

Much like the child of God who is awaiting the return of The Eternal Boaz, we have been left with hands and hearts full until His return to catch us away. Which begs the question, why is it that we act so empty in both hands and heart? Our Eternal Boaz has seen fit to bless us abundantly with His promise of redemption in our hearts and His provision of barley in our hands.

Boaz was concerned that Ruth's hands not be empty, so he blessed her. Our Eternal Boaz is concerned in the same way for us. We are awaiting His return: He has given us sufficient provision to last until He comes back.

The testimony of our lives sends a message about our Eternal Boaz to those around us. What are people hearing about the Eternal Boaz by the way you walk before them? Empty walking and living is a disgrace to our Eternal Boaz.

Think about it . . .

Be still and know. . .

Ruth 3:18 Then said she, Sit still, my daughter, until thou know how the matter will fall: for the man will not be in rest, until he have finished the thing this day.

Naomi's response was significant. She understood the message from God in the barley, which He had Boaz send. God used Boaz's kindness to indicate the changes He brought in her life since she left Moab. Gone are the days of a broken heart as she buried both husband and children. The word "Mara – bitter" has disappeared from her speech. No more accusations are heard of how the hand of The Almighty was against her, nor do we hear how the Lord made her empty.

Naomi's testimony has morphed throughout this book as we are given snapshots of her spiritual development. Her words, *"sit still, my daughter, until thou know how the matter will fall:"* reveals these changes.

She had been through enough to know that the hand of the Almighty had not made her bitter. Instead, He made her better (1:20). She now could see that He exchanged her emptiness for fullness (1:21). Furthermore, she now declared that His testimony did not oppose her, but rather, had opened her eyes (1:21). Now, having been through the harvest with Boaz and Ruth, Naomi now could say, "He did not afflict me, He affected me for good" (1:21).

When Ruth came home after gleaning with Boaz, (2:20) we see more of Naomi's spiritual progress. Naomi made it clear Jehovah was being kind to them. He was not trying to kill them. Naomi was changing from a woman of self-pity to a woman of praise.

Now, at the end of the third chapter, we see yet another change in her spiritual development. This change indicates having learned that it is better to wait for God to move, than it is to move things one's self. She and Elimelech had made this mistake. Naomi had been through enough at this point to know God was in control. She knew enough to counsel Ruth. *"It is better to wait on Boaz than to work things out for yourself."* As it should be with every believer, Naomi grew enough to put her confidence in Him, instead of complaining about Him.

Child of God, it is always better to wait on our Eternal Boaz to arrange our lives. Any attempt to arrange your life's order will only bring frustration. Today, look back at all He has done for you. Has He not brought you through enough just to trust Him today? Then listen to Naomi's advice that comes from experience. *"Sit still, my daughter, until thou know how the matter will fall:"*

Think about it . . .

Grace and new beginnings. . .

Ruth 3:18 *Then said she, Sit still, my daughter, until thou know how the matter will fall: for the man will not be in rest, until he have finished the thing this day.*

After Naomi and Ruth's arrival to Bethlehem, no less than eight times is Ruth called *"my daughter."* Five of those times the phrase was spoken by Naomi. Each time marked a moment of grace and indicated their new beginning. Those who have studied the patterns of numbers used in the Bible and their significance teach that "eight" is the number of new beginnings and "five" is the number of grace. Truly, Ruth and Naomi's story is marked with grace and new beginnings.

When Ruth left out of their house to find grace in the eyes of unknown harvest field-hand, she heard Naomi say, "Go my daughter." When Ruth returned with the good new of Boaz being that field owner who would not only let her glean once, but asked her to return to no other field but his, Naomi said, "It is good my daughter." The third moment Ruth heard this phrase of grace and new beginnings was when Naomi determined that she would seek rest for Ruth in the kinship of Boaz.

The fourth instance Naomi spoke this precious phrase came when she wondered as Ruth came into the house at dawn. Ruth entered with barley in her hand and Boaz in her heart. Naomi saw all this and questioned whether she arrived solely as "my daughter" or as Boaz's betrothed. The last recorded occasion when Naomi used this phrase is reserved for a moment of counsel in grace and new beginnings. She told Ruth to be still "my daughter" and let Boaz work things out. From these occasions the child of God learns that the fabric of new beginnings is always hemmed with the fringes of His grace.

There was something special about Ruth. Her testimony of virtue endeared her to the heart of Mahlon, Naomi, the townspeople, and Boaz. No other person in the Bible is labeled as *"my daughter"* more than Ruth. She had a virtue that displayed her true heart. She tended to draw out the best in people as they sought the best for her.

Though a small phrase, "my daughter" brings an opportunity for the child of God to realize that every new beginning in life is brought about by His grace. The slave owner John Newton certainly learned Ruth's lesson of grace and new beginnings. His poetic testimony in the song we know as **Amazing Grace** phrases Naomi's lesson for Ruth.

Amazing grace! (how sweet the sound)
That sav'd a wretch like me!
I once was lost, but now am found,
Was blind, but now I see.

'Twas grace that taught my heart to fear,
And grace my fears reliev'd;
How precious did that grace appear,
The hour I first believ'd!

Thro' many dangers, toils and snares,
I have already come;
'Tis grace has brought me safe thus far,
And grace will lead me home.

The Lord has promis'd good to me,
His word my hope secures;
He will my shield and portion be,
As long as life endures.

Yes, when this flesh and heart shall fail,
And mortal life shall cease;
I shall possess, within the veil,
A life of joy and peace.

The earth shall soon dissolve like snow,
The sun forbear to shine;
But God, who call'd me here below,
Will be forever mine.

John Newton

May the phrase "my daughter," bring you reminders of our Eternal Boaz's gift of grace and new beginnings.

Think about it . . .

Rest after redemption. . .

Ruth 3:18 *Then said she, Sit still, my daughter, until thou know how the matter will fall: for the man will not be in rest, until he have finished the thing this day.*

Naomi's words were sure and certain. There would be no way that Boaz could rest until the work of being a Redeemer was done. This was not a day for procrastination. This was not a moment when other things could get in the way of Boaz. He was a man on a mission and Naomi knew it.

How did Naomi know this? Was it the honorable way Boaz treated Ruth at the threshingfloor? Could it have been the barley he sent by way of Ruth? Could Ruth have said something unrecorded in Scripture that settled it in Naomi's mind that Boaz would not be able to rest until the matter was done? Perhaps something in Boaz's behavior reminded Naomi of Elimelech and she knew it would be handled without fail.

Boaz knew God's law. As kinsman-redeemer he would have to be near of kin, able and willing to redeem, and to complete the redemption process. Boaz could have decided to redeem the land of Elimelech without marrying the lady left in Elimelech's family. However, because he loved her, he became the complete kinsman-redeemer. There would be no rest in his heart until Ruth's redemption was done.

Boaz would have no other day in his life like this one. It would require all of his character and resources to make this offering of redemption. Because of love, he would not rest until it was done today.

It is certain Ruth's heart could hardly process it all. Because of Boaz, the widowed Moabite would be able to give a final gift to her deceased husband. This gift was the restored honor, and the hope for his family's name to continue. God's law made the kinsman-redeemer provision for His people. Although she was Moabite by birth, she was Israelite by faith. Ruth knew that the God of Israel was to be praised.

Naomi's confidence in Boaz was not misplaced. He would see to it that the redemption process would be handled that day. She knew that when the sun set that day, their redemption was secured.

One day, about 2000 years ago, when all hope for mankind was lost, Jesus Christ, our Eternal Boaz, went to the cross of Calvary and became our Kinsman-Redeemer. He was Kinsman because He was born of a virgin, He was Redeemer because He was the Son of God. As Redeemer only He could fulfill the law and satisfy God's demand for righteousness with His own righteousness. As Naomi said the earthly Boaz would take care of it in a day, so did our Eternal Boaz for when that day ended, He cried out in victory, "*It is finished.*" Only after the earthly and Eternal Boaz finished their work could they rest.

There would be no rest for Boaz until the work was done in Ruth's life. When the Son finished His work here, we see Him sitting at the throne of His Father. First came our redemption and then came His rest.

Think about it . . .

Sitting at the gate of hope. . .

Ruth 4:1 *Then went Boaz up to the gate, and sat him down there: and, behold, the kinsman of whom Boaz spake came by; unto whom he said, Ho, such a one! turn aside, sit down here. And he turned aside, and sat down.*

The morning that brought the dawn of hope for Ruth also brought a day of commitment for Boaz. Boaz rose early. It would be hard to believe he went back to sleep after Ruth left the threshingfloor. He dressed himself and began a short journey into the city to meet with a kinsman nearer than himself. The thoughts that went through his mind are unknown. However, having second thoughts or hesitancy were not among his thoughts as the text indicates that he went to the city and sat in the gate.

From the days of Moses and the giving of the law in Deuteronomy, God made provision for Boaz and Ruth's legal matters. Any decision with legal significance was held in the gate of a city. Here, the elders and city officers would convene and render just decisions for the people.

Boaz waited in this gate of hope for the redemption of the widow and ultimately for the redemption of the world. Boaz arrived at the city gate and sat down to wait. Boaz's time of waiting at the city's gate is unknown. Naomi's statement to Ruth that Boaz would handle it today, coupled with Boaz's decision to leave promptly for the gate of the city, helps us to know that he was willing and able to be the kinsman-redeemer for Ruth.

Any who have sat by hope's gate know how slowly time passes. Ruth was home sitting and waiting for news of redemption. Boaz was in the gate of the city waiting to offer himself as a redeemer. Naomi sat waiting for hope to fully dawn in her heart, as her husband's nearer relative would decide the fate of their land and the heritage of her husband's name. The world yet to come, including our own generation, waited for the answer that day as the redemption of all mankind sat just outside hope's gate.

Our Eternal Boaz sat in Heaven's gate, our gate of hope, waiting for the time of our redemption to come. Our hope arrived in the fullness of time as the Consolation of Israel was virgin born and presented in a temple in Jerusalem. Jesus' ascension to Heaven now places Him as sitting at the right hand of the Father, who is our Gate of Hope. While we await the final redemption of our bodies to be with Him. (Romans 8:23)

Let us not despair as we wait for the final redemption. Many men do not know of the redemption of the soul. They sit by a gate called hopelessness, without the knowledge of Jesus, our Kinsman-Redeemer. In the next 24 hours will you tell someone at the gate of hopelessness about Heaven, our Hope and our Goel?

Think about it . . .

Marked for redemption. . .

Ruth 4:1 *Then went Boaz up to the gate, and sat him down there: and, behold, the kinsman of whom Boaz spake came by; unto whom he said, Ho, such a one! turn aside, sit down here. And he turned aside, and sat down.*

Boaz swiftly went to the only place in the city of Bethlehem where he was sure to meet this nearer kinsman, at the gate. The gate in the Old Testament times was of great significance to its citizens. The gate of every city was a place of commerce, trade and legal decisions.

When one sought to buy or sell land they would come there. If a servant in Israel wanted to serve his master forever, he would come to the city's gate and tell the judges. (Exodus 21:6) In turn, the master would take the servant to the door of the city. He would use an awl and drive it through his ear to indicate this servant volunteered to serve his master's family forever.

On this day, he came to the city's gate like a servant in some respect. He came voluntarily and committed to serve the family of Elimelech forever. He came fully surrendered to whatever the day would bring in the matter of redeeming Elimelech's land and to marrying Ruth.

Boaz was no stranger in the gate of the city. This day Boaz would stand and confess his desire to redeem the darling of his harvest and heart. He would call upon another to do his part. One not called by name, only known as "such a one." "Such a one" had first claim to the land of Elimelech and to take Ruth, the Gentile gem as his wife. If he would not, Boaz would stand at the door of the heart of Ruth and ask for the awl to mark his heart as her's forever.

Similarly, our Eternal Boaz took a voluntary journey for our redemption. When the law, which had first right to us, could not redeem us after thousands of sacrifices, He stood and said, "I will redeem them." He took upon Himself our sin and substituted His righteousness as payment for the redemption of the world. The nail prints and piercing in His side reveal the mark of the awl as our Eternal Redeemer.

The redemption He provides is for all who will come by faith to Him. There is salvation in no other but Him. Any attempt to provide your own redemption will meet with failure and destruction. His offer of redemption stands today. Are you a "redeemed Ruth?" Rejoice today in the fact that our Eternal Boaz stood and redeemed us.

Think about it . . .

The meeting of the kinsmen. . .

*Then went Boaz up to the gate, and sat him down there: and, behold,
the kinsman of whom Boaz spake came by; unto whom he said, Ho,
such a one! turn aside, sit down here. And he turned aside, and sat
down.* Ruth 4:1

The matter of Ruth's redemption should not be discussed
without fully appreciating this moment. This simple meeting
in the gate of Bethlehem would affect generations to come.
Its effect will be seen in Jewish wedding ceremonies and
blessings. Reaching farther abroad, their meeting would
restore the line of the Messiah. This one simple conversation
would do more than redeem a woman, it would make way for
the redemption of the world.

Boaz's seat in the gate gives a wonderful picture of Old
Testament society. The gate of the city provided the venue for
all matters social, legal, and official. Boaz was not a stranger
in this place. Although he may have come here previously for
matters of the harvest he had never been here for matters of
the heart.

From Boaz's seat in the gate of the city he spotted the nearest
kinsman as he entered the city. He called out to him, "*Ho,
such a one! turn aside, sit down here.*" The nearest kinsman is
not specifically named in our text. This protected him and his
family from potential embarrassment from failing to provide
redemption for Ruth. The very invitation by Boaz brought
together the one who could be kinsman-redeemer with the
one who would be.

The nearest kinsman had every legal right to the land and
the ladies of Elimelech's family. The decision fully belonged
to the nearer kinsman's. There was no debate that it was his
choice to do so, but would he?

What the nearest kinsman decided is fully known. Yet, consider this powerful image in your mind. The nearest kinsman and a near kinsman sat together discussing the hope and heritage of the family of Elimelech. Their meeting is more than a reunion. It is a meeting of redemption. The nearer kinsman is a picture of the Law. Boaz is a picture of grace. Together they sit in the gate of the city.

The very image of Boaz and his relative sitting together casts a shadow to the cross. It was the day where the Law of Moses and the grace of God met together. They met just outside the gate of a city on a hill called Calvary. The outcome of their decisions affected the line of the Messiah and the redemption of the world.

The Holy Spirit saw to it that the picture of Boaz and the kinsman would have its New Testament explanation.

> *"For the law (Ruth's nearest kinsman) made nothing perfect, but the bringing in of a better hope did (Boaz); by the which we draw nigh unto God."* Hebrews 7:19

> *"For the law (Ruth's nearest kinsman) having a shadow of good things to come, (Boaz) and not the very image of the things, can never with those sacrifices which they offered year by year continually make the comers thereunto perfect."* Hebrews 10:1

Rejoice today in the gracious provision of redemption by The Eternal Boaz. His redemption is not limited to one family, Elimelech's, but for the whole world. Have you accepted his gracious redemption?

Think about it . . .

Witnesses to the redemption. . .

Ruth 4:2 *And he took ten men of the elders of the city, and said, Sit ye down here. And they sat down.*

With the nearer kinsman seated Boaz sought ten men of the city's elders to be witnesses to this moment of redemption. From the book of Genesis forward, God taught His people the use of witnesses to establish any matter. You will read in the Old Testament accounts about animals, rocks, altars, pillars, and people used as a witness.

A witness was sought to establish integrity, secure property, initiate the death penalty, or to prove an accusation. The law of God showed that any matter would be established between two or three witnesses. The calling of these ten witnesses certainly would play a future role in the worship and weddings of Israel. A synagogue will not function unless a quorum of ten is reached. Jewish weddings need ten witnesses.

Yet, there are occasions when more witnesses are called. On an occasion when Abraham wanted to prove he had dug a well to the King of Gerar, he gave seven lambs as a witness. A multitude of people in Joshua's day became witnesses to their commitment to the One True God, however, the impact of the twelve witnesses, ten elders and the two involved parties, would certainly make this a significant moment.

Ordinarily, there would be only a group of two or three witnesses for a matter of a kinsman-redeemer to buy land. Yet, Boaz chose five times the minimum requirement. The elders of the city must have wondered what was so important that ten witnesses were needed. This could not just be a matter of the harvest; this had to be a matter of the heart. Jewish writings indicate that Ruth's Moabite heritage was the reason Boaz sought for ten men. Securing these witnesses would make clear her conversion to Jehovah and the redemption by Boaz.

Boaz would waste no time. he had a promise to fill, and the love of his heart was waiting for an answer. He asked these ten elders of the city to sit beside him and the nearer kinsman. This gesture made every man an equal in stature and status. The men would listen eagerly as something was on Boaz's heart. Knowing the family relationship of these men, and the recent events in Boaz's field, it would be easy to think they were going to witness the redemption of Elimelech's land.

Yet, their witness of this redemption would not solely meet the minimum requirement of the law. Today these ten would witness a level of redemption that exceeded the law's limit. This moment of redemption would allow them to enter a realm of redemption characterized solely as one of grace.

The cross stands witness of our Eternal Boaz's redemption for the world. All who see it fully know well that not only did He meet the legal requirement of redemption, He exceeded it and offered redemption of love. His redemption reveals His grace to mankind. When He could have rejected man, He redeemed them. When He could have met the legal requirement and paid the penalty, He exceeded it. His redemption by grace made us joint heirs with Himself. All who believe know well that His redemption knows no limit; it will reach the lowest sinner. To what person will you be witness today of His offer of redemption?

Think about it . . .

Repentance and redemption. . .

Ruth 4:3 *And he said unto the kinsman, Naomi, that is come again out of the country of Moab, selleth a parcel of land, which was our brother Elimelech's*

Boaz begins; he selects his words wisely. He is not speaking to the witnesses; he is speaking to the nearer kinsman. He begins with the word, "Naomi." Naomi, this charming woman of Bethlehem was known as pleasant or delightsome. The nearer kinsman knew fully of whom he spoke.

He said to the kinsman, "*Naomi, that is come again out of the country of Moab...*" The small town of Bethlehem knew of Elimelech's departure to find provision in Moab. Although a decade ago, it would be hard to forget the day they watched them leave for Moab, home of the enemies to God's people. The family of Elimelech would suffer great loss in his decision. He would die; his sons married Moabite women and died. Heartache and disappointment would seize his family until news of bread from Bethlehem arrived.

Boaz spoke of Naomi's return, not of her husband's removal from Bethlehem. Naomi's return is what brought about the reward of redemption. Boaz made it clear, she had come home again. The word used in Scripture is precise. It was the turning away from something and facing a new direction. There would have been no redemption had there not been a turning from Moab. This kind of turning is called repentance.

Many today want the blessing of redemption without returning. You cannot live with one foot in Moab and the other in the heart of Boaz. The reward of returning is redemption. Remaining in a place like Moab was a reward; it is the reward of regret. It is interesting to ponder that the people who left in a famine to seek provision suffered more than those who remained in the famine. There is a greater blessing in remaining during a famine than if you depart. Many a church member should learn this lesson when life's famines arise. Stay with God in the place He last had you. You will suffer more seeking your own provision instead of waiting for His provision.

Naomi came back from her Moab. She lost everything and came home and found The Almighty still cared for her. How about you? Was there a time when you once walked closely with Him in the land of His provision? Did you leave in the midst of a famine? Why not return? Naomi would tell you plainly, "Moab will drain you of your delights." Why not come home and find His reward?

Think about it . . .

The declaration of redemption. . .

Ruth 4:3,4 *And he said unto the kinsman, Naomi, that is come again out of the country of Moab, selleth a parcel of land, which was our brother Elimelech's And I thought to advertise thee, saying, Buy it before the inhabitants, and before the elders of my people. If thou wilt redeem it, redeem it: but if thou wilt not redeem it, then tell me, that I may know: for there is none to redeem it beside thee; and I am after thee. And he said, I will redeem it.*

With the twelve men seated, Boaz spoke. These men gathered to give witness to what will transpire between Boaz and "Such a one." Boaz spoke carefully of real-estate and relationships. His announcement of the sale of property would give clear indication to the witnesses why they were there.

Boaz's words point out he had specific knowledge of Naomi's intentions. This knowledge came either from his midnight meeting with Ruth or in an unrecorded visit with Naomi; however, he gleaned the knowledge, he knew what he wanted to do. He was there to make known to the nearer kinsman that Elimelech's wife wanted to sell land and he, being the nearer kinsman, should buy it.

What burden must have been in Boaz's heart as he knew what he was doing but did not know the outcome. Boaz knew he desired the nearer kinsman to step out of the way. He wanted "such a one," to allow him to become the kinsman-redeemer to Elimelech's land and Mahlon's wife.

Boaz's announcement is much like what Paul wrote to the Roman believers. "For what the law could not do, in that it was weak through the flesh, God sending his own Son in the likeness of sinful flesh, and for sin, condemned sin in the flesh." (Romans 8:3) This very truth is what Boaz put on display for the witnesses. He stood and made his declaration of what must be done. In doing so he revealed what the nearer kinsman could not do. His announcement also brought to light his availability to be a kinsman-redeemer.

Jesus Christ did the same for mankind. The Law could not save man, "it was weak through the flesh." However, the Sender of the Law became the Saviour of Love. He stood in our place to become our Kinsman-Redeemer. His offer to be Kinsman-Redeemer is available even today. His extension of redemption is for all? Is He your Kinsman-Redeemer? Have you told someone today of His announcement for their redemption?

Think about it . . .

The decision of redemption. . .

Ruth 4:4 *And I thought to advertise thee, saying, Buy it before the inhabitants, and before the elders of my people. If thou wilt redeem it, redeem it: but if thou wilt not redeem it, then tell me, that I may know: for there is none to redeem it beside thee; and I am after thee. And he said, I will redeem it.*

Boaz made it understandable for the nearer kinsman. The nearer kinsman had to make a decision. Boaz wanted him to decide and make his declaration of redemption in the presence of these ten witnesses.

Boaz wanted the nearer kinsman to know that if he was not going to become kinsman-redeemer for Elimelech's family that he was willing to do so. He stated, *"If thou wilt redeem it, redeem it: but if thou wilt not redeem it, then tell me, that I may know: for there is none to redeem it beside thee; and I am after thee."*

You have to wonder as Boaz said the words what was going through his mind. Was it thoughts of panic or peace? Did he ponder upon the worst or the best? Ruth's heart and hope rested in him. Nothing else mattered now. He had made his statement and the decision of redemption was in the hands of the nearer kinsman.

The nearer kinsman, it seems enchanted by the possibility of obtaining good land, responded immediately. His statement came without delay, "I will redeem it."

Oh how the heart of Boaz could have fallen! That one statement seemed to change everything. In the will of God, the things that appear to be "negatives" are oftentimes His "positives" for us, just in disguise.

How do you handle the disappointments that come as you follow God's Word? Do you struggle with bad news and those who bear it? Take heart fellow servant. *"The steps of a good man are ordered by the LORD: and he delighteth in his way."* (Psalms 37:23) How delighted are you in His way?

Think about it . . .

The difficulty of redemption. . .

Then said Boaz, What day thou buyest the field of the hand of Naomi, thou must buy it also of Ruth the Moabitess, the wife of the dead, to raise up the name of the dead upon his inheritance. Ruth 4:5

The nearer kinsman made his decision known. He would redeem the land of Naomi; it was the right thing to do. Their kinsman's wife was widowed and the law opened the door for them to help her. Boaz spoke up quickly as the thought was just settling into the heart of the nearer kinsman that he could become the owner of Elimelech's land.

Boaz reminded him of the full responsibility of being kinsman-redeemer. The nearer kinsman's redemption could not be for just one part of the law, that is the redemption of the property. He had to redeem the converted widow from Moab.

Deuteronomy 25:5-6 gives the fullest explanation of Boaz's reminder to the nearer kinsman. "*If brethren dwell together, and one of them die, and have no child, the wife of the dead shall not marry without unto a stranger: her husband's brother shall go in unto her, and take her to him to wife, and perform the duty of an husband's brother unto her." And it shall be, that the firstborn which she beareth shall succeed in the name of his brother which is dead, that his name be not put out of Israel.*"

This provision is called the Levirate principle. God's law protected Ruth and in the fullest sense, the messianic line. Ruth's decision to follow Naomi and her God brought her back to Bethlehem. By returning, she came under the provision and protection of the Levirate law. Conversely, this meant that Orpah's decision to remain in Moab with her people and their gods excluded her from this protection.

Now, the nearer kinsman had to make his decision; it was difficult for him. It is clear he wanted the wealth of the land, but not the wife. The nearer kinsman thought solely on how he would benefit from this transaction. However, Boaz's thoughts were solely of how Ruth would benefit. Boaz's redemptive action was one of the law and of love. Boaz knew everything about her; yet, he loved her.

Ruth's redemption was not without difficulty. She was Moabite by birth. Yet, she was Israelite by faith. To marry a woman with a racial inequality but spiritual equality set the stage for a specific kinsman-redeemer. The difficulty in Ruth's redemption was in finding the right redeemer. The nearer kinsman was not the right one.

However, Boaz was the right redeemer. His mother was Rahab the harlot from Jericho and his father a prince named Salmon. He was qualified in his heritage and his heart to be the kinsman-redeemer for Ruth.

The nearer kinsman was called by Boaz to step in and redeem. He could not. So Boaz made himself available to be Ruth's kinsman-redeemer.

Jesus, our Eternal Boaz, did for us what the law could not fully do. The law could not forgive our sin, it could only cover it. The law, as Paul wrote, was our schoolmaster to bring us to Christ and His grace. Christ revealed the inability of the law to redeem and displayed his ability to redeem the world.

Christ's redemption is available still today. He offers it for all. Did you tell someone yesterday? Will you tell someone today? Have you expressed to Him today your gratefulness for His redemption? He chose you, loved you, redeemed you. What will you do for Him today.

Think about it . . .

Ruth, the object of his redemption. . .

Ruth 4:5 *Then said Boaz, What day thou buyest the field of the hand of Naomi, thou must buy it also of Ruth the Moabitess, the wife of the dead, to raise up the name of the dead upon his inheritance.*

Boaz made it known to the nearer kinsman the extent of this particular redemption. The childless marriage of Mahlon to Ruth, along with her adoption of the God of Israel, and return to Bethlehem made this redemption unique. This would not be a simple redemption of property but would involve someone willing to take a Moabite wife.

Yes, Naomi owned the land, but the land by inheritance would be Ruth's. There could be no ordinary redeemer for this multiple redemption. There must be someone who was qualified and willing to step in and forsake all self interest and become kinsman-redeemer. Boaz was that man. He shared with the nearer kinsman the redemption was more than just land, there was a special lady who needed redemption too.

Boaz knew that this would filter any "typical" redemption. Ruth could not be ignored in the redemption. The kinsman-redeemer in this case would have to see Ruth as the object of his redemption. He would have to overcome her nature as a Moabite and give her a new name. A kinsman-redeemer would have to see Ruth as the reward in this redemption.

Ruth had none to carry on the family name of her husband. God's law stated that no Israelite family name should be extinguished. This made a way for families to keep their inheritance within a family. Deuteronomy 25:6 establishes this principle. *"And it shall be, that the firstborn which she beareth shall succeed in the name of his brother which is dead, that his name be not put out of Israel."*

The child of God can fully identify with Ruth's status as we consider our own pitiful state. Our birth and background was marred. We had nothing to offer our Eternal Boaz; however, because of His love for us, we became the object of His redemption. He has given us rewards abundant since then, all by His grace. Because of Calvary we know how Ruth must have felt all of her days after this offer of redemption.

Think about it . . .

Memories of Moab. . .

Ruth 4:5 *Then said Boaz, What day thou buyest the field of the hand of Naomi, thou must buy it also of Ruth the Moabitess, the wife of the dead, to raise up the name of the dead upon his inheritance.*

Boaz spoke with precision as he shared with the nearer kinsman full extent of the type of redemption that was needed. His words certainly carried the weight of the complications surrounding the redemption of Ruth. He spoke of her birthplace, bitter experiences, and background. The nearer kinsman knew this redemption would be complex; however, Boaz knew it was his calling.

Naomi, whose name means "delightsome" and Ruth whose name means "friend" make a wonderful pair in this book where the sin of man meets the grace of God. Yet, you cannot miss the distinct mentioning of Moab in light of the redemptive work in this text.

Now as Boaz stands in the place of their redemption the mentioning of Moab to Naomi and Ruth would speak volumes to their hearts. At one point in Ruth's life Moab meant home. It was the place she met her husband and married. Moab was also the place where she buried her husband. Naomi saw Moab as the place that memorialized the mistake that took her husband, heritage and heart. Naomi saw it as a place of draining of her delight and the filling of her heart with discouragement.

Naomi and Ruth carried a heavy weight as Moab held the tombs of their husbands. Though they buried their men in Moab, burying their memories was more difficult. There is no doubt the memories of Moab were painful and ever present.

Redemption has a way of taking the memories of a painful past and making them into a pleasant present. If you are a child of God you have a Moab time in your past. Your redemption means Moab should remain in the past and the pending marriage supper of the Lamb should become your focus.

A believer gets into trouble when they spend more time affected by their past then they do their future. What about you?

Think about it . . .

Nearer, but not able. . .

Ruth 4:6 *And the kinsman said, cannot redeem it for myself, lest I mar mine own inheritance: redeem thou my right to thyself; for I cannot redeem it.*

The nearer kinsman was now in a difficult situation. Just a moment ago before the elders of the city, he agreed to redeem the property. Now when the full conditions of the redemption were learned he realized that he could not do it.

He spoke in the hearing of all the elders. "I cannot redeem it for myself, lest I mar mine own inheritance: redeem thou my right to thyself; for I cannot redeem it." The nearer kinsman's words confessed his inability and inadequacy to redeem.

The very confession brought the desired conclusion for Boaz and his bride to be. When the nearer kinsman announced he could not be the kinsman-redeemer that meant he passed the responsibility of redemption to Boaz. He stated he had a right to redemption; he was just not the right redeemer. So, he relinquished his right to Boaz.

The hindrance to Ruth's redemption by the nearer and legal kinsman came because of self-interest. His inheritance meant there were those to whom he already was responsible, his own family. He could own more property, but he could do nothing with the precious gem from Moab.

The nearer kinsman did what was right. He passed the right and responsibility of redemption to Boaz. This critical decision brought into our view God's plan for the redemption of man. The line of succession for the Messiah came through Boaz and Ruth.

The Messiah's birth was necessary for the redemption of the world. The law was a nearer kinsman to mankind; however, the law could not save mankind. Christ's death on the cross brought before the witnesses of the world his offer of redemption. Mankind does not have to sit and figure out a way to redeem himself, nor does he have to keep the points of the law to secure his redemption. Christ's death on the cross made the redemption of the world possible.

The surrender of the nearer kinsman meant Boaz could now provide Ruth's redemption. Ruth's life was about to change once again. The days of wondering how to survive would now be exchanged for a lifetime of joy.

For Naomi, Moab's miseries would just become a distant memory of past mistakes. For Ruth, Moab would be a reminder of what she was before Boaz's redemption. Boaz would see Moab as a staging ground for God's will for his life. Boaz's redemption changed Ruth forever. Although her nearer kinsman could not redeem her; Boaz agreed to do so.

The believer should realize our Moab is the life of sin we were in before our Eternal Boaz's redemption. Our decision to forsake Moab and it painful memories have rewarded by His gracious redemption. What the law would not do, Christ did for us.

Think about it . . .

The shoe of redemption. . .

Ruth 4:7-8 *Now this was the manner in former time in Israel concerning redeeming and concerning changing, for to confirm all things; a man plucked off his shoe, and gave it to his neighbour: and this was a testimony in Israel. Therefore the kinsman said unto Boaz, Buy it for thee. So he drew off his shoe.*

The Bible is God's very words. It has no better commentary than itself. God saw fit to explain what would be familiar in its context but for generations to come might not be easily recognized. Its imagery is powerful in a world that knows only court documents, attorneys, and law suits.

When a transaction occurred for the sale of property or when men bartered in order to make the deal final, the one whose property transferred ownership would pull off his shoe and give it to the new owner. It was the "signing of the paperwork" in today's vernacular.

There would be no mistaking the essence of the scene if you were standing in the marketplace watching a man pull off his shoe. The journey home for the new owner is worthy of mention. What good is a walk with one shoe? It depends on who is looking at it. To the releasing owner it meant he would never forget it as he journeyed home with one shoe removed. The remaining shoe was a shoe of reminder.

To the redeeming owner it would never be forgotten as he carried home a shoe of redemption. It was not one he would wear. It was a shoe to carry to portray that what he received he once did not have. Scripture does not tell us what an owner did with the third shoe when he arrived home. It could have been displayed or merely stored. Either way it was a testimony of redemption.

The law mentions a situation where a childless widow could go to her deceased husband's brother. If he refused to marry her, the widow could go to the elders in the city's gate. She could remove his shoe, the shoe of rejection, and spit in his face. She would also call him a name of humiliation. From that day forward the man's name would be called, "The house of him that hath his shoe removed."

What others might call just an old shoe was not how Ruth would look at that shoe. The shoe would always be displayed on the mantle of her heart. Seeing it would bring joy and relief. She would be reminded of the day of her redemption. It was a day that marked the redemption of her heart and hope.

Like the three views of the shoe, the child of The Eternal Boaz has a symbol or testimony of their redemption. It is the cross of Calvary. Some may look at the cross and see it as a testimony of rejection. Others may see the cross as a testimony of remembrance. Yet, to the child of God who has stood at the empty cross sees it as a testimony of redemption, their own. May you be mindful of its significance and salvation that came from the cross of Calvary.

Think about it . . .

The dawn of Ruth's redemption. . .

Ruth 4:8 *Therefore the kinsman said unto Boaz, Buy it for thee. So he drew off his shoe.*

Boaz and Ruth waited for these words since midnight. Although in his heart Boaz was resigned to whatever the day would bring forth, he knew full well he desired to redeem Ruth's inheritance and marry her.

At this same moment, two women sat at home pondering when the news would arrive and what would it be? Boaz would be able to tell them what had transpired that day by his words; however, few words would have to be spoken to Ruth. She looked for one thing; does he have shoe? "Naomi, is he carrying a shoe, the shoe of my redemption?"

The shoe she looked for meant little to anyone else but her. The arrival of Boaz and the shoe he might carry would mark the dawn of her redemption. She would treasure this day always.

Ruth's waiting would be over shortly. Naomi would wonder no more. Boaz was as good as on his way to the house to proclaim that the work was done and redemption's price was paid. He would arrive to what was now his home and declare his status as her Goel.

When the dawn of redemption breaks across the horizon of the heart it brings with it a new day and a brand new ending.

Many people spend this life trying to go back and make a new start. Those who have been redeemed would declare it is better to make a new end. Redemption has a way of silencing the past and making that brand new end.

Calvary marks the place of redemption and points to the One who paid redemption's price. Similarly, our Eternal Boaz, when the work was done on the cross and our sin debt paid, gathered the keys of death, hell and the grave. He took them, the symbolic show and went to his father's house and declared that redemption's work was done.

Many in this world have yet to hear of the redemptive work of Calvary. Why not take the shoe of your redemption and proclaim salvation to a lost and dying world?

Think about it . . .

The selflessness of redemption. . .

Ruth 4:8 *Therefore the kinsman said unto Boaz, Buy it for thee. So he drew off his shoe.*

The man, who spoke so quickly, now speaks solemnly. "Buy it for thee." Surely the embarrassment of his greed swelled him. Yes, he wanted the land, but he did not want the lady from Moab. Boaz cared little for the land, he desired the lady. The simple truth of it exists that when we care for things to the neglect of people, we are greedy.

The honesty in this moment must not be overlooked. The man would not redeem Ruth because it would affect his plans and purpose. He valued his needs above her needs. He cared more for his desires than hers. He esteemed his goals as more important than her needs for a Goel.

A real Goel does not place himself above another. He makes himself a servant. He cares little for his own wealth and wants. He sees the value of the other as greater than the investment required.

The spiritual relevance of the nearer kinsman is explained well by Paul, "For what the law could not do, in that it was weak through the flesh, God sending his own Son in the likeness of sinful flesh, and for sin, condemned sin in the flesh" Romans 8:3. The nearer kinsman was weak, however, God sent Boaz who was able and willing to redeem Ruth.

Paul later wrote of Jesus, the Eternal Boaz, "But made himself of no reputation, and took upon him the form of a servant, and was made in the likeness of men." Philippians 2:7 Redemption requires a selfless redeemer. Jesus is that selfless Redeemer. The writer of Hebrews said ". . .*who for the joy that was set before him endured the cross, despising the shame, and is set down at the right hand of the throne of God.*" Hebrews 12:2.

If you are one who is relying on fulfilling the law or doing good deeds, beware you are relying on what is weak. It cannot and will not redeem you. Redemption is only available through what Christ did on the cross. What are you trusting for your redemption; His work or yours?

Think about it . . .

Ye are witnesses. . .

Ruth 4:9 *And Boaz said unto the elders, and unto all the people, Ye are witnesses this day, that I have bought all that was Elimelech's, and all that was Chilion's and Mahlon's, of the hand of Naomi.*

A crowd had gathered now around these twelve men. Boaz personally gathered eleven of them for this moment of redemption; however, it was not every day a resident of Bethlehem sought to redeem a Moabite woman. Certainly, there were hushed whispers in the gate of the city.

Many in the city knew about Ruth. The town buzzed with excitement when Naomi returned with this Moabite girl. They wondered why she came home with Ruth and without her Elimelech and two boys. The word quickly spread throughout the town. They watched Ruth with amazement how her heart was drawn to her mother-in-law. They saw how selflessly she served to provide. They learned by observation of her conversation and conduct. Now they gathered to see what would be the future of this Moabite by birth and Israelite by faith.

Boaz spoke to those invited and all who showed interest. "Ye are witnesses this day." Yes, they were the legal witnesses who would bear record of this event. They were there to answer anyone's question as to how Boaz married Ruth. Just as the town learned quickly of their return, they will shortly learn of their redemption.

This event was certain to be remembered. Some would speak of it in days to come because they were bound legally to do so when dispute would arise. If someone ever doubted Ruth's redemption, the proper witnesses could be consulted and the truth would be learned. If accusation were made as to her right in Israel, the many townspeople present could quickly bear witness of her redemption. If anyone asked Boaz or "Such a One" they too would tell the story of how Boaz set aside all that he had and was to redeem this one. Yes, any of these three groups could bear record of her redemption.

The child of God is blessed with witnesses that bear record of their redemption. If we were to question the validity of our redemption we have three witnesses who were there. John wrote in his first epistle of these three witnesses. *"For there are three that bear record in Heaven, the Father, the Word, and the Holy Ghost: and these three are one."* 1 John 5:7

The Father bears record because He made your invitation for redemption possible. The Word stands as the record of the truth of our redemption. The Holy Ghost stands as witness to our redemption for He was at work in our lives bringing us to Him down the path of conviction and showing us our need of redemption. Our redemption may be question, but it can never be doubted. We have three perfect Witnesses in Heaven of our redemption; however, if someone were to doubt, remember, *"If we receive the witness of men, the witness of God is greater: for this is the witness of God which he hath testified of his Son."* 1 John 5:9

If you are among the redeemed, Heaven has recorded it in the witness of the Father, Son, and Holy Ghost. Your redemption is settled. Do not spend another moment fretting over what He has done for you. It is time you build a bridge over your doubts and get over it.

Think about it . . .

I have. . .

Ruth 4:9 *And Boaz said unto the elders, and unto all the people, Ye are witnesses this day, that I have bought all that was Elimelech's, and all that was Chilion's and Mahlon's, of the hand of Naomi.*

Boaz informed the invited and the interested witnesses the extent of this redemption. Although "Such a One" could offer a partial redemption; Boaz came with full redemption. God's law would be met in Boaz. No other could offer redemption.

His offer of redemption made clear his position and power. *". . .I have bought all that was Elimelech's, and all that was Chilion's and Mahlon's, of the hand of Naomi."* The land was Elimelech's. His death transferred the land by way of inheritance to Mahlon and Chilion. When the boys died, the land transferred to the Naomi. However, with Ruth being the wife of Mahlon she would receive the land from Naomi upon her death. Yet, one more problem remained. Elimelech's family name would be extinguished from the earth; this is a clear violation of God's law. (Deuteronomy 25:6)

The potential extinguishing of Elimelech's family meant The Messiah's birth line hung in the human balance. Boaz's decision to redeem the land and the lady meant that Elimelech's family name would continue. Boaz's redemption of *"all that was Elimelech's"* meant the birth line of the Eternal Boaz was now secure. Like Boaz offered full redemption for the land and the lady, Christ offered full *"redemption through his blood, even the forgiveness of sin."*(Colossians 1:14)

Satan's attempt to bruise the heel of the Messiah was thwarted once again. The decision of Boaz to redeem signaled to Satan his plan to extinguish the line of the Messiah failed. Make no mistake, it was Satan who tempted Elimelech to move to Moab. Yet with man's failure God had a plan of redemption both with the earthly Boaz and The Eternal Boaz.

Just as Boaz took care of what was needed in this redemption. Jesus took care of mankind's redemption with his death, burial, and resurrection over 2000 years ago. The educated elite might say his redemption is not for all. However, rest assured, His redemption is for whosoever shall call on His name for redemption. Are you amongst the redeemed?

Think about it . . .

Moreover redemption . . .

Ruth 4:10 *Moreover Ruth the Moabitess, the wife of Mahlon, have I purchased to be my wife, to raise up the name of the dead upon his inheritance, that the name of the dead be not cut off from among his brethren, and from the gate of his place: ye are witnesses this day.*

In the previous verse Boaz said, *". . .I have bought all that was Elimelech's, and all that was Chilion's and Mahlon's, of the hand of Naomi."* That could have been sufficient but he did not stop there. He clarifies and completes the redemption with the word, "moreover."

The idea of this special word, used only once in this book, indicated he had more to say about his offer of redemption. Boaz desired to redeem and restore the line of the family of Elimelech. Unlike "Such a One," Boaz was more interested in Ruth than he was the real estate of Elimelech. Boaz's redemption met the minimum requirements and then exceeded them with his "moreover" redemption.

His "moreover" redemption took what might have been an ordinary redemption and made it extraordinary. His "moreover" redemption included her heritage, hurts, and heart. She would no longer live with the problem of her heritage; she would not carry the burden of grief and guilt in regard to her hurts. She would not have to face the emptiness in her heart of poverty and pity.

Boaz took all that Ruth was and redeemed her. She no longer needed to fret about tomorrow; it was covered in the redemption. She would not have to consider the trouble of being a Moabite; it was covered in the redemption. She did not have to concern herself with having nothing to offer him; it was covered in his gracious redemption.

Every citizen of earth must come to know that The Eternal Boaz offered his "moreover" redemption outside the gate of Jerusalem. Christ's righteous death on the cross not only met the requirement of the law; it provided "moreover" redemption for a lost world. The New Testament details this "moreover redemption" in Colossians 1:13-14. *"Who hath delivered us from the power of darkness, and hath translated us into the kingdom of his dear Son: In whom we have redemption through his blood, even the forgiveness of sins:"*

The "moreover" grace of The Eternal Boaz covers anything that could stand in the way of the world's redemption. The world needs the message of redemption in this very hour. It is necessary that every tribe and tongue hear of his redemption. Redemption cannot come through this world's religions, philosophies, and governments. It is only through the work of the Eternal Boaz they can find the redemption from their heritage, hurts, and heart.

While Ruth never was a witness to her own redemption, she was at the house awaiting word that the work of Boaz was done. Yet, when the news reached her she realized there was no need to live without his redemption, adoption, and invitation to be his bride.

Many today are searching and waiting for such a message. A messenger must be dispatched at once to tell them of The Eternal Boaz's redemption, adoption, and invitation.

Will you be a messenger of His redemption today?

Think about it . . .

The Moabitess . . .

Ruth 4:10 *Moreover Ruth the Moabitess, the wife of Mahlon, have I purchased to be my wife, to raise up the name of the dead upon his inheritance, that the name of the dead be not cut off from among his brethren, and from the gate of his place: ye are witnesses this day.*

Five times in this book have we have heard the phrase "Ruth the Moabitess." It seems that no matter how pleasant her present they attached her past to it in this manner, "Ruth – the Moabitess." However, today this will change for her. From today she will be called the bride of Boaz. Although her heritage was formerly Moabite, because of her faith's confession and heart's commitment the present will now override the past.

Ruth's socially imposed title give us insight to the times in which she lived. She was a visitor to Bethlehem. The inhabitants of the city knew she was an outsider. The tendency amongst such a close knit group was to use a title that would distinguish her from another. The only problem with this is that Ruth was seeking to identify more with her beliefs, not her background.

Boaz's wedding announcement would give Ruth a position and title that would override her past. A review of the text chronologically shows the usage of "the Moabitess" title. It was used in moments of introduction (1:22), identification (2:2), instruction (2:21) and inspection (4:5). However, the last use of this title that anchored her to the past is used in a wedding invitation – her own.

His announcement of grace will erase and evict the reminder of Ruth's racial identification. It introduced a title of a romantic identification. In Boaz's announcement and invitation the Moabite one becomes the married one; a widow becomes a wife, and the poor one becomes the purchased one.

For the child of God this section of Scripture brings a peaceful moment of reflection. We, who were once outcasts and alienated from God, had a title that anchored us to our past – sinner. However, because of the invitation signed with His blood to be part of his bride we now have a new title – sinner saved by grace.

Look closely at something else in this moment of reflection and see the titles we as believers use with people who come into our fellowship. We identify them more with their past and not their position in Christ. This social sin of labeling God's people by their race, past relationships, and positions is wrong. Even at times more subtly we excluded on the basis of birthplace, background, or bank accounts. We strive to open our hearts to sinners, but to the saved we are clannish. The announcement of Boaz's purchase changed Ruth's designation by others. Shouldn't the announcement of The Eternal Boaz's purchase change our designation of others? If the purchase of our redemption changed God's view of man, shouldn't yours change too?

Think about it ...

The wife of Mahlon. . .

Ruth 4:10 *Moreover Ruth the Moabitess, the wife of Mahlon, have I purchased to be my wife, to raise up the name of the dead upon his inheritance, that the name of the dead be not cut off from among his brethren, and from the gate of his place: ye are witnesses this day.*

Our only clue in the whole book to whom Ruth was married occurs in this verse. Much had happened since she gave her heart to Mahlon. They married just after the death of Elimelech. They had ten years together before his death.

She was once his wife, now she was his widow. She once treasured moments with him, now she can only treasure his memories. The day they buried her Mahlon, they buried her heart. Ruth's hope for children and her husband's name to continue was lost as both brothers perished at that time.

Today, the widow of Mahlon becomes the wife of Boaz. This announcement demonstrated the devotion of Boaz to Ruth and his duty to God. While Ruth waited for the arrival and announcement of Boaz; Boaz was preparing a place in his home and heart for her. His address in the city gate made clear his intentions and invitation. Ruth would be his wife.

Her heritage, husband, and heartaches which devalued her worth to others made her more precious to Boaz. His love for her when she could provide him nothing was a true demonstration of grace. He did not see her as she was, he saw her in what she could become.

Our Eternal Boaz did the same for mankind. He announced his intention and declared his invitation with His death, burial, and resurrection. He instructed His disciples He was preparing a place for them in His Father's house. To those who are children of God by faith, He is our Bridegroom and we are His bride. He desired us though unlovely and worthless. Because of His grace He looked beyond our fault and saw our need.

Is there someone in the harvest field where you work that needs to know of the unconditional love of The Eternal Boaz? Do you know someone defeated by their past? Do you know someone overwhelmed with guilt and despair? Today, take them to the empty cross and empty tomb. Tell them of our Eternal Boaz who will prepare for them a place in Heaven when they accept his price of redemption for them.

Think about it ...

The riches of redemption. . .

Ruth 4:10 *Moreover Ruth the Moabitess, the wife of Mahlon, have I purchased to be my wife,*

Boaz carefully shared with all who listened, Ruth's benefits in his redemption. Boaz wanted them to know he knew what he was doing. He desired for them to know that his redemption came with benefits. Although he was aware of all these things, he wanted them to know.

He announced his knowledge and acceptance of Ruth's race and past relationships. These were not a hindrance to him. His mind was made up. He would be her Goel. It did not matter what might devalue her to another redeemer; he had her potential in mind, not her past. While "Such a one" desired the land for his harvest, Boaz desired the lady for his heart.

The motive in Boaz's heart becomes quite clear as he continued to speak. Boaz sought the very best for his kinsman Elimelech. Since Elimelech died, his sons were the rightful heirs. The death of Elimelech's sons changed the placement of the inheritance. Naomi was rightful owner of the land.
Yet, there was no way for her to carry on the family's name. This problem clung to Naomi's heart from the time she departed Moab.

On Naomi's return to Bethlehem she mentioned to Orpah and Ruth that she had no other sons for them to marry to continue the family name so it was not extinguished. She declared to them in Ruth 1:12-13. *"Turn again, my daughters, go your way; for I am too old to have an husband. If I should say, I have hope, if I should have an husband also to night, and should also bear sons; Would ye tarry for them till they were grown?..."* The continuance of her husband's name and the certainty of her future in the land of Israel were the cause of her concern; however, in Boaz's all her concerns were met.

Boaz sought to redeem all that was part of the household of Elimelech. The marriage to Ruth distinguished him as one who sought to be obedient to the laws of God. The marriage also displayed his character as one who valued commitment to family both immediate and extended.

Boaz wanted nothing less than to continue the family line of Elimelech. He stated his intention was *"to raise up the name of the dead upon his inheritance, that the name of the dead be not cut off from among his brethren, and from the gate of his place."* Boaz had Ruth's best interest in mind as he pursued Ruth's redemption.

Ruth benefited from Boaz's redemption. He offered her his heart when no other would. He offered her a home when none else could. He offered her a heritage when it seemed impossible. Yet, best of all, he presented her with a happily ever after she could find in none else than Boaz. What Mahlon, her husband, and "Such a one," her nearest kinsman, could not provide she found in Boaz.

Similarly, The Eternal Boaz offers to mankind the riches of His redemption. His redemption offers mankind His heart, a heritage, and a hereafter. The New Testament declares to you that His redemption comes exclusively through His blood. It provides the forgiveness of your past, fullness of His promises, and forever in His presence.

Yes, His redemption has riches. Paul reminded us of what God said to Isaiah. ". . .*Eye hath not seen, nor ear heard, neither have entered into the heart of man, the things which God hath prepared for them that love him.*" (1 Corinthians 2:9) The riches of His redemption are more than what we could imagine. Why not pause this day and reflect and relish in the riches of your redemption. Then, in your conversations with God throughout the day, praise him for the riches of your redemption.

Think about it ...

Witnesses this day. . .

Ruth 4:10-11a *Moreover Ruth the Moabitess, the wife of Mahlon, have I purchased to be my wife, to raise up the name of the dead upon his inheritance, that the name of the dead be not cut off from among his brethren, and from the gate of his place: ye are witnesses this day. And all the people that were in the gate, and the elders, said, We are witnesses*

Boaz invited ten witnesses to the gate to listen to his announcement of redemption. Yet, more came as word quickly spread through this quiet village amongst those that passed through the gate. This crowd gathered to listen.

What they heard was an unprecedented announcement. They had not witnessed, nor would their generation see again the redemption of a Moabite. The next time Scripture will record a similar redemption will be with our Eternal Boaz.

Boaz made it clear. Ruth was to be his wife and they would have a son. He would honor his relative Elimelech and his sons, Mahlon and Chilion and redeem all that belonged to them.

However, Boaz chose to end his announcement with five words that held them accountable to what they had heard and seen of the day of Ruth's redemption. Boaz knew a day might come to their quiet hillside village where one might question his marriage to a Moabite. This gathering and all who would hear of what happened in the life of Ruth would know that Boaz chose to redeem all that was Elimelech's.

He did not select or elect the preferable elements of Elimelech's house to redeem. He chose to redeem all that belonged to Elimelech. This included Elimelech's indebtedness, the individuals and the inheritance connected to it.

Boaz made sure the invited and interested witnesses knew they had a responsibility in redemption. They were to bear witness of this event. They were to tell those with questions about Boaz's redemption that they knew what happened, because they had been commissioned as witnesses by Boaz.

The elders who were invited and the crowd that was interested made a commitment to Boaz and vicariously to Ruth. They committed that they would be witnesses of the position, pledge, and purchase of Boaz.

Your redemption enlists you to be a witness of His redemption in the same areas. Our Eternal Boaz was in the position to provide our Redemption. In the garden of Eden He made a pledge to be that Redeemer. On Calvary's cross he made the purchase to offer Redemption through His blood. Soon after, outside the gate of Jerusalem on a mountain called Olivet, our Eternal Boaz commissioned 11 men, representatives of His church, to be witnesses of His redemption. Have you turned your world upside down with the message of His redemption?

Think about it ...

Sharing joy. . .

Ruth 4:11 *And all the people that were in the gate, and the elders, said, We are witnesses. The LORD make the woman that is come into thine house like Rachel and like Leah, which two did build the house of Israel: and do thou worthily in Ephratah, and be famous in Bethlehem:*

The elders and the others in the gate replied to Boaz in accepting their responsibility in unison. It is interesting to consider that only the ten had to be in agreement, yet all of them said they would be witnesses.

This response indicates that the citizens from Bethlehem were delighted and thrilled at what had taken place. God had opened a place in their heart for Ruth.

God's opening of their heart took place over time. Ruth's accompanying Naomi home from Moab along with their arrival in Bethlehem gave an opportunity for the townspeople to be hospitable. Ruth's attitude and activities indicated to the people though her conception made her Moabite, her conversion made her Israelite.

In Chapter Two of Ruth, we learned that Boaz had the information presented to him about Ruth's demeanor, duty, and devotion with Naomi. This information certainly came from the residents of Bethlehem. Their interest in Ruth is confirmed by their gathering in the city gate and by their getting involved in the witnessing of such a gracious redemption.

They did not stop with just the promise of involvement as witnesses of this transaction. They added to their promise a pronouncement of a blessing on the union between Boaz and Ruth. This blessing whether spoken in unison, or by different individuals in the crowd, indicated their desire for Boaz and Ruth to be fruitful.

Not a selfish word was recorded in Scripture by any in the crowd. No words of envy were spoken. Gathered there that day were a people with a genuine joy for Ruth's redemption and the wedding that would take place. Ruth's tomorrows would never be the same; they rejoiced in God's goodness shown through Boaz to Ruth.

There are people today in our churches who are delighted when God is blessing them; however, when God blesses another in an extraordinary way they can't be happy. This is not the way it was in Bethlehem. Yet, is it that way in your church?

When others around you are experiencing the goodness of God, what is your response? Are you able to share in the enjoyment of others? Do you enjoy their blessing only as long as they do not fare better than yourself?

Think about it ...

A blessing to remember. . .

Ruth 4:11-12 *And all the people that were in the gate, and the elders, said, We are witnesses. The LORD make the woman that is come into thine house like Rachel and like Leah, which two did build the house of Israel: and do thou worthily in Ephratah, and be famous in Bethlehem: And let thy house be like the house of Pharez, whom Tamar bare unto Judah, of the seed which the LORD shall give thee of this young woman.*

The crowd responded to the wedding announcement with a most unusual benediction. This is not the first blessing in the book. There have been seven benedictions before this one. (1:8-9; 2:4, 12, 20; 3:10) Three of them originated from Naomi. The other three came from Boaz. The other benediction was spoken by Boaz's workers. This eighth benediction is unique. This blessing is from the townspeople upon Boaz and Ruth.

The manner in which the benediction came is not expounded in Scripture. It seems unlikely that they all had a memorized script from which they quoted. It seems more spontaneous as if one said something and then another chimed in with their blessing.

Perhaps someone in the crowd spoke up and said, "*The LORD make the woman that is come into thine house like Rachel and like Leah.*" Perhaps another said, "*which two did build the house of Israel.*" Yet another of the gathered witnesses may have cried out, "*and do thou worthily in Ephratah*" and another, "*and be famous in Bethlehem."* For just a moment there is silence. Then someone called out, *"And let thy house be like the house of Pharez, whom Tamar bare unto Judah, of the seed which the LORD shall give thee of this young woman."*

Scripture is silent in the manner by which the benediction came; however, the message they spoke is not silent. This was a blessing to remember. It brought to remembrance God's goodness on the children of Israel in blessing them by fulfilling His promise to Abraham.

Their blessing placed honor upon the two women whose maternal efforts gave Jacob the sons who became the tribes in Israel. The townspeople's blessing remembered another woman, Tamar, Judah's wife. They knew to which tribe Boaz belonged; he was of the tribe of Judah. Without Pharez, Tamar's son, there would be no Boaz.

While it was a blessing that remembered their heritage, it also expressed their honor for Boaz and Ruth. They wished the fruitfulness that came to the house of Israel because of the Rachel, Leah, and Tamar be repeated. They desired that God, in the same manner, would honor this union and bless them with children.

The blessing from the residents of Bethlehem gives believers a wonderful example of encouragement. When Boaz and Ruth chose to do what was right, the townspeople responded with words of support. This couple chose to honor God's Word and they were met with encouragement.

Do you know someone who is trying to obey and honor God's Word in his life? Why not seek him out and offer a blessing of encouragement in his life. It may be in marriage or possibly ministry where he is making his stand. His commitment to God to do right makes him stand out.

Why not stand with and support him with encouragement? Why not give him a blessing to remember?

Think about it ...

A woman of His making. . .

Ruth 4:11-12 *And all the people that were in the gate, and the elders, said, We are witnesses. The LORD make the woman that is come into thine house like Rachel and like Leah, which two did build the house of Israel: and do thou worthily in Ephratah, and be famous in Bethlehem: And let thy house be like the house of Pharez, whom Tamar bare unto Judah, of the seed which the LORD shall give thee of this young woman.*

The people gathered in the gate of the city, knew very well that this was a special day. Their presence at the gate and their pledge to give witness both point the importance of this day. Their prayer for God's blessing on the couple is worthy of close examination. The townspeople's prayer was simple. They prayed for fruitfulness, favor, and fame for Boaz and Ruth.

In their prayer three women are mentioned. Their mentioning is not by happenstance; each of them shared a significant role in this moment. The people wanted God to do for Boaz and Ruth like He did for the house of Israel through these women. They knew if it weren't for the hand of God making these women fruitful, the twelve tribes of Israel would not be as they knew them. Each Israelite, standing in the gate of Bethlehem, knew the importance of each woman's role in their very own existence.

Their understanding of Israel's history and their own family's heritage made a special place in their hearts for Rachel, Leah and Tamar. Each woman had a unique story known to the dwellers in Bethlehem. They remembered Rachel for her barren womb that was blessed. Leah, Rachel's sister, was remembered for the rejected heart that was rewarded. Tamar, the wife of Leah's grandson, was mentioned as the forgotten wife remembered. In the days ahead we will look at each story of these women. For now let the focus remain on God's making of these women.

The people cried out, *"the Lord make the woman. . .."* They wanted Ruth to be a woman of His making. They knew God made these three women, not solely in the matter of creation, but He made them unique for His purpose and His praise. Were these women perfect? Certainly not! However, they were women whose hearts were toward the Lord God of Israel and he blessed them. The townspeople knew Ruth had a heart that was toward God and therefore knew Ruth could be a woman made by God for His purposes and praise.

What about you? Are you a person of your making or His? Have you allowed God to make you into what He desires? He can take your heart, man or woman, and uniquely make you suitable for His purposes and praise. Have you placed yourself before the Almighty God for His making? The people's cry for Ruth should be the cry of our own heart, "Lord make me whatever you would have me be."

Think about it ...

Builders of the house of Israel. . .

Ruth 4:11 *And all the people that were in the gate, and the elders, said, We are witnesses. The LORD make the woman that is come into thine house like Rachel and like Leah, which two did build the house of Israel: and do thou worthily in Ephratah, and be famous in Bethlehem:*

The people of Bethlehem cried out for God to make Ruth like Rachel and Leah. They revered Jacob's favored wife, Rachel, and her sister, Leah, as the builders of the house of Israel. Their mentioning is not without significance to the newly announced marriage of Boaz and Ruth.

These women were valued in Bethlehem for several reasons. Together the sisters gave birth to the sons that made up the tribes of Israel. As Israelites, the people of Bethlehem were directly affected by these two sisters. Their understanding of Israel's history and their own family heritage made a special place in their hearts for Rachel and Leah. Rachel, the younger of the two sisters, died in Ephratah, the original name for Bethlehem, giving birth to Benjamin. She was buried just outside the city's gate just a short walk from where they were standing.

The desire of the townspeople was to see Ruth to be the builder of the house of Elimelech. They desired that God would make her union with Boaz fruitful. They wanted God to make Ruth like Rachel, one of the co-builders of the house of Israel. This title, "builder of the house of Israel," revealed the position of honor Rachel and Leah held in their hearts though several generations later.

Rachel was the object of Jacob's affection. He loved her deeply even so to the rejection of Leah, her sister. God saw this inequity and made Leah's womb fruitful and Rachel's womb barren. Rachel's womb remained empty until her sister had given Jacob six sons and a daughter.

Rachel desired children to the extent she pled with Jacob, "give me children or else I die." Jacob knew that he was not in control, for it was God who made women fruitful. It was after her plea for children to her husband, God remembered Rachel. His favor brought fruitfulness to Rachel. She gave birth to Joseph. A few years later she gave birth to her second son Benjamin. Jacob loved the sons of Rachel dearly; they both were living reminders of his love for her.

Ruth's role was clear in the minds of the people. She was redeemed by Boaz for a purpose. She was to bring forth a son to prevent the family name from being extinguished.
As one who is redeemed by the Eternal Boaz we should be careful to remember our responsibility. Our adoption in the Eternal Boaz's family creates a responsibility to be builders of the house of God. We are to be fruitful first in the places close to our heart and home; then we are to be fruitful in the places that are hard to reach.

Many a believer rejoices in their redemption; yet, the same ones are reserved in reaching others with the message of the Eternal Boaz.

When was the last time you led someone to Him with His message of redemption? How often do you tell men of the Eternal Boaz? May you strive to be a builder of the house of God.

Think about it ...

A prayer for favor and fame. . .

Ruth 4:11 *And all the people that were in the gate, and the elders, said, We are witnesses. The LORD make the woman that is come into thine house like Rachel and like Leah, which two did build the house of Israel: and do thou worthily in Ephratah, and be famous in Bethlehem:*

Boaz listened as the people spoke. Each one shared his prayerful cry and desires for Bethlehem's newest couple. One by one people in the crowd amongst the invited and interest gave his heart's best to Ruth and Boaz. None could know the joy sensed in his heart as he heard them share prayers for fruitfulness, favor, and fame. Surely, he could not wait for the opportunity to share these matters for the heart with Ruth.

The prayerful desire of the people brought out two interesting phrases. They said, *"and do thou worthily in Ephratah, and be famous in Bethlehem."* Boaz and Ruth had the well wishes and prayers of the people in Bethlehem.

It is interesting to combine their reminiscing of Rachel with the mentioning of Ephratah. Ephrathites were the original inhabitants of the city which is now called Bethlehem. Their desire was for the couple to do well in the name of the old city. This was logical as the couple sought the old ways of kinsman-redemption and Levirate restoration.

They desired for Boaz and Ruth to both honor their ancestors name but also their virtues. It was honorable for a man to set aside whatever would be exclusively his inheritance and share it with another. It was virtuous for a man to lay aside his best for one who needed his best. It was upright for Boaz to take Ruth and restore the family name of his kinsman Elimelech.

The people also desired that they be famous in Bethlehem. Little did they know the notoriety that would come to this couple and to the little town of Bethlehem. Although in this time of the Judges when every man did what was right in his own eyes. Here stood a man who was doing what was right in God's eyes. The townspeople wanted them to find distinction and to be renowned for Boaz's redemption and Elimelech's restoration by Boaz and Ruth.

A reading of the Bible reveals the desires of the townspeople favor and fame were fully met. A whole book of the Bible was devoted to the act of one man, Boaz. His very deed illustrated a greater act of redemption by our Eternal Boaz. Bethlehem became well known for it hospitality for taking in strangers and hosting them in time of birth, with this couple and Joseph and Mary.

The people's desire for Boaz and Ruth should be our own desire. They wanted them to honor their spiritual heritage and make a name for their homeland. It must be our chief aim to honor our spiritual heritage in our choices and as we face life's challenges. While many today seem quite content to seek fame for themselves, it should be the desire of the child of God to seek to bring attention to the homeland of Heaven.

Our lives must bring to God glory and honor in every area. Did your decisions yesterday bring honor to God and bring to others an awareness of His salvation? Will everything you do today bring that honor and awareness?

Think about it ...

Reflections of faith...

Ruth 4:11-12 *And let thy house be like the house of Pharez, whom Tamar bare unto Judah, of the seed which the LORD shall give thee of this young woman.*

Tamar's story, was not one of which little girls would dream. Her story was more of an ugly reality. Yet, it directly affected this moment in the gate of Bethlehem.

Tamar married a man named Er; his father was Judah. He was a wicked man, and God killed him. So following the same principle which Boaz now followed, Judah told his other son Onan to marry Tamar. Through a most humiliating experience to Tamar, he refused. As with all selfish and mean acts the Lord observed this He slew him like his brother, Er.

Judah told Tamar to wait at her father's house until his other son, Shelah grew up. He would then have his son follow the same principle to raise up seed for the family name not to be extinguished; however, Judah did not honor his word. Tamar, through an act of deception, was found to be with the child of Judah, her father in law. When it was discovered Judah confessed that Tamar had been more righteous than he had been.

Tamar, though scarred by the events of being married to a wicked man, rejected by another, and refused by yet another, sought to make sure that the family name of her husband was not extinguished. She gave birth to twins whose names were Pharez and Zarah. According to the census of Israel in the book of Numbers, the population of the sons of Judah, including the house of Pharez, grew to over 76,500. Without Tamar the house of Pharez would not have existed, nor could all of Bethlehem's citizens gathered to witness, as Boaz, the grandson of Pharez four generations removed, offered to redeem Ruth.

The words of the townspeople were more than just matrimonial blessings. They were reflections of faith in a God who brought justice to injustice. They believed in a God who accepted those who were rejected and refused. They had confidence that God could bring fruit to any barren womb. They knew that all things worked together for the good for those who loved God.

The people of Bethlehem spoke as if the matter of a son born to Boaz and Ruth was settled. They wanted the house of Boaz to be like the house of Pharez. Their knowledge of the past gave them their faith for their present. These children of Israel knew the painful story of the house of Pharez and its vague similarities to Boaz and Ruth. Yet, their reflections of faith gave them comfort and challenged them.

The people of Bethlehem knew, what God had done before He could do again. They knew God could give seed to Boaz through the fruit of Ruth's womb. They knew God honored those who honored His Word. What have you seen God do in the past? Have you developed your faith to the place where you can take God at His Word? Pause a moment today. Look for the reflections of faith in the pool of your life's experiences since Calvary. Whatever you are facing today do not let it get you disheartened. Turn your heart around and trust Him!

Think about it ...

Boaz returns for his bride. . .

Ruth 4:13 *So Boaz took Ruth, and she was his wife: and when he went in unto her, the LORD gave her conception, and she bare a son.*

Boaz's arrival back to Naomi's house is without description but certainly not without drama. He had instructed Ruth to go home. When she left the threshingfloor he gave her provision to share with Naomi. Naomi quickly understood all that was underway and told her to wait until she knew how everything would go.

Naomi sought to encourage Ruth while waiting. She said Boaz wouldn't rest until the matter had been dealt with both legally and emotionally. Ruth's waiting for the arrival of Boaz must have been filled with anxiousness and anticipation. Her future rested in his word. She merely had to live on the words of Boaz until she saw him again.

Ruth knew that he went to secure her redemption. She was to live on his provision and live by his promise until he returned. His return was imminent. Images of when he would return and what would it would be like could have played in her mind. No matter when it was she needed to be ready for his arrival.

The last 24 hours had been dramatic to say the least. She went through the cleansing process for presenting herself to Boaz. She went through the emotional high and low of hearing he would redeem her, but there was another who had first right to the inheritance of the land of Elimelech and these ladies who remained. She spent a short night on the threshingfloor and quickly left before dawn to avoid tarnishing her virtuous reputation. Now, she waits for the arrival of her kinsman-redeemer.

Boaz left the city gate; he headed to Naomi's house. Yet, no longer was it Naomi's; it was his now by right of purchase. He clutched the shoe from the nearer kinsman who decided the redemption was beyond what he was willing to pay. Each step toward Naomi's house brought the realization of redemption.

What would the look be on their faces? He had secured their future and they could be with him for the rest of their days.

He desired Ruth's heart and sought to honor her and her husband's family by not allowing their name to be extinguished from the families Judah's tribe.

Finally the house was in sight. Did he call out to Ruth or knock at the door? Was she watching for him? Did she sense his arrival? Did he stand at the turn in the path and hold up the shoe? Did he stand in the doorway and hold up the shoe for them to see? Perhaps these things are kept from us so the focus would be on the redemption and the redeemer.

The words are simply stated for us, "*So Boaz took Ruth, and she was his wife.*" It is sure that the arrival of Boaz was welcome. The shoe he carried symbolizing the act was legally satisfied was certainly treasured. However, the greatest treasure of the day was the one held in their hearts; they were going to grow old together and with the blessing of God, they would have a son and the family's name would be restored.

The shadows cast toward the New Testament are abundant as we reach this verse. We too, are a bride waiting for the return of our Redeemer. He has given us His promise and provision. He promised to return for his bride, the church. He gives us provision for living while we wait His arrival. Are you ready for His return? Has the time waiting for Him brought discouragement or even distraction? His return is imminent; He will come. You must occupy yourself in His business until He arrives.

Do you anticipate His arrival as Ruth did with Boaz? May we follow the New Testament teaching about this matter and, "*. . .love His appearing.*"

Think about it ...

The battle. . .

Ruth 4:13 *So Boaz took Ruth, and she was his wife: and when he went in unto her, the LORD gave her conception, and she bare a son.*

God made a promise to mankind in the Garden of Eden of a Messiah. Since the promise was made, Satan sought to attack God's creation in order to disrupt the line of The One that would crush his own head. One such attempt by Satan to destroy the line of the Messiah is seen in his attack on the family of Elimelech. Satan attacked Elimelech, who stood at the head of the line of the Messiah. Then, with the death of all the living males in the family line of the Messiah, Satan could extinguish the hope of the Messiah.

Ruth's redemption was the very will of God and all of Satan's army could not prevent it. This day, Satan lost a battle in his war to prevent the birth of the Messiah; however, the last battle in this war would be waged in this little town of Bethlehem in a few generations. Satan would enlist rulers, inn-keepers, and politicians to prevent the birth of Christ. Yet, he would fail miserably and Jesus Christ, our Kinsman-Redeemer, would be born to provide redemption for the world.

Jesus, our wealthy relative, by His birth in the family of mankind, generously gave himself for the redemption of the world. His virgin birth and sinless life uniquely qualified Him. His sacrificial death was the price he paid for the redemption of the family of man. His resurrection gave him the keys of death, hell and the grave. He alone is the only way mankind can be redeemed.

Are you among the redeemed? Is your family? Are your neighbors and co-workers?

The greatest story we could ever tell is the story of redemption by our Eternal Boaz.

Think about it ...

The birth. . .

Ruth 4:13 *So Boaz took Ruth, and she was his wife: and when he went in unto her, the LORD gave her conception, and she bare a son.*

Their first days surely were filled with the joy of any newly wedded couple. Rays of love splashed across their home as they began in earnest to establish their new home together. Laughter and smiles were abundant as they shared stories of their thoughts of what once was and what would be in their future. There was no question; they were in love!

Their marriage was not one entered into with reluctance; rather it was one with rejoicing. This redeemed bride and her kinsman-redeemer sought to share their love and seek God's blessing in conception. They desired a son to continue the family name of Elimelech and Ruth's deceased husband, Mahlon. This desire was honorable in the eyes of God and man.

In yesterday's reading we saw as hard as Satan fought, God is overall and reigns supreme. His Sovereign hand oversaw and orchestrated the events of Boaz and Ruth's lives to bring them down His aisle of grace. Their meeting was not by chance; it was by divine appointment and it would be the same with the fruit of their union.

Who would have thought a generous act several thousand years ago by a wealthy relative toward an impoverished, childless widow would play such an important role in the redemption of the world? Yet, it did. Redemption is the very heart of God. He allowed nothing to prevent making redemption available to all of mankind in all ages. He blessed Boaz and Ruth with a son, thirty generations later as He blessed the family of man with the virgin birth of Jesus, the Messiah.

The blessing of the birth of a son to Boaz and Ruth highlights a clear truth. God is in control in the matters of redemption and reproduction of mankind. Man cannot redeem himself, nor can he reproduce without God. God desires to redeem every man without exemption or exclusion. He still gives heritage even today in the reproduction and adoption of children today, through both He receives the glory.

Our focal verse today states it clearly; '*and when he went in unto her, the LORD gave her conception, and she bare a son.*" It is no wonder that as Satan fought against their union, God would bless it and give them conception, and at that a son. Four generations later God used their great-great grandson Solomon to write, in Psalms 127:3 "*Lo, children are an heritage of the LORD: and the fruit of the womb is his reward.*"

Perhaps you are aware of someone who is having a baby. Why not use it as a reminder to tell others of God's redemption available to all men? Let us thank God today for His grace and goodness toward us. It is easy when reading a verse like this one today to understand what John wrote in the New Testament. "*We love him, because he first loved us.*" 1 John 4:19

Think about it ...

God's remembrance, redemption, and reward. . .

"And the women said unto Naomi, Blessed be the LORD, which hath not left thee this day without a kinsman, that his name may be famous in Israel." Ruth 4:14

The community of Bethlehem learned of the birth of a child to Boaz and Ruth. The women in the city, who had known Naomi, came to her house to rejoice in the wonderful news. It would seem their rejoicing should be toward Boaz and Ruth. After all Boaz and Ruth were the parents; however, their praise is directed toward the child's grandmother. Their rejoicing in this way reveals the impact of the kinsman-redemption on the community.

Memories of Bethlehem's famine a decade ago and the accompanying sorrows found little grasp on their hearts in the birth of this little lad. A son had been born. God had remembered Naomi Yes, Naomi! Although Ruth was the mother, Naomi represented her deceased husband Elimelech. It was Elimelech's line that had been remembered, redeemed, and rewarded by the redemption of Boaz.

The redemption by Boaz was comprehensive. He purchased to himself all that was Mahlon's, Chilion's, and Elimelech's. Naomi, as the child's grandmother, was burdened by all that had taken place. Naomi's past with her husband's departure, which brought his death, was nullified because of Boaz's redemption. Naomi's pain in her heart was lifted as she saw the Almighty bless her, and she realized the He had not dealt bitterly with her as she had accused Him. Naomi's potential, because of Boaz's redemption, was before her. His redemption restored hope and renewed her happiness.

God had been gracious to Naomi; she and her neighbors knew it. These same neighbors who had heard her bemoan God's forgetting, forsaking, and fierceness, now arrive to raise the banner of rejoicing over the heart and home of Naomi. They rejoiced in God's remembrance, redemption and reward toward Naomi.

The word of the neighbors must have struck a chord of remembrance in Naomi's hearing. Long gone were the days where she in desperation accused God in the presence of her neighbors upon her return from Moab. You remember she said, *"Call me not Naomi, call me Mara: for the Almighty hath dealt very bitterly with me. I went out full, and the LORD hath brought me home again empty: why then call ye me Naomi, seeing the LORD hath testified against me, and the Almighty hath afflicted me?"*

The Eternal Boaz reminded Naomi, through the visit of the women, of His grace and goodness. She was reminded of the Father and Friend she had in Heaven. She was not alone. She had been remembered, not forgotten. She had been redeemed, not forsaken. She had been rewarded, not fined by the fierceness of God.

You know the redemption offered by The Eternal Boaz offers is the same today. It is the bemoaning of believers that isolates them from recalling that the mercies of the Lord endure forever. As Naomi had a Friend in Heaven that remembered, redeemed, and rewarded her, so do believers today. His redemption erases our painful past and gives us potential we never knew. When the events of a million yesterdays seek to restrain you remember, it is His redemption that makes us valuable. *"In whom we have redemption through his blood, even the forgiveness of sins:"* Colossians 1:14

Think about it ...

Without a kinsman. . .

Ruth 4:14 *And the women said unto Naomi, Blessed be the LORD, which hath not left thee this day without a kinsman, that his name may be famous in Israel.*

The words of the women of Bethlehem to Naomi were precious in her hearing. Just listen to the clarity and confidence with which they spoke. *"Blessed be the LORD, which hath not left thee this day without a kinsman, that his name may be famous in Israel."* They told Naomi she had not been left without a kinsman. For this, God's name was to be blessed.

What would have things been like if Naomi had been left without a kinsman-redeemer? Elimelech's name would have just been a memory, not linked to the Messiah. Naomi would have died lacking and alone. Hopelessness and hurt would have been nursed in her home until her dying day. Ruth would have lived exiled from hope and joy. Had it not been for Boaz being their kinsman-redeemer they would have lost their lands to "such a one" who wanted the land but not the ladies. We know that Naomi was not left without a kinsman-redeemer.

God had orchestrated the events of the lives of many to bring about His will. It was God's will from the Garden of Eden to bring a Kinsman-Redeemer to the world, The Messiah. Naomi's friends reminded her on this most special of days, the birth of her first grandchild, she had a kinsman who changed her future.

Have you ever paused to ponder what your life would be like had you been left without a Kinsman-Redeemer? Where would you be today? Had you been left without a Kinsman, your eternal home would not be the same. You would have an emptiness that would never be filled. Love and security would only be wishful thinking in your heart. You would never know about His grace being made perfect in weakness. You would never know what forgiveness meant.

Yes, we are the better having a Kinsman-Redeemer! However, today there is neighbor of yours that may not know there is a Kinsman-Redeemer. He lives without the knowledge that God will forgive his sinful past. Even in regions beyond your neighbor there are millions who know not of our Kinsman-Redeemer. We must tell them, today!

Think about it ...

Famous in Israel. . .

Ruth 4:14 *And the women said unto Naomi, Blessed be the LORD, which hath not left thee this day without a kinsman, that his name may be famous in Israel.*

The women in Naomi's home town knew how special this day was. Ruth had conceived by her kinsman-redeemer, Boaz. Today she gave birth to a son. The townspeople understood it was the hand of God which brought this to pass. No other, but God, would see to it in such a manner.

The words of the women merely echo the initial blessings issued at the gate of the city where the proclamation of Ruth's redemption was made. The gathering on that auspicious day about a year ago had its own blessing for Boaz. *"The LORD make the woman that is come into thine house like Rachel and like Leah, which two did build the house of Israel: and do thou worthily in Ephratah, and be famous in Bethlehem."* Now the women who knew Naomi best gathered to see this precious child. To these women, Boaz and Ruth's child represented God's grace.

Their words represented the very thoughts of their heart. They desired ". . .that his name may be famous in Israel." For Boaz playing the part of the kinsman-redeemer, they wanted more than their tiny village, often overshadowed by Jerusalem, to know it. They desired all Israel to know it.

Yet, little did they realize just how famous the name of Boaz would become. Boaz, son of Rahab the harlot, kinsman-redeemer to all that was Elimelech's, father to a son which restored the family line of Elimelech, great-grandfather to King David, great-great-grandfather to the world's wisest king, and one of the 42 mentioned in Scripture in the line of the Messiah become famous in all of Israel and the world.

They wanted Israel to know the graciousness and goodness that Boaz extended to the most unlikely candidate for redemption in all of Israel. Their desire for Boaz to stand out and be recognized by all Israel was appropriate. When a kinsman-redemption like this is done, everyone should know about it.

Similarly, we should desire the same thing for our Eternal Boaz. His redemption of our pitiful state and status should be declared around the world. The fame of his goodness and grace should reach every heart on earth. It is the responsibility of the redeemed to proclaim His glory among the heathen. We are to bring news of His redemption to all and we do this with our going and giving. How much going and giving have you done lately?

Think about it ...

Benefits of redemption. . .

And he shall be unto thee a restorer of thy life, and a nourisher of thine old age: for thy daughter in law, which loveth thee, which is better to thee than seven sons, hath born him. Ruth 4:15

The women's voices continued to praise Boaz for his value as a redeemer and the redemption he brought. Naomi listened as her well wishers brought words of comfort and courage.

Certainly her heart was renewed as these her friends, friends who stood with her in the famine of her life, reminded her of the blessings of Boaz's redemption.

They knew that Boaz would be the complete redeemer that Naomi needed. Naomi no longer stood alone, her friends knew she needed to hear that, especially on a day when so much was happening in her heart and home.

Naomi's friends told her that they knew Boaz would be a restorer and nourisher in her life. Naomi grew accustomed to living alone and struggling to make it. Boaz's commitment to redemption meant he would bring new life to this grandmother. Boaz would see to it she would never lack again.

Redemption had many benefits. Boaz brought more to her than just a name. He brought meaning to life. He made things new. He took that which was lifeless and gave it life. Such work was not to be ignored and Naomi's neighbors knew it. They knew that Boaz would supply and sustain Naomi for life. His redemption meant Naomi would know replenishment of her need as she never knew. This day was a blessed one. Naomi's friends helped her hear and see the benefits of Boaz's redemption.

The child of God would do well to visit this verse in light of the redemption by our Eternal Boaz. We too have benefits that go beyond our redemption. He is both our Restorer and Nourisher.

David, great grandson to Boaz and Ruth, would write to this same affect, "Bless the LORD, O my soul, and forget not all his benefits:" Psalms 103:2 His writings in this Psalm reveals that the benefits of redemption are abundant. His redemption brings to us forgiveness, healing, deliverance, crowns of lovingkindness and tender mercies, satisfaction, and renewing.

You probably will be busy today. It seems that is how life goes. Why not determine right now to live the next 24 hours with the benefits of redemption on your mind instead of the burdens of responsibility? Your days will be brighter and your loads a lot lighter.

Think about it ...

"Turn your eyes upon Jesus, look full in His wonderful face, and the things of earth will grow strangely dim, in the light of His glory and grace."

Helen H. Lemmel

Ruth, Naomi's daughter-in-love. . .

Ruth 4:15 *And he shall be unto thee a restorer of thy life, and a nourisher of thine old age: for thy daughter in law, which loveth thee, which is better to thee than seven sons, hath born him.*

The women rejoiced with Naomi. They shared testimonies with this new grandmother who was trying to assimilate the events of the day with the past dozen years or more. Her friend spoke of God's goodness in supplying Boaz. They told of their confidence that Boaz would be all Naomi needed to live out her days in peace and joy; however, at the end of our focus verse today they turn their testimony of praise to the mother of the baby, Ruth.

The town knew of Ruth. It was not everyday a Moabite would convert from idolatry to God. Furthermore, it was not common to see a Moabite move to Bethlehem, however, Ruth was no ordinary Moabite. No, she was a Gentile gem, cultivated by God from the sands of Moab, for the Messiah's crown.

The testimony of her conversion became well-known to the residents of Bethlehem. You may remember Ruth's words to

Naomi. *"And Ruth said, Intreat me not to leave thee, or to return from following after thee: for whither thou goest, I will go; and where thou lodgest, I will lodge: thy people shall be my people, and thy God my God: Where thou diest, will I die, and there will I be buried: the LORD do so to me, and more also, if ought but death part thee and me."* Ruth 1:16-17

The testimony of her redemption was well-known. Almost a year had passed since Boaz stood in the gate and proclaimed his offer of redemption. Yes, the women of Bethlehem knew Ruth's heritage and they knew her heart. She loved Naomi and was committed to staying with her until death parted them.

The women praised Ruth to Naomi. *"Thy daughter in law, which loveth thee, which is better to thee than seven sons, hath born him."* Their tribute testifies of Ruth's value and their esteem of her. She may have been the subject of a few whispers amongst the women in the town, perhaps even amongst some of these. However, they watched her movements and motives. They realized she was one of them, not by the heritage of her birth but rather by heritage of her faith.

Ruth maintained a proper relationship to Naomi. She did not become envious of Naomi's friends praise on this the day of birth of her first born son. She knew that this was a matter of God's hand blessing all of them. She did not seek to take anything away from this moment with pouting or worrying whether she would be recognized. She just held her baby and knew The Almighty had been gracious to her, and He knew she had been faithful. Ruth's contentment brought her beyond the realm of being Naomi's daughter-in-law to being her daughter in love.

The women of Bethlehem announced Ruth's value was greater than having seven sons. If Naomi had one son it was certainly special, however, if she had seven sons it would have distinguished Naomi as a mother with great value. In that culture sons represented security, sustenance, and continuance of the family line; however, Ruth's quiet faithfulness distinguished her amongst the women of Bethlehem. Her worth to Naomi was greater than if Naomi had given birth to seven sons.

Only God would take a Moabite and make her more valuable than a mother having seven sons. Only God would raise her estimation amongst women in that city who may have first decried her and now praise her. Ruth's value was not tarnished by her words or actions. She was faithful and God honored her.

What situation are you facing today? God does see and He knows where you are. You need to purpose in your heart to make yourself valuable to Him. He will increase your value over time in the eyes of others. What is your testimony amongst your neighbors? What is your testimony amongst your in-laws?

Think about it ...

A babe in Bethlehem. . .

Ruth 4:16 *And Naomi took the child, and laid it in her bosom, and became nurse unto it.*

Time must have stood still as this widowed grandmother sat with her grandson. The voices of the women of the city are silent. It is just a grandmother, her grandchild and her daughter in love, Ruth. Images of yesterdays began to fill her mind as she held the most precious of children, her own grandchild. The birth of this moment represented over a dozen years of labor in Naomi's life. Scripture gives us this pause in the narrative to fully consider the facets of this moment.

Naomi now held in her hands, the heart of her husband, and the life of her son. Certainly tears from the heart were abundant. A sweet innocent child had come to their family by the Hand of God. Words would come later. This was a moment for cherishing the scrapbook of the heart.

What a picture we see in our verse today! A woman who thought she would go to her grave alone. She could not provide a child to continue a family name for her husband. The disgrace of their departure and deaths in Moab left her defenseless and in despair. Each step home on her 67 mile journey seemed to seal her fate. She was the sole representative of her husband and she had no way of continuing the family line. No matter what she could do on her own it would not be enough. Yet, somehow God took her repentant return and brought redemption and restoration to her life.

These words say it all. "She took the child and laid it in her bosom." She was able to take the child because the Almighty's hand had not been fierce against her but rather faithful to her. Her accusation that He had dealt very bitterly with her is silenced. She learned a valuable lesson in life; the only difference between bitter and better is the letter I.

When she took the child, it spoke volumes to Ruth. Ruth a Moabite, and Boaz, the son of Rahab the harlot, had been granted a son by God. Racially the child represented cultures, communities, and conduct all cause enough to raise walls of prejudice, however, when Naomi took the child she took all that he was and accepted him because of love. The placement of the baby in her bosom silenced all opposing voices that could be raised. This was a child of grace.

God's favor had been extended to her. The great lengths God had gone to by moving Heaven and earth to bring a son to stand in the family line of Elimelech touched her heart. She placed the baby near her heart and embraced more than just a child; she embraced hope in swaddling clothes and held on to the promise of a bright tomorrow.

Our God has done the same for the family of man today. He saw us in our pitiful state distant and away from Him. On our own there was no way we could come to Him; so, He came to us. We were marred by our condition, culture, and conduct. He saw our hearts condition and drew us to Himself and loved us. We were no prize to Him, yet, His choice to love us while we were yet sinners; that is a wonderful gift.

His gift goes beyond a child in a manger. It extends to a cross where your sin payment was made. Redemption comes when the price has been paid. Have you accepted His offer of redemption? If not, do so today. If you have accepted His redemption, then tell someone today!

Think about it ...

Connected at the heart. . .

Ruth 4:16 And Naomi took the child, and laid it in her bosom, and became nurse unto it."

The relationship between Ruth and Naomi was sealed on their trip to Bethlehem. On that journey of faith Ruth selflessly and unconditionally pledged her heart to her Mother-in-law. She promised to remain with Naomi. Wherever life's events brought them they were connected, connected at the heart. Ruth's pledge said only death would part their relationship.

Yet, even in death Ruth pledged to be buried by her mother-in-law. Naomi had buried all the family she had since marriage to Elimelech. Yet, Ruth would not allow her to be buried without family. She committed that day to be buried in the land of Naomi's God and people.

Ruth's love for her Mother-in-law was one of honor and of the heart. Naomi represented the sole living connection to her deceased husband. Ruth was the last link to Naomi's deceased husband and son. The bond between Naomi and Ruth was one that connected them at the heart.

The new life that followed redemption was now secure in the bosom of Naomi. This little lad could not yet know how valuable he was to these two women. Naomi and Ruth never knew that when they discussed the impossibility of Ruth's marrying a son of Naomi, when they left Moab, would unfold as this did.

Yet, here in Naomi's bosom is the fruit of God's uniting a near kinsman with a childless widow who could restore the line of the Messiah. Naomi, without recorded words, pledged from the heart to Ruth, "I will be the nurse to this child." I will faithfully nourish and support this child's development; he is my son. She committed to her daughter-in-law; the child of your womb is the child of my heart. From their journey to Bethlehem Naomi became Ruth's Mother in love. This moment only solidified that emotional connection as Naomi held the future in her hands; a future that would have been lost were in not for redemption.

Your redemption has connected you to the heart of God. His love for you is beyond human description. He loved us though we were hopelessly and desperately useless to Him; however, He saw in us what He could make us and loved us. He came to earth expressed His love of Calvary's cross and freely offered His Redemption to all mankind. Yes, redemption connects our heart to Him. It is a universal connection; no matter the background, behavior, or burdens He will redeem even to the uttermost.

Naomi became nurse to the child because of love. Perhaps today there is someone in your church family you have brought to the Lord that needs someone to faithfully nourish and support their spiritual development. You are connected at the heart to them. Do not allow other things to stand in your way to nurse a convert in their walk with the Lord. Rare is the person who will ignore a newborn baby and not pause to express their affection for this new life.

We should do the same for the spiritual newborns around us; to whom will you become a spiritual nurse today?

Think about it ...

A name from the neighbors. . .

Ruth 4:17 *And the women her neighbours gave it a name, saying, There is a son born to Naomi; and they called his name Obed: he is the father of Jesse, the father of David.*

Considering the manner of the people of God, it would seem likely that these events in the previous three verses have taken place within the first eight days of the newborn's birth. Jewish law required that the baby would be circumcised and also typically named. It would be likely that the neighbors of Naomi had come on this auspicious occasion to rejoice with the redeemed family of Elimelech.

Naomi's neighbors observed the events in the life of Naomi, Ruth, and Boaz. They saw God bring the wandering Naomi home. They beheld the loving way Ruth has helped Naomi and her faithfulness in Boaz's field. They witnessed the redemption of all that was Elimelech, Mahlon's and Chilion's.

Truly this was the hand of God at work in their little town. They could hardly contain their blessings and congratulations. The joy of the moment coupled with their enthusiasm, the crowd cried out, "'There is a son born to Naomi' and they called *him Obed.*" The name was not a family name to them. He was not named after Elimelech or Boaz. Obed is a name which literally means, serving. The word describes his action, serving, more than his position, as a servant.

The neighbors saw Obed's arrival as there was a special task for him. He would be serving. He would serve God as he restored hope in the hearts of the little town of Bethlehem. He would serve as the symbol of the grace found in the law of God. Obed's birth marked a moment in time where the people recognized God's hand at work in their midst, in that he served.

In their cries to name Obed, it is interesting to see the women announce that there is a son born to Naomi. They knew it was Ruth who conceived of Boaz. They knew it was Ruth who delivered a son. Yet, they cried out, *"There is a son born to Naomi."* Their cry merely indicated their heart. As Naomi drew Obed to her bosom, so they were drawing Obed to their collective bosom. They saw Naomi had been blessed by God with a grandson and vicariously a son to continue the line of Elimelech and the greater line of the Messiah.

The law of God that made provision for Boaz to be kinsman-redeemer, also revealed itself in Obed to be a law of grace. The son that was born into the family of Elimelech now stands at the head of the line of the Messiah. Obed was serving. He was serving the God who promised Abraham, Isaac, and Jacob theirs would be a great nation from whom the Messiah would come.

Is there an "Obed" quality in your life? Are you serving? Is God content with your serving? You were redeemed to serve. Failure to serve disgraces your redemption. Why not make it your prayer today to please Him in the way you are serving?

Think about it ...

He is the father. . .

Ruth 4:17 *And the women her neighbours gave it a name, saying, There is a son born to Naomi; and they called his name Obed: he is the father of Jesse, the father of David.*

The gospel according to Ruth concludes as it began; in the most ordinary of ways. We began with the story of a man with two sons, and we conclude with his genealogy. However, as we have seen throughout this book, no small decision is an isolated event. Every decision has future consequences. It is the grace of God that brought a different end to the family of Elimelech after a fateful decision he made.

The narrative section of this book ends with a statement that reveals the restoration of what appeared to be a disruption in the lineage of the Messiah. The unnamed writer of this book makes Obed's link to the Messiah clear. *"He is the father of Jesse, the father of David"* Jericho's harlot and Moab's Children joined the line of the Messiah in the redemptive birth of Obed.

Obed, standing at the head of the Messianic line will pass the baton of the Messiah's lineage to Jesse. Jesse would then hand the baton to his son, David. David's city Bethlehem would host the birth of the Messiah. David's throne would become the Messiah's throne and to His Kingdom there would be no end.

Yes, God took what seemed impossible and when there was no hope of a child being born to restore the Messianic line, and God rose up Boaz as kinsman-redeemer. To Boaz and Ruth He gave Obed. The birth of Obed in Bethlehem symbolizes to generations later the faithfulness of God to keep His word to bring about the redemption of man.

God's sovereign hand worked in the life of Elimelech and all his progeny to bring glory to His name. What is that little thing over which you fret today? Can He who aligned all of the details in the life of Elimelech mistakes and all not do the same for you? Obed was the father of Jesse, Is God your Father?

Think about it ...

A heritage of grace. . .

Ruth 4:18-22 *Now these are the generations of Pharez: Pharez begat Hezron, And Hezron begat Ram, and Ram begat Amminadab, And Amminadab begat Nahshon, and Nahshon begat Salmon, And Salmon begat Boaz, and Boaz begat Obed, And Obed begat Jesse, and Jesse begat David.*

The ending of this beautiful story of God's grace and goodness concludes with a genealogical record of ten men. As with all genealogies they serve as a link to our heritage. God saw fit to place this genealogical record in Ruth's story because it helps us discover His righteousness, riches, and redemption.

His righteousness is seen in bringing justice to injustice in the life of Pharez's mother. His riches of grace are seen in sparing Boaz's mother, a harlot from Jericho. His redemption is seen the work of Obed's father as he stood to serve as kinsman-redeemer to a Moabite.

The story behind this genealogy cannot be told by singling out one person but rather looking at each man by the light of the others. It is wise to remember that the future is brightest when seen through the past. Like most men, each man listed had no idea the affect his life would have on generations to follow. Yet, each man fulfilled a most vital role in the plan of God. He used each in the path of redemption that leads to the cross.

The heritage of grace begins with Pharez. His father Judah had three other sons, Er, Onan, and Shelah. Er, like his father, married a Canaanite girl whose name was Tamar. Er was so wicked; God killed him. Since Tamar had no children, she appealed to Judah for Onan to give her seed to continue the family line. He refused, and God killed him. Afterward, Judah promised Tamar when his youngest son grew older, he would marry her. Shelah grew up and Judah did not keep his word. This frustrated Tamar and through her own act of deception was found with child of Judah. Convicted by his immorality and deception Judah confessed his wrong and praise Tamar for being more honorable he was. Tamar bore a son and his name was Pharez.

Pharez's birth violated God's law. In Deuteronomy 23:2 God wrote, "*A bastard shall not enter into the congregation of the LORD; even to his tenth generation shall he not enter into the congregation of the LORD.*" God's law was clear. If a child were born of illegitimate parentage that it would take ten generations to cleanse this line before that family could enter the congregation of the Lord.

The ten generations following Judah's sin were Pharez, Hezron, Ram, Amminadab, Nahshon, Salmon, Boaz, Obed, Jesse, David. In this line of men we see a glimmer of God's grace in the fifth generation. The Old Testament Chronicler states that Nahshon became a prince of the children of Judah. In the seventh generation, Boaz stood and became kinsman-redeemer. In the tenth generation, God has king for his people, David. In David the generational line is cleansed and he is able to enter the congregation of the Lord. With David's kingship the door is opened for the Messiah to sit on the throne of David.

The Messiah's authenticity and arrival is the real story of this genealogy. His coming was sought by many generations. His human heritage came through Judah's line represented by these ten men. Included in this line were men who made mistakes. We even see men whose wives were of questionable origin. Yes, His heritage is a heritage of grace.

Ruth's story should remind you that those who are marred, scarred, and discarded are all welcome in the family of God. The account of Ruth's redemption reveals the men of all nations are welcome in the family of God. Pharez's mother and his father's wife were both Canaanites. Rahab was from Canaan, and Ruth from Moab. Their multinational heritage and sin-stained lives find a welcome inclusion in the line of the Messiah. Ruth's testament reveals; all men from all nations are able to find their redemption in His righteous blood.

God's righteousness demanded a righteous death to pay for the sin of man. The law was inadequate to save the family of man. Like 'Such a One' who could not redeem all that was Elimelech's, so the law could not redeem man to God. However, Jesus Christ is our Eternal Boaz stood in the gate and said, "I will redeem them." His blood payment on the cross satisfied God and the provision for man's redemption was made.

All men, of all nations, will find in The Eternal Boaz their redemption. Yes, the genealogy that concludes the book of Ruth is a heritage of God's grace and mercy. It points to the path that leads from the little town of Bethlehem to the cross of Calvary. Have you accepted his redemption? Are you telling others of it?

Think about it ...

Conclusion. . .

This book is a wonderful testament to how small decisions in a narrow place end up affecting generations to come. It would be wise to ponder your decisions in light of these things. It is no wonder that Obed's great grandson could review his family's history and write under the inspiration of the Holy Spirit, *"Trust in the LORD with all thine heart; and lean not unto thine own understanding. In all thy ways acknowledge him, and he shall direct thy paths."* Proverbs 3:5-6

Think about it ...

Epilogue

The Book of Ruth is another wonderful reminder that our Lord God holds sway over the affairs of men and will work His divine will, even without the recognition of men. It is doubtful that any of the characters of this story were cognizant of the workings of Jehovah through their lives. Some decisions were made from desperation, some from principle. As Naomi determined to return to Bethlehem-judah and Ruth chose to forsake the gods of her homeland and cling to Jehovah, the Lord was putting eternally chosen pieces together. As Boaz stood to follow the precepts of God and assume the position of kinsman-redeemer, the lineage of the Divine promised from Genesis 3:15 was carried to the next stage. Today we enjoy the blessing of salvation from our eternal Kinsman-Redeemer, Jesus Christ, because men and women chose to follow the Word of God, perhaps not knowing at the time just how far and how wonderfully God would use them. It behooves us as believers in this hour to do the same.

Dr. Larry M. Groves
Faith Baptist Church
Indianapolis, IN

Notes from Author...

I am grateful to my dear friend, Dr. Larry Groves. It was his prompting and encouragement that brought about this devotional series.

I dedicate this work to my wife Kimberly and son, John. They encouraged, listened, and helped me in this three year quest.

I appreciate those who helped edit and shape this volume.
    Bonny Lorenzo
    Sharon O'Malley
    Tammy Funston
    Mark O'Malley

Cover design by:
    Vanessa Valentine - Valentine Designs

For additional copies:

John M. O'Malley
PO Box 1374 Kings Mountain, NC 28086
704-730-1440

Online:

www.OMalleyBooks.com